B 48905

THE EUROPEAN
CONVENTION ON
HUMAN RIGHTS

BY

FRANCIS G. JACOBS

Professor of European Law
in the University of London

CLARENDON PRESS · OXFORD

1975

Oxford University Press, Ely House, London W. 1

GLASGOW   NEW YORK   TORONTO   MELBOURNE   WELLINGTON
CAPE TOWN   IBADAN   NAIROBI   DAR ES SALAAM   LUSAKA   ADDIS ABABA
DELHI   BOMBAY   CALCUTTA   MADRAS   KARACHI   LAHORE   DACCA
KUALA LUMPUR   SINGAPORE   HONG KONG   TOKYO

ISBN 0 19 825370 2

© *Oxford University Press 1975*

First published in 1975
Reissued in paperback 1980

*Printed in Great Britain
by Billing & Sons Limited,
Guildford and London*

PREFACE

It has been said that the European Convention on Human Rights has generated a greater volume of writing than any other legal text except the E.E.C. Treaty. Yet there is at present no up-to-date, systematic work on the Convention available in English—or indeed in any other language apart from Norwegian: and the English translation of Professor Castberg's book comes too late to be cited, except in the bibliography.

I wish to record my thanks to Dr Andreas Khol, formerly a colleague in the secretariat of the European Commission of Human Rights, for reading the whole of the manuscript, for much generous help and encouragement, and for criticisms that were always constructive. My thanks also to Miss Susan Cox who, in her spare time, typed and re-typed successive versions of the manuscript, and remained cheerful throughout.

November 1974   F. G. JACOBS

CONTENTS

PART I

PART II: RIGHTS

PART III: RESTRICTIONS

PART IV: REMEDIES

PART I

INTRODUCTION

The subject of this book brings together two threads which, however precariously, have brought developments in the ordering of international society that can only be described as spectacular if compared with the situation in 1945. One of these threads is European integration on a level to serve not only technical needs and economic interests, but also to embody a system of liberal values which crystallize centuries of political development.

The second is a new concern, despite grim reality, in relations between States both within and beyond Europe, for the protection of human rights. The international protection of human rights has of course many other dimensions, but it has been most fully and systematically developed under the new law which is the subject of this book. European integration, also, has many other facets, but both the construction of the European Communities, and co-operation in various fields among the States of Western Europe, have been progressively based on a set of ideas and values of which the system described here is the most complete expression.[1]

After the Second World War, European movements arose, simultaneously and spontaneously, throughout the European democracies. They arose in response to the threat to fundamental human rights and to political freedom which had all but overwhelmed the European continent in the War, and which reappeared after the War in new forms of totalitarianism. The most significant immediate results of the International Committee of Movements for European Unity, and of its Congress at The Hague in May 1948, were the foundation of the Council of Europe on 5 May 1949 and the drafting by its Member States of the Convention for the Protection of Human Rights and Fundamental Freedoms of 4 November 1950, generally known as the European Convention on Human Rights.

---

[1] See Sørensen, 'The Enlargement of the European Communities and the Protection of Human Rights', *European Yearbook*, 1971, 3.

The Convention reflected the concerns and objects of this novel international organization, as set out in its Constitution, the Statute of the Council of Europe. In the Preamble to the Statute, the Contracting States reaffirmed 'their devotion to the spiritual and moral values which are the common heritage of their peoples and the true source of individual freedom, political liberty and the rule of law, principles which form the basis of all genuine democracy'.

The aim of the Council of Europe was, and remains, 'to achieve a greater unity between its Members for the purpose of safeguarding and realising the ideals and principles which are their common heritage and facilitating their economic and social progress',[1] and this aim was to be pursued 'through the organs of the Council by discussion of questions of common concern and by agreements and common action in economic, social, cultural, scientific, legal and administrative matters and in the maintenance and further realisation of human rights and fundamental freedoms'.[2]

Given the concern of the Council of Europe with parliamentary democracy, it was appropriate that the organs of the Council of Europe should include not only a Committee of Ministers, its executive organ, consisting of the Minister for Foreign Affairs of each Member State, or his deputy;[3] but also the first European parliamentary organ, the Consultative Assembly, comprising members of the Parliaments of the Member States.[4]

Another feature unique in the history of international organizations was the requirement in Article 3 of the Statute that every Member State 'must accept the principles of the rule of law and of the enjoyment by all persons within its jurisdiction of human rights and fundamental freedoms'.

Under Article 8, a Member State which has seriously violated Article 3 of the Statute may be requested by the Committee of

---

[1] Article 1(a) of the Statute. There are at present eighteen Member States of the Council of Europe: Austria, Belgium, Cyprus, Denmark, the Federal Republic of Germany, France, Greece, Iceland, Ireland, Italy, Luxembourg, Malta, the Netherlands, Norway, Sweden, Switzerland, Turkey, and the United Kingdom. All the Member States of the Council of Europe have now ratified the Human Rights Convention. One State, Greece, denounced the Convention and withdrew from the Council of Europe in 1969 (see below, p. 27), but was readmitted to membership, and re-ratified the Convention, in 1974.

[2] Article 1(b).   [3] Articles 13 and 14.

[4] Articles 22 and 25.

Ministers to withdraw from the Council of Europe and, if it does not comply, may be expelled. It was in consequence of proceedings started under this provision, following an initiative in the Consultative Assembly, that Greece announced in 1969 its withdrawal from the Council of Europe and denounced the Human Rights Convention.[1]

The uniqueness of these provisions lay in the fact that questions of human rights fell traditionally within the domestic jurisdiction of States, and were of concern to international law only if the interests of another State were affected, as for example by the treatment of its nationals.

History had all too convincingly demonstrated the inadequacy of those traditional concepts of international law and State sovereignty which made the protection of the individual the exclusive prerogative of the State of which he was a national. His rights may require protection, above all, against his own State—and the values of democratic government require a collective guarantee—for there are no boundaries to the denial of liberty. The creation of the Council of Europe and the adoption of the Human Rights Convention are an acknowledgment that the protection of human rights cannot be separated from the very existence of independent European States.

The principle of respect for human rights had been established in international law by the Charter of the United Nations.[2] The Universal Declaration of Human Rights, adopted by the General Assembly of the United Nations on 10 December 1948, proclaims as a 'common standard of achievement' an extensive list of human rights, which, although the Declaration is not legally binding as such, is an authoritative guide to the interpretation of the Charter.[3]

---

[1] See below, p. 269.

[2] See the relevant provisions of the United Nations Charter cited in Brownlie (ed.), *Basic Documents on Human Rights*, Oxford, 1971, p. 93 *et seq.*

[3] See Brownlie, op. cit., p. 106. While the Declaration itself is not a binding instrument of international law, the principles it enshrines may acquire legal force as the 'general principles of law recognized by civilized nations' under Article 38(1) (c) of the Statute of the International Court of Justice, or as customary law reflecting the general practice of States (cf. Article 38(1) (b) of the Statute), or even as 'a peremptory norm of general international law' (*jus cogens*), i.e. a norm accepted and recognized by the international community of States as a whole as a norm from which no derogation is permitted (cf. Article 53 of the Vienna Convention on the Law of Treaties).

Further work in the United Nations, which led to the adoption in 1966 of two Covenants, the Covenant on Economic, Social and Cultural Rights and the Covenant on Civil and Political Rights, showed that a distinction had to be drawn between two different classes of fundamental rights. Social and economic rights, although they appear in the Universal Declaration, are less universal in the sense that they constitute standards to be attained, depending on the level of economic development. They require action by governments, whereas civil and political rights often require protection against executive action. Within the Council of Europe, social and economic rights are the concern of the European Social Charter, which provides for progressive implementation and for supervision by the examination of periodic reports on progress achieved.

The European Convention on Human Rights guarantees, for the most part, civil and political rights: the right to life, liberty, and security; freedom from inhuman or degrading treatment, slavery, servitude, and forced labour; the right to a fair trial; freedom of conscience, of speech, and of assembly. However, Article 1 of the First Protocol, which protects property rights, and Article 2 which guarantees the right to education, are limited exceptions to this principle.

Section I of the European Convention spells out, generally in more detailed form, most of the basic civil and political rights contained in the Universal Declaration, while the First and Fourth Protocols guarantee certain further rights and freedoms.[1]

The rights set out in the Convention and Protocols are thus derived essentially from the Universal Declaration. For the purpose of an instrument which was to be binding in law, the content of these rights was often made more specific, and the circumstances in which limitations might legitimately be imposed on their

---

[1] The First Protocol has been ratified by all the eighteen States Parties to the Convention except Switzerland—see above, p. 2 n. 1—the Fourth Protocol by ten States (Austria, Belgium, Denmark, the Federal Republic of Germany, France, Iceland, Ireland, Luxembourg, Norway, and Sweden). The Second Protocol, which confers on the Court of Human Rights the power to give advisory opinions on the interpretation of the Convention, has been ratified by all the States Parties to the Convention except France. All States Parties to the Convention have ratified the Third Protocol, which amends the procedure of the Commission (see below, p. 251), and the Fifth Protocol, which amends the procedure for election of members of the Court and of the Commission.

exercise were spelt out. The rights guaranteed, and the restrictions permitted, are the subject of Part II and III of this book.

However, the most important, and the most original, feature of the European Convention is the system it established for the protection of the rights guaranteed.

The Convention created two organs 'to ensure the observance of the engagements undertaken by the High Contracting Parties': the European Commission of Human Rights and the European Court of Human Rights.[1] The primary function of these organs is to deal with applications brought against the States Parties by other States or by individuals under Article 24 or 25 of the Convention.[2]

Under Article 24, any State Party to the Convention may refer to the Commission any alleged breach of the provisions of the Convention by another State Party.

Under Article 25, the Commission may receive applications from any person, non-governmental organization or group of individuals claiming to be the victim of a violation by one of the States Parties of the rights set forth in the Convention, provided that the State concerned has declared that it recognizes the competence of the Commission to receive such applications. Such declarations may be made for a specific period, and may be renewed. All but five States Parties to the Convention, Cyprus, France, Greece, Malta, and Turkey, have made such declarations, in most cases for a limited period. All but four (Cyprus, Greece, Malta, and Turkey) have also recognized, under Article 46, the compulsory jurisdiction of the Court.[3]

If an inter-State or individual application is declared admissible by the Commission, the final decision on the question whether there has been a breach of the Convention is taken by the European Court of Human Rights, if the case is referred to it, or else by the Committee of Ministers.

Finally, the Convention also institutes, under the control of the Secretary General of the Council of Europe, an embryonic form of the reporting procedures found in other international human

[1] Article 19.
[2] The Convention also confers certain functions on the Committee of Ministers of the Council of Europe, on the Secretary General and, in the election of members of the Commission and the Court, on the Consultative Assembly.
[3] See *Collected Texts*, 9th ed., 1974, Section 6(b).

rights instruments, notably in the Conventions of the International Labour Organisation, and in the European Social Charter.[1]

Both Article 24 and Article 25 introduced striking innovations by the normal canons of international law. A State bringing an application under Article 24 is not required to prove itself, even indirectly, a victim of the alleged violation of human rights; or even to establish an 'interest' in the proceedings.[2]

The States parties are indeed presumed to have a collective interest in the maintenance of human rights, and the guarantee created by the Convention is a collective guarantee, not based on subjective rights nor on reciprocity. The conditions for bringing an inter-State application are therefore entirely novel by comparison with the classic system of State responsibility, which implies that the plaintiff State is the injured party, even if only through the person of one of its nationals. Under the system of collective guarantee introduced by the Convention, any State party can bring an application under Article 24, without itself or its nationals being victims of the alleged violation.[3] It may do so, for example, purely on humanitarian grounds.

Article 25, in making provision for the direct right of action of the individual before an international organ against his own or another government, was an even greater innovation. Thus, pressure on the United Kingdom Government to recognize the right of individual petition, before its finally did so in 1966, was long resisted on the ground that it would be contrary to the accepted doctrine that States, not individuals, were the proper subjects of international law.[4]

The provisions in the Convention for inter-State and individual applications are broadly similar; the most important differences are in the rules relating to admissibility.[5] It will be noted, also, that a State may refer to the Commission 'any alleged breach' of

[1] Article 57 of the Convention. See generally Khol, *Zwischen Staat und Weltstaat*, Vienna, 1969; and on the International Labour Organization see Landy, *The Effectiveness of International Supervision: Thirty Years of I.L.O. Experience* . . . , London, New York, 1966.

[2] Contrast in this respect the judgment of the International Court of Justice in the South West Africa Case, Second Phase, ICJ Reports 1966, p. 6 at 18 ff. See further on inter-State applications under Article 24 of the Convention Walter, *Die Europäische Menschenrechtsordnung*, Köln, 1970, 48–98.

[3] As happened, for example, in the Greek Case: see below, p. 26.

[4] See *Yearbook* 2, 546; *Yearbook* 3, 610.

[5] See below, p. 222.

the provisions of the Convention, and not only violation of the rights 'set forth'.[1] However, all inter-State applications to date have been concerned with alleged violations of the rights set out in Section I.

More important is the fact that an applicant State can rely on an alleged incompatibility of the respondent State's law or practice in general with the provisions of the Convention; it is not required to adduce evidence of the existence of individual victims.[2]

An individual applicant may also allege that a law is incompatible with the Convention, but he must then go on to show that that law, as applied to him, has violated his rights. In fact individual applications have frequently raised questions of the compatibility with the Convention of major national legislation, e.g. the language laws in Belgium,[3] and the immigration laws in the United Kingdom.[4]

THE EUROPEAN COMMISSION OF HUMAN RIGHTS

The function of the Commission, as of the Court, is 'to ensure the observation of the engagements undertaken' by the States parties to the Convention (Article 19). The formulation is very broad, but the functions of the Commission are limited in several ways.

First, its tasks are exhaustively listed in the subsequent provisions of the Convention. These tasks are, briefly, as follows:

1. To examine the admissibility of applications[5] by individuals (Article 25) or States (Article 24). For reasons which will be considered below, the great majority of applications under Article 25 have been rejected as inadmissible; of some 6,000 applications examined by the end of 1973, only about one hundred had been declared admissible, and this figure includes several groups of cases raising the same issues.

Most applications have been rejected as inadmissible on one of three of the various grounds laid down in the Convention: that the complaint is 'incompatible with the provisions of the

---

[1] See below, p. 233. [2] See below, p. 227.
[3] See below, pp. 170 and 268. [4] See below, p. 33.
[5] The term 'application' is generally used rather than the term 'petition' found in Article 25 since the latter term implies a relationship of seeking an *ex gratia* remedy rather than one of legal rights and obligations. An application under Article 25 initiates as of right proceedings under international law.

Convention',[1] in particular that the right invoked is not among those guaranteed by the Convention; that domestic remedies have not been exhausted,[2] i.e. that the complaint has not been brought before the national authorities, if necessary to the highest instance; or that the complaint is 'manifestly ill-founded'.[3] The conditions of admissibility are discussed in Part IV. Often, before deciding on admissibility, the Commission obtains the observations of the respondent Government, and the observations of the applicant in reply. This procedure, which may be quite full in complex cases, is also examined in Part IV.

2. Where the Commissions finds an application admissible, it is required by Article 28 to establish the facts of the case and, at the same time, to place itself at the disposal of the parties with a view to securing a 'friendly settlement' of the case. If a settlement is reached, that is the end of the case.

3. If no settlement is reached, the Commission draws up a report on the facts and states its opinion as to whether there has been a breach of the Convention (Article 31). The final decision whether there has been a breach is then taken by the Committee of Ministers, or, if the case is referred to it, by the European Court of Human Rights. The Commission also has certain functions in proceedings before the Court (below, p. 264).

Thus, the Commission cannot examine a situation *ex officio* but can act only if an application is made by a State party under Article 24; or under Article 25, at the instance of a 'person, non-governmental organisation, or group of individuals' claiming to be the victim of a violation of the rights guaranteed. On the other hand, once a complaint has been brought before it, the Commission has the power, and indeed the duty under Article 19, to examine *ex officio* whether the complaint raises issues under the Convention other than those indicated by the applicant.[4]

DECISION OF THE EUROPEAN COURT OF HUMAN RIGHTS OR THE COMMITTEE OF MINISTERS OF THE COUNCIL OF EUROPE

The final decision on a case which has been declared admissible by the Commission, and which has not resulted in a friendly settlement, is taken either by the European Court of Human

---

[1] Article 27(2).   [2] Articles 26 and 27(3).   [3] Article 27(2).
[4] Neumeister case, 'Judgment of the Court', p. 41; *Yearbook* 11, 822–4.

Rights or by the Committee of Ministers. The Commission's report, which is transmitted to the Committee of Ministers, contains only its 'opinion' as to whether there has been a violation, and is not legally binding. Within three months of the transmission of the report to the Committee of Ministers, the case may be referred to the Court. It may be referred by the Commission or by the respondent State, or by a State whose national is alleged to be a victim.[1] In an inter-State case, it may also be referred by the applicant State,[2] but, in an individual application under Article 25 of the Convention, the individual applicant has no power to refer the case to the Court. If the case is referred to the Court, a new stage in the procedure opens, when the Commission, and the States concerned, are represented, but the individual applicant has no *locus standi*.[3] The judgment of the Court is final and binding, and its pronouncements on the interpretation of the Convention have greater authority than interpretations contained in the opinions of the Commission, and will normally be followed by the Commission.

If a case is not referred within three months to the Court, the final decision is taken by the Committee of Ministers, which normally endorses the Commission's opinion without any fresh investigation of the merits of the case.[4]

GENERAL SCOPE OF THE CONVENTION

Article 1 provides that 'The High Contracting Parties shall secure to everyone within their jurisdiction the rights and freedoms defined in Section I of this Convention.'

Section I of the Convention contains, in Articles 2 to 18, a list of the rights and freedoms guaranteed, similar to and indeed partly modelled on the Universal Declaration of Human Rights. The whole of Section I, however, does not in terms impose any obligations on States; it takes the form of a declaration of rights. It is Article 1 which transforms this declaration of the rights of individuals into a set of obligations for the States which ratify the Convention.

Writers have differed on the nature of the guarantee. Some have argued that there is an obligation to incorporate the actual

---

[1] Article 48. [2] Ibid.
[3] See below, p. 264. [4] See below, p. 268.

9

text of the Convention, or of Section I at least, into domestic law.[1] There is no dispute, however, that domestic law must give full effect to the rights guaranteed by the Convention; and the Contracting States have in fact chosen to implement its guarantees by different methods, according to their own constitutional practices.[2] Thus the Convention has the status of domestic law in Germany and of constitutional law in Austria. In France the Convention has an intermediate status, higher than ordinary legislation but lower than the Constitution. In the United Kingdom it has not been enacted as such and therefore does not have the force of law.

The question by what means the rights are implemented may in the end be a matter of legal technique; though certainly some techniques may be more effective than others. The protection of the individual is plainly more effective if the substantive rights guaranteed by the Convention can be enforced by the national courts.[3] Where the rights are not expressly enacted in domestic law, or cannot be invoked before the domestic courts, there is no alternative to the European procedure.

Whether or not they incorporate the actual text of the Convention into domestic law, States are obliged, by appropriate means, 'to ensure that their domestic legislation is compatible with the Convention and, if need be, to make any necessary adjustments to this end'.[4] Further, the terms of Article 57 show that domestic law must be such as to 'ensure the effective implementation' of all the provisions of the Convention.

This does not, however, exhaust the effect of Article 1. States are liable for violations of the Convention which may result not only from legislation incompatible with it, but also from acts of all public authorities, at every level, including the executive and

[1] See Golsong, 'Die europäische Konvention zum Schutze der Menschenrechte und Grundfreiheiten', *Jahrbuch des öffentlichen Rechts*, Bd. 10, 1961, pp. 123–57, and Buergenthal, 'The effect of the European Convention on Human Rights on the internal law of member States', in *The European Convention on Human Rights*, British Institute of International and Comparative Law Supplementary Publication No. 11, 1965, 57 f., and for the opposite view Partsch, *Die Rechte und Freiheiten der europäischen Menschenrechtskonvention*, Berlin, 1966, 272 f., and Sørensen, *Human Rights in National and International Law*, ed. Robertson, Manchester, 1968, at pp. 11–31.

[2] See Buergenthal, pp. 79–106.

[3] See below, p. 215.

[4] De Becker, *Yearbook*, 2, 234.

the courts. The double aspect of Article 1, requiring States to implement the Convention, on the one hand, and not to infringe it, on the other, explains their obligation to 'secure' the rights guaranteed to everyone 'within their jurisdiction'. Clearly these words do not mean that States are not liable for violations committed by them outside their territory; such an interpretation would be manifestly unreasonable, and would misconstrue the function of Article 1. A State must be responsible for its own violations of the Convention, wherever they are committed; but it can be responsible for securing human rights in the sense of implementing them by the necessary legislation, only within its jurisdiction.

A difficult question is how far a State is responsible for violations of the rights guaranteed by the Convention, committed within its territory by private persons. Where Section I of the Convention is enacted as part of domestic law, or can be invoked before the domestic courts, a limited effect on third parties[1] may be allowed, since Section I does not itself confine liability to the State. On the European level, however, the Commission can only deal, under Article 25, with an application by an individual claiming to be a victim of a violation by one of the Contracting Parties. If the violation is by a private individual, therefore, a State may have fulfilled its obligations if its law adequately protects the rights guaranteed and provides for an effective remedy in the event of such violation.[2]

The precise extent to which a State may be liable for the conduct of a private individual must ultimately depend on the terms of the individual Articles of the Convention, and must be examined separately in relation to each of the rights guaranteed. We shall thus consider below, for example, how far the conduct of a lawyer may involve the responsibility of the State in relation to its duty to provide a fair trial;[3] how far the State is liable, in

[1] See for this effect on third parties (Drittwirkung) in national law, as well as on the European level, Eissen, 'La Convention et les devoirs de l'individu' in *La protection internationale des Droits de l'Homme dans le cadre européen*, Paris, 1961, 167; id., 'The European Convention on Human Rights and the duties of the individual' in *Acta Scandinavica Juris Gentium*, 1962, 230; id., 'La Convention européenne des Droits de l'Homme et les obligations de l'individu: une mise à jour', in René Cassin, *Amicorum Discipulorumque Liber* III, Paris 1971, 151.

[2] See below, p. 227.   [3] See below, p. 101.

relation to trade union freedoms, for the acts of private employers;[1] and how far the rights relating to education are guaranteed where children are educated at private schools.[2]

What is clear is that the State must provide for a remedy for any violation, whether committed by it or by a private individual. For Article 13, by providing in effect that it should not be a defence that the violation was committed by a person acting in an official capacity, presupposes that it cannot be a defence that it was committed by a private individual.[3]

TEMPORAL SCOPE

'Under a generally recognised rule of international law, the Convention only governs for each Contracting Party those facts which are subsequent to the date of its entry into force with regard to the Party in question.'[4] The Convention, therefore, can have no retroactive effect.

The Convention entered into force, in accordance with Article 66(2), after ratification by ten States; this figure was achieved on 3 September 1953. The First Protocol entered into force on 18 May 1954, and the Fourth Protocol on 2 May 1968. For any State ratifying the Convention and Protocols after these dates, they enter into force on the date of ratification.[5] An application cannot relate back to an event earlier than the entry into force of the instrument in question in respect of the State against which the application is brought, unless that event has consequences which may raise the question of a continuing violation.[6]

On the other hand, the acceptance of the competence of the Commission, under Article 25, to deal with individual applications, has in principle a retroactive effect. So if an alleged violation is subsequent to the entry into force of the Convention in respect of the State concerned, but prior to its declaration under Article 25, the Commission will be competent *ratione temporis*.[7] Similar considerations apply to declarations accepting the compulsory jurisdiction of the Court.[8]

Acceptance of the Commission's competence under Article 24

---

[1] See below, p. 227.   [2] See below, p. 175.
[3] See below, p. 216.   [4] 343/57, *Yearbook* 2, 412 at 454.
[5] See Article 66(3) of the Convention, Article 6 of the First Protocol and Article 7(1) of the Fourth Protocol.
[6] See below, p. 243.   [7] See below, p. 230.   [8] See below, p. 262.

to deal with inter-State cases is not optional, but follows automatically from acceptance of the Convention. If the respondent State had ratified the Convention, it does not matter that the applicant State was at the date of the event in issue not itself a Party to the Convention.

The point was illustrated in the Pfunders case, brought by Austria against Italy. Six young men had been convicted of murdering an Italian customs officer in the German-speaking part of South Tyrol, an area which was the subject of a long-standing dispute between the two countries. The Austrian Government alleged that the criminal proceedings in the Italian courts were not compatible with the provisions of Article 6 of the Convention, which lays down rules concerning the proper administration of justice and the protection of the rights of persons charged with criminal offences. The Italian Government objected that the Commission was not competent *ratione temporis* to deal with the case, since although Italy was a party to the Convention at the date of the proceedings in question, Austria had not ratified the Convention at that time.

The Commission, in rejecting this objection, found it inconsistent with the fundamental character of the Convention. The Human Rights Convention is not based, as are most other treaties, on reciprocity, and does not involve a mutual exchange of rights and obligations by the Contracting Parties. Its object is to set up an independent legal order for the protection of individuals.

Relying, in particular, on the wording of the Preamble, the Commission stated that 'the purpose of the High Contracting Parties in concluding the Convention was not to concede to each other reciprocal rights and obligations in pursuance of their individual national interests but to realize the aims and ideals of the Council of Europe, as expressed in its Statute, and to establish a common public order of the free democracies of Europe with the object of safeguarding their common heritage of political traditions, ideals, freedom and the rule of law.'[1]

Hence 'the obligations undertaken by the High Contracting Parties in the Convention are essentially of an objective character, being designed rather to protect the fundamental rights of individual human beings from infringement by any of the High Con-

[1] 788/60, *Yearbook* 4, 116 at 138.

tracting Parties than to create subjective and reciprocal rights for the High Contracting Parties themselves.'[1]

TERRITORIAL SCOPE

Although, under Article 1, the Contracting States guarantee the rights and freedoms defined in Section I to everyone within their jurisdiction, this guarantee may be subject to certain territorial limits.[2] This follows from the so-called 'colonial' clause in Article 63, which provides that a State may, by means of a declaration, extend the Convention to all or any of the territories for whose international relations it is responsible. But for this Article, it would have been clear that the Convention extended, by the mere act of ratification, to all such territories. It has already been shown that the wording of Article 1 does not introduce any territorial limitation to the Convention. It is introduced, therefore, only by implication in Article 63, which runs counter to the whole scheme of the Convention, and which can be explained by historical circumstances of little relevance today.[3]

Thus it is quite clear that the State may be responsible for the acts of its officials abroad. It is responsible, for example, for the acts of its diplomatic and consular representatives. In one case, the Commission accepted that the acts of the German consul in Morocco could make the Federal Republic liable under the Convention.[4] It justified its decision on the narrow ground that the nationals of a State are, in certain respects, still within its jurisdiction, even when domiciled or resident abroad. The decision is certainly correct, but the reasoning is not satisfactory. No distinction should be made between nationals and others; it could not seriously be maintained that a State is liable under the Convention for the acts of its diplomatic and consular officials abroad towards its nationals, but not towards aliens. As we have seen, the significance of the expression 'within their jurisdiction' in Article 1 is quite different. It does not mean that a State is liable only for violations committed within its territory, or outside its territory if committed against its nationals. Such an interpretation would be

[1] At 140.
[2] 1065/61, *Yearbook* 4, 260 at 268, see below, p. 232 and cf. p. 186.
[3] See Robertson, *Human Rights in Europe*, p. 109, and below, p. 232.
[4] 1611/62, *Yearbook* 8, 158 at 168.

contrary to the whole system of the Convention. Subject to Article 63, the State is responsible for breaches of the Convention wherever they are committed.

Under Article 63, the United Kingdom has extended the Convention to a number of dependent overseas territories, and the Netherlands has extended it to Surinam and the Netherlands Antilles.[1]

When such territories become independent, the declaration automatically lapses, and it is unnecessary to denounce the Convention in respect of the territory concerned under Article 65(4). On independence, of course, the State which has made the declaration ceases to be responsible for the international relations of the new State; and there can be no question of the new State remaining a party to the Convention by the law of State succession, since the Convention is confined, by Article 66(1), to Members of the Council of Europe.[2]

A declaration under Article 63 may also lapse for a different reason. The Convention was extended by Denmark to Greenland, for whose international relations it was responsible at the time; but subsequently, in 1953, Greenland became part of metropolitan Denmark, so that the Convention automatically applied to Greenland irrespective of the declaration.

PRINCIPLES OF INTERPRETATION

When considering the general scope of the Convention, it is appropriate to discuss the principles which should be applied in interpreting its provisions. This problem, although it has been the subject of *obiter dicta* by the Commission and the Court, has rarely been examined in any depth. The most systematic approach is to be found in the Commission's report on the Golder case, which raised a difficult and fundamental question of interpretation on whether the Convention guarantees the right of access to the courts.[3]

A preliminary issue on the interpretation of the Convention is how far the general rules of treaty interpretation, as expressed

[1] See *Collected Texts*, 9th edn., section 6(c).
[2] See Eissen, 'The Independence of Malta and the European Convention on Human Rights', *British Year Book of International Law* (1965–6), p. 401, and 'Malawi and the European Convention on Human Rights', *British Year Book* (1968–9), p. 190.
[3] See below, p. 90.

most authoritatively in the Vienna Convention on the Law of Treaties,[1] are applicable to the European Convention on Human Rights. The relevant provisions of the Vienna Convention are sufficiently general to give some guidance but must be applied with caution in view of the special features of the European Convention.

Thus, the European Convention being equally authentic in the English and in the French text, where these texts differ the mean-

[1] Articles 31–3:

SECTION 3. INTERPRETATION OF TREATIES

Article 31

General rule of interpretation

1. A treaty shall be interpreted in good faith in accordance with the ordinary meaning to be given to the terms of the treaty in their context and in the light of its object and purpose.
2. The context for the purpose of the interpretation of a treaty shall comprise, in addition to the text, including its preamble and annexes:
   (*a*) any agreement relating to the treaty which was made between all the parties in connexion with the conclusion of the treaty;
   (*b*) any instrument which was made by one or more parties in connexion with the conclusion of the treaty and accepted by the other parties as an instrument related to the treaty.
3. There shall be taken into account, together with the context:
   (*a*) any subsequent agreement between the parties regarding the interpretation of the treaty or the application of its provisions;
   (*b*) any subsequent practice in the application of the treaty which establishes the agreement of the parties regarding its interpretation;
   (*c*) any relevant rules of international law applicable in the relations between the parties.
4. A special meaning shall be given to a term if it is established that the parties so intended.

Article 32

Supplementary means of interpretation

Recourse may be had to supplementary means of interpretation, including the preparatory work of the treaty and the circumstances of its conclusion, in order to confirm the meaning resulting from the application of article 31, or to determine the meaning when the interpretation according to article 31:
   (*a*) leaves the meaning ambiguous or obscure; or
   (*b*) leads to a result which is manifestly absurd or unreasonable.

Article 33

Interpretation of treaties authenticated in two or more languages

1. When a treaty has been authenticated in two or more languages, the text is equally authoritative in each language, unless the treaty provides or the parties agree that, in case of divergence, a particular text shall prevail.
2. A version of the treaty in a language other than one of those in which the text was authenticated shall be considered an authentic text only if the treaty so provides or the parties so agree.

ing which best reconciles the texts, having regard to the object and purpose of the treaty, must be adopted.[1]

The Commission's report on the Golder case suggests that account should be taken of two features, in particular, of the European Convention when a question of interpretation arises. First, it provides for a system of international adjudication, while the general rules of treaty interpretation have evolved primarily as guides to interpretation by the parties themselves.[2] Hence, as indicated in the passage from the Pfunders case cited above,[3] its provisions should be interpreted objectively; for '. . . the obligations undertaken by the High Contracting Parties in the Convention are essentially of an objective character, being designed rather to protect the fundamental rights of individual human beings from infringement by any of the High Contracting Parties than to create subjective and reciprocal rights for the High Contracting Parties themselves'.

Secondly, any general presumption that treaty obligations should be interpreted restrictively since they derogate from the sovereignty of States is not applicable to the Human Rights Convention. This follows indeed from the last words of Article 31(1) of the Vienna Convention which provides that 'A treaty shall be interpreted in good faith in accordance with the ordinary meaning to be given to the terms of the treaty in their context and *in the light of its object and purpose.*' Thus the Court of Human Rights stated in the Wemhoff case that it was necessary 'to seek the interpretation that is most appropriate in order to realise the aim and achieve the object of the treaty, not that which would restrict to the greatest possible degree the obligations undertaken by the Parties'.[4]

---

3. The terms of the treaty are presumed to have the same meaning in each authentic text.

4. Except where a particular text prevails in accordance with paragraph 1, when a comparison of the authentic texts discloses a difference of meaning which the application of articles 31 and 32 does not remove, the meaning which best reconciles the texts, having regard to the object and purpose of the treaty, shall be adopted.

[1] Article 33(4) of the Vienna Convention; cf. Wemhoff case, 'Judgment of the Court', paras. 7 and 8; *Yearbook* 11, 796 at 800–2.

[2] See Jacobs, *The International and Comparative Law Quarterly*, 1969, 318 at 341–3.

[3] See above, p. 13.

[4] 'Judgment of the Court', para. 8.

These two features of the European Convention suggest that a further conclusion may be drawn as to the appropriate principles of interpretation: that the interpretation of the Convention must be 'dynamic' in the sense that it must be interpreted in the light of developments in social and political attitudes. Its effects cannot be confined to the conceptions of the period when it was drafted or entered into force. Thus the concept of degrading treatment, in Article 3, may be interpreted to include racial discrimination, even though this might not have entered the minds of the drafters of the Convention;[1] and the protection of privacy under Article 8 must be developed to meet new technological developments which were not envisaged twenty-five years ago.[2] Many other examples will be met in subsequent chapters: changes in the concept of the family, of education, of forced labour, or of trade union freedom. It cannot be objected that this approach to interpretation extends the obligations of the Contracting States beyond their intended undertakings. On the contrary, this approach is necessary if effect is to be given to their intentions, in a general sense. They did not intend solely to protect the individual against the threats to human rights which were then prevalent, with the result that, as the nature of the threats changed, the protection gradually fell away. Their intention was to protect the individual against the threats of the future, as well as the threats of the past.

It follows that even more caution is necessary than usual in relying on the preparatory work of the Convention.[3] Preparatory work is notoriously unreliable as a general guide to treaty interpretation, and is hence treated only as a supplementary means of interpretation in Article 32 of the Vienna Convention. But because of the special features of the European Convention, it should be invoked, if at all, as a guide to the general intentions of the Parties, as indicated above, rather than to delimit strictly the scope of the Articles. This, too, is in accordance with the real purpose of the Convention.

The preparatory work was legitimately invoked by the Commission to show that the provision that 'Everyone shall be free to leave any country, including his own', does not entitle a convicted

---

[1] See below, p. 36.

[2] See below, p. 126. Cf. the Belgian Linguistic Case, 'Judgment of the Court', p. 32; *Yearbook* 11, 832 at 860.

[3] Cf. the Report of the Commission in the Golder case, para. 46.

prisoner to leave the country in which he is lawfully detained.[1] The contrary interpretation would lead, in the words of Article 32 of the Vienna Convention, to a result which is manifestly absurd or unreasonable. On the other hand, in the Lawless case, the Court refused to resort to the preparatory work to interpret a provision which was sufficiently clear.[2]

Because of the limited value of the preparatory work, little account is given of it in this book. Nor is much attention paid to the provisions of national constitutions or of other international instruments which, although they may be of similar purport, are differently worded and must be construed in a different context. It may of course be valuable to refer to such instruments in certain cases: for example, to refer to the relevant Conventions of the International Labour Organisation, as the Commission has done, when interpreting Article 11 of the Convention on the same matters. This may be necessary to avoid inconsistent interpretations of similar guarantees by different international institutions. In the future, efforts will also be necessary to avoid divergent interpretations of the United Nations Covenants and regional arrangements for the protection of human rights.[3] Here, as in the application of the European Convention in those European States where it has the force of law, the work of the European Commission and Court may provide some guidance.

On the other hand, the standards adopted for interpreting the European Convention may sometimes differ from those applicable to other international instruments. This is because the interpretation of the European Convention may legitimately be based on a common tradition of constitutional law and a large measure of legal tradition common to the Member States of the Council of Europe.[4] Thus the Commission has relied as a guide to the scope of the rights guaranteed by the Convention, on comparative surveys of the laws of the Member States: the laws relating to vagrancy,[5] for example, or legislation on the right to respect for family

[1] See below, p. 184.

[2] Lawless case, para. 14 of 'The Law', *Yearbook* 4, 430 at 466.

[3] Cf. below, p. 276.

[4] Cf. Scheuner, 'Comparison of the jurisprudence of national courts with that of the organs of the Convention . . .', in *Human Rights in National and International Law*, ed. Robertson, Manchester, 1968, 214 at 220 f.

[5] See Appendix IV to the Commission's Report on the Vagrancy cases, 'Outline of Vagrancy legislation in force in European countries'.

life,[1] or on various aspects of criminal procedure.[2] Again, to decide what is 'reasonable' or what is 'necessary'—two terms which occur frequently in the Convention—or what constitutes 'normal' civic obligations,[3] reference may be made to the general practice of the Member States of the Council of Europe. There may thus be a conflict between two legitimate aims of interpretation: to avoid inconsistencies with other international instruments, and to develop the protection of human rights in Europe on the basis of a common European law.

[1] See below, p. 138.   [2] See below, p. 112.   [3] See below, p. 44.

PART II: RIGHTS

ARTICLE 2

The right to life

The opening words of Article 2(1) provide that 'Everyone's right to life shall be protected by law.'

The right to life is in an obvious sense fundamental. Its scope, however, is uncertain in respect of laws permitting for example, certain forms of abortion and euthanasia. Neither the Court nor the Commission has had occasion to determine at what point, for the purposes of Article 2, human life begins or ends.

It would have been more consistent with the general pattern of the Convention if Article 2(1) had opened with the words 'Everyone has the right to life,' following Article 3 of the Universal Declaration. The requirement in Article 2 of the Convention that 'Everyone's right to life shall be protected by law' carries a different emphasis, but does not seem to affect the substance of the rights guaranteed under the Convention. Articles 1 and 13 show that the obligations of the authorities in any event include the duty to provide legal guarantees against violations by others, as well as the duty to respect the rights themselves.[1] But the terms of Article 2 directly put in issue legislation which may not sufficiently protect the right to life.

Under the Convention, however, such legislation cannot be challenged in an application brought under Article 25 unless the applicant can show a sufficient interest.[2] An early application was directed against a Norwegian law which provided for the interruption of pregnancy under certain conditions.[3] The applicant asked the Commission to decide, first, whether the 'right to beget offspring is an inalienable human right or if not, under what conditions and circumstances this right might be forfeited'; and secondly, 'whether human rights are fully applicable to the human embryo from the time of conception,[4] or if not, at what stages in the development of the human individual' these rights arise.

[1] See above, p. 11.   [2] See below, p. 229.   [3] 867/60, *Yearbook* 4, 270.
[4] See the Interamerican and Central American Conventions, Article 2. Cf. the American Convention on Human Rights, Article 4.1.

The Commission was unable to examine the extremely pertinent questions raised by the applicant, as he had not claimed to be a victim of the law in question. It held that it was not competent, in such an application, to examine in the abstract the conformity of this law with the Convention.

This does not mean, of course, that the Commission is never competent to question the conformity of national legislation with the Convention. On the contrary, in a case where the applicant could claim to be a 'victim' as required by Article 25,[1] or in an inter-State application under Article 24,[2] this would have been directly in issue before it. The Commission's decision should be taken to mean only that an application under Article 25 is not admissible unless the applicant satisfies the condition that he claims to be the victim of a violation.

In societies which are increasingly conscious of the problems of over-population, other forms of birth control may also raise problems under Article 2, as well as under Article 12[3] of the Convention. These problems have not yet been ventilated before the Commission; it has, however, stated in an unpublished decision[4] that an operation for sterilization might, in certain circumstances, involve a breach of Article 2.

The legalization of euthanasia, which would seem *prima facie* contrary to the express terms of the first sentence of Article 2 as well as falling outside the exceptions permitted by that Article, might raise the difficult question how far the consent of a victim may negate what would otherwise be a violation of the Convention. In principle, it would seem that the fundamental character of the rights guaranteed by the Convention, and the element of public interest, would exclude the possiblity of any form of waiver of those rights.[5]

Provision for the death penalty is expressly reserved in the second sentence of Article 2(1), which provides that 'No one shall be deprived of his life intentionally save in the execution of a sentence of a court following his conviction of a crime for which this penalty is provided by law.' In practice, capital punishment, at least in peace time, has almost disappeared among the Contracting States. With the progress of penal reform there can be no

[1] See below, p. 228. [2] See below, p. 233.
[3] See below, p. 164. [4] 1287/61.
[5] See below, pp. 44, 57.

doubt that the death penalty, in certain forms or in certain cases, might amount to 'inhuman or degrading . . . punishment' contrary to Article 3. The express reservation for the death penalty in Article 2(1) cannot be interpreted as permitting any form of death penalty for any offence. Otherwise the absurd consequence would follow that punishment could be contrary to Article 3 only if it did not involve the ultimate penalty.

This argument is of general importance in construing the relations between different articles of the Convention. The fact that the death penalty is expressly preserved by Article 2 does not mean that capital punishment may not in certain circumstances be contrary to Article 3. But it does show that the death penalty *as such* is not prohibited by Article 3.

The relation between Articles 2 and 3 is similar to that between Articles 4 and 9. The wording of Article 4 shows that States are not obliged under the Convention to recognize objections to compulsory military service on grounds of conscience. Consequently, Article 9, which protects the right to freedom of thought, conscience and religion, cannot be interpreted as giving an absolute right of conscientious objection. The refusal to recognize conscientious objectors might, however, in certain circumstances infringe Article 9, or that Article taken together with Article 14.[1] The same reasoning applies to Articles 2 and 3. It cannot be inferred, from the mere fact that Article 2 allows for the death penalty, that such a penalty cannot in any circumstances be contrary to Article 3. The conclusion, therefore, must be that while the death penalty as such is not contrary to the Convention, it may well be so in particular cases the scope of which cannot be determined in advance.

Among the factors to be considered, in deciding whether the death penalty, in particular circumstances, was contrary to Article 3, would be whether it was disproportionate to the offence, and the form and circumstances of the execution. Thus, even if a capital sentence were not considered disproportionate to the offence in a particular case, a degrading form of execution, such as execution in public, might be contrary to Article 3.

Article 2(2) provides that deprivation of life shall not be regarded as inflicted in contravention of this Article when it

---

[1] See below, p. 144.

results from the use of force which is no more than absolutely necessary:

(a) in defence of any person from unlawful violence;

(b) in order to effect a lawful arrest or to prevent the escape of a person lawfully detained;

(c) in action lawfully taken for the purpose of quelling a riot or insurrection.

In a case where a woman complained that her husband had died from a shot fired by a policeman in the course of disturbances, the Commission found that, even if the shot was fired by a policeman, there was no reason to suppose that the killing had been intentional; the Commission appears to have considered that it was therefore unnecessary to examine whether the killing might have been lawful under Article 2(2) (c).[1] Nor did it rely on Article 2(2) (a), although it followed the finding of the Belgian court that the policeman 'must be considered to have acted in lawful self-defence'. To rely on either of these provisions, of course, the Commission would have had to find that the force used was 'absolutely necessary'.

This reasoning is not satisfactory; it adopts altogether too narrow an interpretation of Article 2. The Commission appears to have assumed that the entire content of the obligation contained in the first sentence is exhausted by the second sentence, i.e. that 'Everyone's right to life shall be protected by law' means only that 'No one shall be deprived of his life intentionally'.

The purpose of the second sentence of Article 2(1), however, is not to state exhaustively the content of the right to life.[2] Its purpose is to provide for a particular application of the general principle and to allow for a limited exception, namely the death penalty. It is clear from the wording of Article 2(2) that the Article is not limited to cases of intentional killing. The language of Article 2(2), which refers to deprivation of life that 'results from' the use of force in specified circumstances, is the same as in Article 15, which refers to deaths resulting from lawful acts of war, and could not be more clearly intended to cover deaths caused inadvertently. It makes no sense, therefore, to exclude the application of this provision on the ground that the killing was not intentional.

[1] 2758/66, *Yearbook* 12, 174.

[2] Compare the similar structure of Article 1 of the First Protocol, below, p. 165.

24

The effect of Article 2 is thus to protect the individual against any intentional taking of life, with the sole exception of the death penalty, and also against the unintentional taking of life, with the exceptions specifically listed in Article 2(2).

In the Irish Case,[1] the Irish Government alleged violations of Article 2, among others, referring to deaths said to have been caused in Northern Ireland by the security forces of the United Kingdom Government in 1971 and 1972, including the deaths of thirteen persons in Londonderry on 30 January 1972 ('Bloody Sunday').

The disturbances in Northern Ireland which broke out again in 1969, and threatened the outbreak of full-scale civil war, had led the United Kingdom Government to declare that there was a public emergency in Northern Ireland, and to inform the Secretary-General of the Council of Europe, in accordance with Article 15, of emergency powers which had been brought into operation at various dates, including the power to detain without trial.[2] Article 15 allows the Contracting States, in time of war or other public emergency threatening the life of the nation, to take measures derogating from their obligations under the Convention, but no derogation is permitted from Article 2 except in respect of deaths resulting from lawful acts of war.

The Commission, however, declared inadmissible the allegations under Article 2, holding that it could not deal with them unless and until it were shown, as required by Article 26, that the domestic remedies available under the law of Northern Ireland had been exhausted. It was true that this rule did not apply where the compatibility with the Convention of 'legislative measures and administrative practices' was in issue.[3] The Irish Government had alleged that there was such an administrative practice in the present case, but had not offered substantial evidence. The case thus gives no specific guidance to the interpretation of Article 2 but shows that the Commission will be reluctant, naturally enough, to accept without good reason allegations that a government has *prima facie* been guilty as an administrative practice of violating the right to life.

[1] 5310/71, *Collection of Decisions* 41, 3.
[2] See *Yearbook* 1, 50, *Yearbook* 12, 72–4 and *Yearbook* 14, 32.
[3] See below, p. 237.

ARTICLE 3

Inhuman or degrading treatment or punishment

Article 3 provides that 'No one shall be subjected to torture or to inhuman or degrading treatment or punishment'. That is the extent of the Article; only in this Article are there no qualifications or exceptions, no restrictions to the rights guaranteed. The fundamental character of the Article is shown also by the fact that, in common with Articles 2, 4(1), and 7, no derogation may be made from its provisions under Article 15 even in time of war or public emergency.

While Article 3 must be read as a whole, its individual elements can to some extent be separately analysed. In the Greek Case, more than three hundred pages of the Commission's Report dealt with alleged violations of Article 3 by the Greek Government after the revolution of 21 April 1967.[1] The Commission analysed the meaning of the provisions of Article 3 as follows:[2]

It is plain that there may be treatment to which all these descriptions apply, for all torture must be inhuman and degrading treatment, and inhuman treatment also degrading. The notion of inhuman treatment covers at least such treatment as deliberately causes severe suffering, mental or physical, which, in the particular situation, is unjustifiable. The word 'torture' is often used to describe inhuman treatment, which has a purpose, such as the obtaining of information or confessions, or the infliction of punishment, and it is generally an aggravated form of inhuman treatment. Treatment or punishment of an individual may be said to be degrading if it grossly humiliates him before others or drives him to act against his will or conscience.

The Commission examined allegations of a variety of forms of ill-treatment, the commonest of which was *falanga* or *bastinado*, but which included also electric shocks, mock executions or threats to shoot or kill the victim, and other forms of beating or ill-treatment[3]. Extensive investigations were made by the Sub-Commission in Greece, and many witnesses examined in Athens, Strasbourg, and elsewhere.

The Commission concluded that torture or ill-treatment con-

---

[1] *Yearbook* 12: The Greek Case, 186–510.
[2] At p. 186.
[3] At p. 500. *Falanga* is defined at p. 499.

trary to Article 3 had been inflicted in a number of cases and that there were reasons for considering that these cases were part of a practice of torture or ill-treatment of political detainees in Greece since 21 April 1967.[1]

In reaching its conclusion as to an administrative practice, the Commission had regard to two criteria: the repetition of the acts concerned, and official tolerance of them. The notion of administrative practice has a double significance. First, at the stage of admissibility, the Commission has held that the rule requiring the exhaustion of domestic remedies does not apply where the conduct complained of constitutes an administrative practice.[2] Secondly, on the merits, the finding of an administrative practice, implying official recognition and acceptance of that conduct, is clearly far more serious than isolated instances of such conduct by individual officials.

The Greek Case is a model case for demonstrating both the possibilities and the political limitations of the international protection of human rights. At the first stages of the proceedings the Greek Government co-operated in the examination of the merits of the case, allowing the Sub-Commission, although not without reservations, to visit Greece and to examine witnesses and some of the places where torture was alleged to have been committed. 'This was a historic occasion for those interested in human rights, for there in Greece a body of foreign jurists heard evidence and confronted alleged torturers with their victims.'[3] Subsequently, however, the Greek Government refused access to certain witnesses, and the Sub-Commission left Greece without completing its task.

Again, in the course of negotiations with a view to reaching a friendly settlement of the case under Article 28 of the Convention, the Government signed an agreement with the International Committee of the Red Cross, giving them access to all detention places in Greece. These facilities were withdrawn after the friendly settlement talks had broken down, apparently over the question of a fixed time-table for the holding of elections and the restoration of democracy in Greece.[4]

Shortly after the adoption of the Commission's Report, Greece

---

[1] At p. 501.   [2] See below, p. 237.
[3] *Amnesty International Report on Torture*, 1973, p. 91.
[4] See below, p. 269.

felt obliged to withdraw from the Council of Europe and to denounce the Convention.[1]

The Commission's analysis of Article 3 quoted above is at first sight questionable in referring to treatment 'which, in the particular situation, is unjustifiable'. It may be doubted whether inhuman treatment is a relative notion, dependent on the circumstances of the case, and whether inhuman treatment could ever be 'justifiable'. This, however, would be to look at the question from the wrong angle. Torture and inhuman treatment are never justifiable, and the definition is misleading if it suggests that they may be. But treatment which may be perfectly justifiable in some circumstances may, in different circumstances, be unlawful. The clearest case is of criminal punishment. A penalty which might be justified for a serious crime could constitute inhuman treatment or punishment if imposed for a petty offence. To this extent at least inhuman treatment is a relative notion.[2]

In the Irish Case, the Commission declared admissible the Irish Government's allegations that persons in custody in Northern Ireland had been subjected to treatment which constituted torture and inhuman and degrading treatment and punishment within the meaning of Article 3 of the Convention and that such treatment constituted an administrative practice. The Commission had regard, in particular, to the techniques for interrogating detained persons, consisting of covering their heads with hoods, obliging them to stand for long periods against a wall, subjecting them to intense noise, depriving them of sleep, and feeding them on a diet of bread and water.[3]

Quite apart from these two inter-State cases,[4] there have been numerous applications by individuals detained in prison or elsewhere, alleging violations of Article 3. It is possible to group these cases in two main categories, according to whether the allegations are of physical ill-treatment or brutality by prison officers or police officers, or of inadequate conditions of detention, lack of medical treatment, and so forth.

The issue of ill-treatment in the form of brutality has frequently been raised but of their nature these complaints are difficult to

---

[1] See below, p. 269. [2] See below, p. 31.

[3] *Collection of Decisions* 41, 3 at 85–7.

[4] Reference may also be made to the First Cyprus case (*Greece* v. *United Kingdom*), *Yearbook* 2, 174.

substantiate, especially in the absence of independent witnesses. Consequently even where the applicant has exhausted domestic remedies these complaints have often been rejected at the stage of admissibility as being manifestly ill-founded. This is an unsatisfactory feature of the working of the Convention, and there might be good reasons to relax the rigorous conditions of admissibility in some of these cases. On the other hand, the very fact that the applicant, even in prison, normally enjoys regular access to the Commission,[1] when his contact with the outside world may otherwise be severely limited, is a salutary safeguard in itself, and may have contributed over the years to the mitigation of abuses.

In one case that was admitted,[2] the Commission finally reached the opinion that the treatment to which the applicant was submitted did not amount to inhuman or degrading treatment within the meaning of Article 3. The applicant had been severely handled by prison officers and was finally put in a strait jacket. The Commission found that there was no evidence of any substantial physical injury as a result of the incident, and that 'Although not conclusive, this is a strong argument in favour of the opinion that the treatment had not been "inhuman" within the meaning of Article 3.'[3] It also took account of the fact that the strait jacket had been used only because of the applicant's violent behaviour.[4]

In the second category of cases, relating to inadequate conditions of detention, lack of medical treatment, etc., the leading individual application is that of Simon Herold v. Austria. The applicant, who was partly paralysed from poliomyelitis, made a number of serious allegations of inadequate medical treatment while he was detained on remand and complained, *inter alia*, that in the course of his treatment he was detained, although not himself mentally ill, in a closed ward of a psychiatric hospital together with a number of violent lunatics, several of whom died in his presence.[5] These complaints were declared admissible by the Commission but after extensive investigation of the facts, a friendly settlement was reached. The Austrian Federal Minister for Justice issued a directive to the Austrian judicial authorities concerning the accommodation in public hospitals of sick or injured prisoners serving sentences or remanded in custody.

---

[1] See below, p. 141.
[2] *Zeidler-Kornmann* v. *Federal Republic of Germany, Yearbook* 11, p. 1020.
[3] At p. 1026.   [4] At p. 1028.   [5] 4340/69, *Yearbook* 14, 352.

In this instruction the Ministry gives notice to all these authorities that 'care must be taken to ensure that the prisoner serving his sentence or on remand is not indirectly subjected to "inhuman or degrading treatment or punishment" when he is transferred to a hospital, since this is expressly forbidden under Art. 3 of the Convention for the Protection of Human Rights and Fundamental Freedoms. . . . In the view of the Federal Minister for Justice the fact that a convicted prisoner or a prisoner on remand is admitted to a closed ward of a psychiatric hospital or to the corresponding installation in a general hospital, although there are no doubts as to his mental health, might constitute such inhuman or degrading treatment or punishment.'[1]

In other cases, the Commission has held, at the stage of admissibility, that the measures complained of, even if established, were not capable of constituting violations of Article 3. Thus the Commission has rejected as being manifestly ill-founded, on the particular facts, complaints of: detention in solitary confinement;[2] the additional penalty of 'sleeping hard' (*hartes Lager*);[3] the taking of a prisoner, in the course of his trial, through a town in handcuffs and in prison uniform.[4]

It seems doubtful whether the distinctions between treatment and punishment, or even between what is inhuman and what is degrading, can be strictly applied in all these cases.

No rigid distinction, therefore, can be drawn between different forms of ill-treatment, and in particular little significance can be attached to the distinction between 'treatment' and 'punishment'. Punishment implies that an offence has been committed, but treatment which would otherwise be contrary to Article 3 is not permissible simply on that ground. Conversely, what is permissible as 'treatment' cannot go beyond what is lawful as punishment; there can plainly be no special protection for offenders. In any event, while the terms used in Article 3 can to some extent be separately analysed, the Article must be read as a whole and the measures complained of, whatever their description, must be

---

[1] Stock-taking note, DH (73) 3, p. 25.

[2] 2479/66, *Yearbook* 10, 368 at 382; 4203/69, *Yearbook* 13, 836 at 860; 6038/73, *Collection of Decisions* 44, 115.

[3] 1505/62, not published.

[4] 2291/64, *Collection of Decisions* 24, 20 at 31. The Commission found the practice 'undesirable' and it appears that it has since ceased.

assessed in each case to see whether, in the context of the Article, they constitute any of the prohibited forms of treatment.

In each case, as always, the facts must be viewed in the light of the circumstances as a whole. Thus the physical condition of the applicant may make treatment which would otherwise be lawful contrary to Article 3; conversely, the applicant's own conduct may exceptionally legitimize a degree of violence which would otherwise be prohibited.

Again, a penalty disproportionate to the offence may constitute inhuman treatment, even though it might be justified in the case of a more serious crime. On the other hand, Article 3 must also be regarded as setting an absolute limit, based on respect for the human person, to what treatment is permissible, regardless of its label, and regardless also of the victim's own conduct. Article 3 should be considered as imposing an absolute prohibition of certain forms of punishment such as, perhaps, flogging, which are by their very nature inhuman and degrading. Within that limit, all the circumstances of the individual cases are relevant.

The Commission has also examined under Article 3 of the Convention many cases in which the applicant complains of his imminent extradition or expulsion by one of the Parties to the Convention. Article 3(1) of the Fourth Protocol[1] provides that no-one shall be expelled from the territory of the State of which he is a national, and the next following Article prohibits the collective expulsion of aliens, but apart from these provisions there is no restriction on extradition or expulsion as such, and, in contrast to the Universal Declaration of Human Rights,[2] there is no right of asylum under the Convention. However, an issue might arise under Article 3 of the Convention if the applicant were liable to suffer inhuman treatment, for example political persecution, in the country to which he is to be sent.[3]

The Commission has not accepted the argument that, if the applicant is sent to a State not party to the Convention, any action which that State may take is outside its competence. Instead, the Commission has recognized that the act of the sending State, which is a contracting party, may itself violate Article 3 in such

[1] See below, p. 184.

[2] Article 14; American Convention on Human Rights, Article 22.7.

[3] 1465/62, *Yearbook* 5, 256; 1802/62, *Yearbook* 6, 462; 2143/64, *Yearbook* 7, 314; 1611/62, *Yearbook* 8, 158; 1983/63, *Yearbook* 8, 228; 3040/67, *Yearbook* 10, 518; 3110/67, *Yearbook* 11, 494; 3745/68, *Collection of Decisions* 31, 107.

circumstances. Thus, the Commission is not concerned with preventing, by indirect methods, a possible 'violation' of the Convention by a State which is not a party; it is the act of the sending State which is in issue if that act of expulsion, while not as such unlawful, may indirectly infringe the Convention. Similarly, under Article 8, if expulsion will result in the separation of close members of a family, such a measure may be contrary to the Convention, although the sending State would otherwise be at liberty to expel an alien at will.[1] The underlying principle in all these cases is that 'although extradition and the right of asylum are not, as such, among the matters governed by the Convention . . . the Contracting States have nevertheless accepted to restrict the free exercise of their powers under general international law, including the power to control the entry and exit of aliens, to the extent and within the limits of the obligations which they have assumed under the Convention.'[2] As will be seen shortly, similar considerations may apply to the refusal of admission of nationals.

In urgent cases of threatened expulsion, it is the practice of the Commission to contact the respondent Government at once, and often the Government has agreed to postpone the expulsion until the Commission has had the opportunity of considering the admissibility of the application. This practice 'protects the applicant against any precipitate or unconsidered action and warns the Government of a complaint which may later, and then too late, show a violation of the Convention'.[3]

Only one such application has been declared admissible.[4] An officer in the Moroccan Air Force, Lt.-Colonel Amekrane, was convicted by court martial and executed on a charge connected with an attempt to assassinate the King of Morocco in 1972. He had arrived in Gibraltar by helicopter on the day of the attack and had asked for political asylum. The Moroccan authorities requested his extradition and on the next day he was sent back to Morocco in a Moroccan Air Force plane.

The application was introduced against the United Kingdom Government by Lt.-Colonel Amekrane's widow in her own name and in the name of her late husband and of her two children, alleg-

---

[1] See below, p. 129.

[2] 2143/64, *Yearbook* 7, 314 at 328.

[3] 'Stock-taking note' (see bibliography), 51; cf. 'Case-law Topics', No. 3, 20–1. On interim measures, see below, p. 222.

[4] 5961/72, *Collection of Decisions* 44, 101.

ing violations of Articles 3, 5(4) and 8. The case was concluded by a friendly settlement, the Government agreeing to pay the applicants an *ex gratia* sum of £37,500.[1]

Although only one such application has been admitted, it is possible to derive from the Commission's decisions some indication of the circumstances in which expulsion may constitute a violation of Article 3. It may do so, of course, where it leads to the gross violation or entire suppression of the applicant's basic human rights.[2] It may do so, also, where it leads to treatment contrary to Article 3 itself, or contrary to other fundamental Articles of the Convention, such as Article 4.[3] Or it may do so where it exposes the person expelled to persecution or discriminatory treatment, by reason of his political opinion, his religion, or his race.[4] Thus the nucleus, but the nucleus only, of a right of asylum may be constructed out of Article 3.

Degrading treatment

The question of the meaning of 'degrading treatment' as a separate concept in Article 3 arose for the first time in one of the most important cases to be heard by the Commission. The background of this case,[5] concerning the immigration of East African Asians to the United Kingdom, must be briefly described.

Before the Commonwealth Immigrants Act 1962, there was no restriction on the entry of Commonwealth citizens to the United Kingdom. Commonwealth citizens comprised on the one hand citizens of the independent Commonwealth countries, who had their own citizenship, and on the other hand citizens of the United Kingdom and Colonies; there was, of course, no separate citizenship for the overseas territories of the United Kingdom which had not yet reached independence. Normally, on independence, the residents of the new State acquired the new citizenship.

In the course of the independence arrangements made for Kenya and Uganda in the early 1960s, however, many of the Asian population retained their British passports and did not acquire the citizenship of the newly independent States. There is some evidence, although it is much disputed, that the United Kingdom Govern-

[1] Council of Europe Press communiqué C(74) 29.
[2] 1802/62, *Yearbook* 6, 463; 3040/67, *Collection of Decisions* 22, 136.
[3] 4314/69, *Collection of Decisions* 32, 96.
[4] 4162/69, *Collection of Decisions* 32, 87 at 95.
[5] *Yearbook* 13, 928. See also 5302/71, *Collection of Decisions* 44, 29.

ment accepted that, in retaining their British passports, they would retain the right to enter the United Kingdom. Most of them had lost that right under the Commonwealth Immigrants Act 1962, but could obtain a new passport after independence which enabled them to enter the United Kingdom without restriction.

Africanization policies introduced by the East African Governments, especially in Kenya and Uganda, resulted in a considerable increase in immigration to the United Kingdom from 1965 onwards, as non-citizens of those countries lost their jobs and their livelihood, and this in turn produced pressures to limit this immigration. These pressures themselves increased the rate of immigration as potential immigrants sought to anticipate the impending ban. Finally, in great haste, the Commonwealth Immigrants Act 1968 was enacted, which effectively deprived the East African Asians of their right to enter the United Kingdom. Broadly speaking, under the 1968 Act, a person retained the right to enter the United Kingdom only if he, or one of his parents or grandparents, had been born in the United Kingdom or had otherwise acquired his citizenship there.

The result of the 1968 Act, whether intended or not, was that the vast majority of the East African Asians who, more especially as the Africanization policy was developed in 1969 and 1970, sought desperately to enter the United Kingdom were precluded from doing so, while the white settler in Kenya, for example, if he had a sufficient connection with the United Kingdom, could continue to enter at will.

In the first group of twenty-five cases to reach the Commission, early in 1970, the applicants had all been initially refused admission to the United Kingdom. They were subsequently, and in most cases after a period of detention, admitted for a limited period. They complained, *inter alia*, of violations of Article 3 of the Convention.

The Fourth Protocol, which provides that no one shall be deprived of the right to enter the territory of the State of which he is a national, has not been ratified by the United Kingdom. The applicants could not therefore rely on any provision directly guaranteeing the right of entry. Equally, their complaint that the immigration law discriminated against them could not be examined under Article 14, since that Article prohibits discrimination only in the enjoyment of the other rights and freedoms guaranteed,

34

which in the case of the United Kingdom did not include the right of entry.

The Commission nevertheless declared the applications admissible under Article 3, holding that 'quite apart from any consideration of Article 14, discrimination based on race could, in certain circumstances, of itself amount to degrading treatment within the meaning of Article 3 of the Convention'; that 'it is generally recognized that a special importance should be attached to discrimination based on race, and that publicly to single out a group of persons for differential treatment on the basis of race might, in certain circumstances, constitute a special form of affront to human dignity.'

Hence, 'differential treatment of a group of persons on the basis of race might be capable of constituting degrading treatment in circumstances where differential treatment on some other ground, such as language, would raise no such question.'[1]

The United Kingdom Government submitted that it had not intended to exclude its citizens permanently from the United Kingdom, but only to regulate the flow of entry. To implement this policy special vouchers mainly intended for East African Asians had been issued under the 1968 Act which entitled the holder with his family to settle in the United Kingdom. Some 1,500 such special vouchers were issued a year, permitting the entry of 6,000 to 7,000 persons, but in the course of the proceedings before the Commission this figure was doubled, and it was subsequently further increased to 3,500 vouchers.

The East African Governments, while depriving the Asian communities of their livelihood and in some cases making their continued residence in East Africa illegal, had not taken any steps to expel them, which would have placed an obligation on the United Kingdom under general international law to admit them. However, in 1972, the President of Uganda announced the expulsion of United Kingdom passport holders. The United Kingdom then accepted its obligation under international law, and admitted over 25,000 Ugandan Asians for permanent resettlement. It continued to refuse to accept other United Kingdom passport holders from East Africa for immediate entry, although, by the time the proceedings before the Commission ended, a majority of them had been admitted.

[1] *Yearbook* 13, 928 at 994.

The case is of course a complex and highly controversial one. Some of the issues could not be fully considered within the framework of the Convention, such as the degree of responsibility of the East African governments, and the social, economic, and political constraints on British immigration policy which may have come close to a situation of *force majeure*.

Quite apart from the merits of this case, however, the Commission's decision on the interpretation of 'degrading treatment' in Article 3 is important as showing that the Convention is not a static instrument, but must be interpreted in the light of developments in social and political attitudes. Racial discrimination may not have been in the minds of the drafters of Article 3 but can clearly be regarded as degrading treatment by the standards of 1970.

ARTICLE 4

Article 4(1) prohibits slavery and servitude; Article 4(2) prohibits forced or compulsory labour. While the prohibitions of slavery and servitude are absolute (and outside any derogation under Article 15), the prohibition of forced or compulsory labour is subject to the exemption of certain forms of work or service expressly permitted under Article 4(3).

The wording of Article 4(1), 'No one shall be held in slavery or servitude', shows that these are conceived of as questions of status;[1] while the provision of Article 4(2) that 'No one shall be required to perform forced or compulsory labour' is intended to protect persons who are at liberty, and excludes 'any work required to be done in the ordinary course of detention'.

1 Slavery or servitude

'Slavery . . . is in essence the condition of being wholly in the legal ownership of another person, while servitude is . . . broader and . . . can cover conditions of work or service which the individual cannot change or from which he cannot escape.'[2]

2 Forced or compulsory labour

Article 4(2) provides that no one shall be required to perform forced or compulsory labour.

[1] See Fawcett, 43.   [2] Ibid.

Article 4(3), however, provides for certain exceptions; it reads:

For the purpose of this Article the term 'forced or compulsory labour' shall not include:

(a) any work required to be done in the ordinary course of detention imposed according to the provisions of Article 5 of this Convention or during conditional release from such detention;

(b) any service of a military character or, in case of conscientious objectors in countries where they are recognised, service exacted instead of compulsory military service;

(c) any service exacted in case of an emergency or calamity threatening the life or well-being of the community;

(d) any work or service which forms part of normal civic obligations.

The expression 'forced or compulsory labour' is taken over from a Convention of the International Labour Organisation, Convention No 29 of 1930, subsequently supplemented by another I.L.O. Convention, the Abolition of Forced Labour Convention of 1957. It seems reasonable to rely, for the interpretation of Article 4, on the work of the I.L.O. organs in defining the term for the purposes of the I.L.O. Conventions,[1] and the Commission has in fact done so.

The problem was first examined by the Commission in the Iversen case.[2]

A law passed in Norway in 1956 provided that dentists might be required for a period of up to two years to take a position in public dental service. Some members of the Opposition had objected to the Bill on the ground that it introduced a compulsory direction of labour which was contrary to the Norwegian Constitution and to Article 4 of the Convention. The Government, however, rejected these arguments and maintained that this direction of labour was necessary to implement a public dental service. The applicant, Iversen, was directed under the Act to take up for one year the position of dentist in the Moskenes district in northern Norway. He eventually accepted the post, but after some months he gave it up and left. He was subsequently convicted and sentenced under the Act, and his appeal was dismissed by the Supreme Court.

In his application to the Commission, he alleged that the Act, and the order assigning him to the district of Moskenes, were

---

[1] See above, p. 15, on the general problems of interpretation.
[2] *Yearbook* 6, 278.

contrary to Article 4 of the Convention. Exceptionally, the Commission's decision on admissibility records a divided vote: it held by a majority of six votes to four that the application was inadmissible. The majority considered that the service of Iversen in Moskenes was not forced or compulsory labour within the meaning of Article 4 of the Convention. However, the majority was itself divided; four members of the majority considered that the service of Iversen in Moskenes was manifestly not forced or complusory labour under Article 4(2), and therefore found it unnecessary to express any opinion on the applicability of Article 4(3), while the other two members of the majority considered that that service was reasonably required of him in an emergency threatening the well-being of the community and was therefore authorized under Article 4(3).

The concept of forced or compulsory labour was analysed by the four members of the majority as follows:

The concept cannot be understood solely in terms of the literal meaning of the words, and has in fact come to be regarded in international law and practice, as evidenced in part by the provisions and application of I.L.O. Conventions and Resolutions on Forced Labour, as having certain elements . . . [namely] that the work or service is performed by the worker against his will and, secondly, that the requirement that the work or service be performed is unjust or oppressive or the work or service itself involves avoidable hardship.[1]

On this analysis the service required of Iversen was held not to be forced or compulsory labour under Article 4(2); the requirement to perform that service was not unjust or oppressive since the service, although obligatory, 'was for a short period, provided favourable remuneration, did not involve any diversion from chosen professional work, was only applied in the case of posts not filled after being duly advertised, and did not involve any discriminatory, arbitrary, or punitive application'.

However, even if the element of oppressiveness could be said to be absent in this case, it is doubtful how far it is a necessary constituent of forced labour as generally understood in international law and practice. The Forced Labour Convention of 1930 in fact defines the term 'forced or compulsory labour', for the purposes of that Convention, simply as 'all work or service which is exacted

[1] At p. 328.

from any person under the menace of a penalty and for which the said person has not offered himself voluntarily';[1] but that Convention did not prohibit such work or service if it forms part of normal civic obligations in a self-governing country, or is exacted in execution of a penal sentence, or exacted in an 'emergency requiring the mobilisation of manpower for essential work of national importance'.

Article 4(3) of the European Convention, as seen above, contains similar provisions.

In the Iversen case, as already stated, the reasoning of the other two members of the Commission who voted for inadmissibility was based on Article 4(3); they held that the service of Iversen was service reasonably required of him in an emergency threatening the well-being of the community. The Norwegian Government had made no substantial submissions on this point but as part of the general background of the case had explained that the northern districts of Norway had a deplorable lack of social services, which seriously affected the social and health conditions of these communities; thus, while there was in Oslo in 1946 one dentist per 650 inhabitants, the ratio in three of the northern provinces was one dentist per 13,000, 6,000 and 5,500 inhabitants respectively. Moreover, adequate dental care was rendered even more difficult by the enormous distances, the difficulties of communication, and the arctic weather conditions prevailing during the winter months.

While these considerations may have made it difficult for the Norwegian authorities to find any alternative practical solution to the problem, it is by no means clear that they are relevant to the provisions of Article 4, which, unlike many of the later Articles, contains no escape clause 'for the protection of health'. The opinion of the two members of the Commission referred to above is open to criticism; for it seems doubtful whether the situation in northern Norway could be described as an 'emergency' or 'calamity' as required by Article 4(3) (c). These terms suggest some sudden overwhelming natural disaster, not the permanent social, climatic, and geographical conditions however serious they may be.

The minority of the Commission was rightly of the opinion that the application was not manifestly ill-founded, and that it

---

[1] Article 2(1). But see Fawcett, p. 47, for the argument that this definition is incomplete as omitting the element of oppression.

should be declared admissible. The minority found that the conditions under which Iversen was required to perform his work, although it was paid and was only for a limited time, did not exclude the possibility of it being forced or compulsory labour, since it was imposed subject to penal sanctions; and that the question of the applicability of Article 4(3) (c) of the Convention required further examination.

It is hard to escape the conclusion that the Commission's decision to reject the application was influenced by political considerations. The case had caused considerable controversy in Norway and the decision coincided with a decision of the Norwegian Government to renew its declaration accepting the Commission's competence under Article 25 for a period of only one year.[1] Although no definite conclusion can be drawn in this case, it is essential for the Commission to avoid creating the impression that pressure can be brought to bear by a Government by the threat of non-renewal.[2]

Prison labour

It has been seen that Article 4(3) (a) excludes from the term 'forced or compulsory labour' 'any work required to be done in the ordinary course of detention imposed according to the provisions of Article 5 of this Convention or during conditional release from such detention'.

In a group of applications[3] from persons detained in various prisons in Germany, the Commission examined the scope of this provision. The applicants complained that during their detention in prison they were subjected to forced and compulsory labour without receiving adequate payment and without being insured under the social security laws.

The Commission has regularly rejected applications by prisoners claiming higher payment for their work or claiming the right to be covered by social security systems.[4] The present applicants, however, raised a new point in complaining also that

---

[1] *Yearbook* 6, 26. See Schermers, 'European Commission of Human Rights: The Norwegian dentist case on compulsory labour', *Nederlands Tijdschrift voor international recht*, 1964, 366.

[2] See below, p. 275.

[3] *Twenty-one detained persons* v. *Federal Republic of Germany*, 3134/67 and others, *Yearbook* 11, 528.

[4] At 552 and cases there cited.

part of the work required of them during their detention was performed on behalf of private firms under contracts concluded with the prison administration; this system, they alleged, constituted a state of slavery for the prisoners concerned. The Commission examined this complaint primarily, however, under Article 4(3) (a), i.e. in relation to forced or compulsory labour. After an exceptionally detailed investigation of the background of this provision, and a survey of the practice in the Member States of the Council of Europe, the Commission found that the form of prison labour of which the applicants complained clearly appeared to fall within the framework of work normally required from prisoners within the meaning of Article 4(3) (a).

It may be thought that the exemption under Article 4(3) (a) of 'work required to be done in the ordinary course of detention imposed according to the provisions of Article 5' can arise only if all the provisions of Article 5 have been observed. In the Vagrancy Cases[1] the Commission had expressed the view that the work that the applicants were required to do was not justified under Article 4 because there had been a breach of Article 5(4). The Court, however, held that while there was a breach of Article 5(4), there was no breach of Article 4 because the vagrants were lawfully detained under Article 5(1) (e).[2]

This is a perplexing decision since Article 5 must be read as a whole, and it would seem that any breach of paragraphs (1) to (4) would render the arrest or detention unlawful. It is not sufficient to say that the detention is justified under one provision of the Convention if it is unlawful under another provision. Nor does Article 4(3) (a) itself differentiate between the provisions of Article 5. On this point, therefore, the view of the Commission is to be preferred to that of the Court.

Military service

Article 4(3) (b) excludes 'any service of a military character' from the prohibition of forced or compulsory labour.

In the 'sailor boys' case'[3] four applicants aged fifteen and sixteen had joined the British army or naval forces for a period of nine years to be calculated from the age of eighteen. They had subsequently applied for discharge from the service but, in spite

---

[1] See below, p. 55. [2] Para. 89.
[3] 3435/67 etc., *Yearbook* 11, 562.

of repeated requests, discharge had been refused. They alleged, *inter alia*, a violation of their right under Article 4(1) not to be held in servitude.

The Commission also considered the case under Article 4(2) but found that any complaint that the applicants' service constituted 'forced or compulsory labour' must be rejected as being manifestly ill-founded in view of the express provision of Article 4(3) (b). That provision, according to the Commission, wholly excluded *voluntary* military service from the scope of Article 4(2); and, by the omission of the word 'compulsory' which appeared in the I.L.O. Convention, 'it was intended to cover also the obligation to continue a service entered into on a voluntary basis.'[1]

The United Kingdom Government submitted that the exclusion of military service in Article 4(3) (b) was to be understood as applying equally to slavery and servitude in paragraph (1). Any argument to the contrary necessarily involved the anomalous conclusion that although no service of a military character can be, under the Convention, forced or compulsory labour, military service may amount to the more oppressive condition of slavery or servitude. The applicants, however, rightly pointed out that the drafters of the article clearly intended that there should be an absolute prohibition against servitude or slavery, but only a qualified prohibition against forced or compulsory labour.

The Commission found that generally the duty of a soldier who enlists after the age of majority to observe the terms of his engagement, and the ensuing restriction of his freedom and personal rights, do not amount to an impairment of rights which could come under the terms 'slavery or servitude'; and that the young age at which the applicants entered the services could not in itself attribute the character of 'servitude' to the normal condition of a soldier.

With regard to the young age of enlistment, the applicants referred to the special protection of minors provided for in all legal systems in respect of 'their own possibly unconsidered engagements'. The Commission pointed out that the applicants' parents had given their consent and that 'the protection of minors in other fields of law consists exactly in the requirement of parental consent and also in the existence of the principle that an engagement entered into by the minor will be void without

[1] *Yearbook* 11 at 594.

such consent but valid and binding if the consent has been duly given'. The Commission did not, however, refer to another element in the protection of minors, frequently found in domestic legal systems, which enables the minor, in certain circumstances, to decide for himself on reaching the age of majority whether to continue or to repudiate his undertaking.

The applications were thus finally rejected as inadmissible but subsequently new Navy Service Regulations were introduced in the United Kingdom under which boy entrants could decide at the age of eighteen to leave the navy after three years adult service, i.e. at the age of twenty-one.

In addition to military service, Article 4(3) (b) also authorizes service required to be performed by conscientious objectors in lieu of compulsory military service. Questions raised by this provision are discussed below in relation to the Grandrath Case.[1]

Civic obligations

Article 4(3) (d) authorizes 'any work which forms part of normal civic obligations'.

The question was raised whether the Austrian system of legal aid was compatible with Article 4 of the Convention.[2]

The applicant, a lawyer practising in Vienna, complained that he was compelled, contrary to Article 4, to act as unpaid defence counsel for a person who lacked the means to pay counsel's fees. Under the legal aid system, a lawyer was required to offer his services and was subject to disciplinary sanctions if he refused to do so. He was paid no fee and was reimbursed for practically none of his expenses. In return for these services, the Government paid annually to the Bar Association a fixed lump sum which was used for charitable purposes, especially for old age pensions for lawyers no longer in practice; but there was no legal right to such benefits.

In the proceedings on admissibility, the Government submitted, *inter alia*, that a lawyer, by voluntarily choosing his profession, accepts the obligation to act under the legal aid system, and that consequently this was not compulsory labour, but a consequence of his own free decision. Further, even if it did constitute

---

[1] Below, p. 145.

[2] *Gussenbauer* v. *Austria*, 4897/71, *Collection of Decisions* 42, 41 and 5219/71, *Collection of Decisions* 42, 94.

43

compulsory labour, it formed part of normal civic obligations under Article 4(3) (d). The applicant replied that the obligation was limited to the legal profession, and within that profession applied only to counsel; consequently it could not be regarded as part of normal civic obligations.

It would seem that, whatever the outcome of this case, the interpretation of 'normal' civic obligations requires a comparison with the practice in comparable professions in other Contracting Parties. Article 4(3) (d) contains the clearest express reference in the Convention to current practice as a standard of interpretation.[1]

Consent

It seems clear that consent cannot make lawful slavery or servitude which would otherwise be prohibited under Article 4(1). In the 'sailor boys' case'[2] the United Kingdom Government argued that an essential feature of servitude is that it has been forced upon a person against his will, in circumstances where he has no genuine freedom of choice.[3] However, Article 4(1) should be construed as prohibiting also the voluntary acceptance of servitude. 'Personal liberty is an inalienable right which a person cannot voluntarily abandon.'[4] Indeed, a proposal to add the qualification 'involuntary' to servitude was rejected by the drafters of the Supplementary Convention on Slavery 1956 and of the United Nations Covenant on Civil and Political Rights precisely on the ground that 'It should not be possible for any person to contract himself into bondage.'[5] This interpretation is further confirmed by the judgment of the Court in the Vagrancy Cases.[6]

However, it is less clear, in view of the terms 'forced' and 'compulsory', whether a voluntary undertaking would exclude the applicability of Article 4(2). It has already been seen that one of the elements of work which is prohibited is its performance by the worker against his will; but the question remains whether a person who has voluntarily accepted an obligation can be compelled to continue in circumstances which, objectively viewed, would constitute forced or compulsory labour.

In the Iversen Case the Norwegian Government contended

---

[1] See above, p. 20.   [2] Above, p. 41.   [3] *Yearbook* 11, 562 at 576.
[4] Report of the Commission in the Vagrancy Cases, 'Publications of the Court', Series B, page 91.
[5] See Fawcett, p. 46.   [6] Below, p. 57.

that the applicant had freely accepted the conditions of service, that he knew of the effect of the Norwegian legislation and voluntarily entered into an agreement with the competent authorities, and in particular that by his conversations with officials in the Ministry for Social Affairs and his consent to being posted in Moskenes, the relation between the applicant and the Ministry had assumed a contractual nature which excluded any application of Article 4 of the Convention.[1] The Commission, however, did not refer to this aspect of the case in its decision.

In the sailor boys' case, however, the Commission appeared to attach great importance to the fact that not only the applicants but also their parents had initially given their consent. This view, again, may be open to doubt in view of the Court's judgment in the Vagrancy Cases and the issues of principle underlying that judgment, which were not fully apparent in the Commission's reasoning.

ARTICLE 5

Liberty of the person

The object of Article 5 is to guarantee liberty of the person, and in particular to provide guarantees against arbitrary arrest or detention. It seeks to achieve this object by excluding any form of arrest or detention without lawful authority and proper judicial control, by spelling out in detail, in paragraph (1), the conditions under which alone a person may be deprived of his liberty, and by providing, in paragraphs (2) to (5), certain rights for persons who have been detained.

The Article first states the general principle that 'Everyone has the right to liberty and security of person'.[2] The meaning of 'security' in this context is uncertain; the question was raised, but not resolved, in the East African Asians cases.[3] On the normal principles of interpretation, the term 'security' should be given a

---

[1] *Yearbook* 6, 308.

[2] The French text reads 'Toute personne a droit à la liberté et à la sûreté'.

[3] Above, p. 33; see *Yearbook* 13, 928 at 996 and cf. 5302/71, *Collection of Decisions* 44, 29 at 46.

meaning independent of 'liberty', but the remainder of the Article is concerned exclusively with deprivation of liberty.[1]

The Fourth Protocol gives additional protection to personal liberty, by limiting further the conditions under which detention is lawful, and by guaranteeing in particular freedom of movement.[2]

I THE CONDITIONS AUTHORIZING ARREST AND DETENTION

Under Article 5(1) of the Convention, no one may be deprived of his liberty unless three conditions are fulfilled. First, it must be 'in accordance with a procedure prescribed by law'.[3]

This means that domestic law must lay down the procedure to be followed by persons authorized to carry out arrest and detention, and that the correct procedure must in every instance be observed. Where, for example, a warrant is required for arrest, the warrant must be in the correct form. Otherwise the arrest will be unlawful under Article 5. Similarly, where force is used in order to effect an arrest, the degree of force used must not exceed that authorized in the circumstances by domestic law. This point seems to have been overlooked by the Commission.[4]

Secondly, as well as complying with the procedural provisions of domestic law, arrest and detention must be authorized by substantive law. With this object, in enumerating, in sub-paragraphs (a) to (f), the six cases in which arrest or detention is permitted, Article 5(1) provides in each case that the arrest or detention must be lawful. Not only must it fall within one of the six specified cases; it must in every instance be authorized by substantive domestic law, in the particular circumstances.

Thirdly, the arrest or detention must fall within one of the six cases. These will now be considered in turn.

[1] See further Golsong, 'Le droit à la liberté de la personne tel qu'il est garanti par l'article 5 de la Convention européenne des Droits de l'Homme', in *Droit pénal européen*, Brussels, 1970, 25 at 30–3.

[2] Below, p. 182.

[3] On the status as 'law' of Nazi legislation, see 4324/69, *Yearbook* 14, 342 at 346; cf. below, pp. 125, 197.

[4] See, e.g. 604/59, *Yearbook* 3, 236 at 242; 4220/69, *Collection of Decisions* 37, 51; and 4225/69, *Yearbook* 13, 864.

(a) *the lawful detention of a person after conviction by a competent court*

As already observed, whether detention is 'lawful' is a matter of domestic law, not the law of the Convention, which would lead to circularity. In this provision, the requirement of lawfulness would seem to embody two separate requirements, although the Commission has not always adverted to both.[1] First, the conviction must be in accordance with domestic law; for if the conviction is not lawful, the detention cannot be. Secondly, the order of detention imposed must be authorized by domestic law for the offence of which the accused has been convicted. Similarly, the court giving judgment must be 'competent' under domestic law.[2]

It is clear that the use of the term 'court' is intended to exclude detention for commission of an offence by decision of an administrative body, although detention by such decision on other grounds is permissible under other provisions of Article 5. The term 'court' in Article 5(1), as in Article 5(4),[3] implies that the authority must possess a judicial character, that is, it must be independent both of the executive and of the parties to the case.

It might have been supposed that 'conviction by a competent court' included a reference to the procedural safeguards of a fair trial guaranteed by Article 6 of the Convention. This would greatly reinforce the protection given by Article 5. The Commission, however, appears to have rejected this interpretation.[4] An applicant complained that a sentence passed by an East German court was enforced in West Germany. After serving part of his sentence in East Germany, he had escaped to the Federal Republic, but the Federal authorities had decided, on the basis of an inter-German judicial and administrative assistance Act, that the remainder of his sentence should be enforced. The Commission, pointing to the growing practice of international judicial co-operation,[5] held that 'competent court' did not necessarily mean a court in the territory of the State where the sentence is served. As for Article 6, the East German courts were outside the Commission's competence

---

[1] Compare the approach of the Court in the Vagrancy cases to Article 5 (1)(e), below, p. 56.

[2] 2645/65, *Yearbook* 11, 322; 4161/69, *Yearbook* 13, 798 at 804.

[3] See below, p. 73.

[4] 1322/62, *Yearbook* 6, 494.

[5] See now the European Convention on the International Validity of Criminal Judgments, 1970 (European Treaty Series, No. 70).

ratione personae,[1] while the West German court which had rejected the applicant's appeal against the enforcement of his sentence had not been concerned with the determination of a criminal charge within the meaning of Article 6, but only with the enforcement of a decision. The Commission pointed out, however, that that court had examined the question whether the decisions of the East German courts in the matter could be criticized from the standpoint of 'respect for the rule of law'.

The Commission's decision opens an unfortunate gap in the system of protection afforded by Articles 5 and 6. The enforcement of foreign judgments appears to be the only exception to the principle that the guilt of a person who is detained under Article 5(1) (a) has been established in the course of a trial conducted in accordance with the requirements of Article 6. Indeed, the Court seems to have assumed in the Wemhoff Case (*obiter*) that there are no exceptions whatever to this principle.[2]

Possibly the view should be adopted that, where a State is requested to enforce a sentence of detention imposed in the requesting State, the court in the requested State which authorizes the enforcement should first be satisfied that all the provisions of Article 6 have been observed.

The issue of what constitutes a court under Article 5(1) (a) was also raised in applications by five Dutch soldiers who complained of certain penalties which had been imposed on them;[3] these cases have been referred to the European Court of Human Rights. All five applicants were conscripts serving in different non-commissioned ranks in the Netherlands Armed Forces. They were punished on separate occasions by their respective company commanders for breaches of the rules of military discipline, and were committed to several days of 'light' or 'aggravated' or 'strict' arrest, or to service in a disciplinary unit. Each applicant had complained to the Complaints Officer about his punishment, and had finally taken his case before the Supreme Military Court which had confirmed the penalties.

All the applicants complained to the Commission, *inter alia*, that the punishments imposed a 'deprivation of liberty' contrary

---

[1] See below, p. 226.

[2] The Wemhoff Case, para. 9 of 'The Law'.

[3] 5100/71 etc., *Collection of Decisions* 42, 61. Cf. the reservation made by France to Articles 5 and 6, below, p. 90.

to the terms and stipulated procedure of Article 5 of the Convention, and that the proceedings before the military authorities, including the Supreme Military Court, did not satisfy the requirements of Article 6 of the Convention.

One of the applicants argued, in particular, that the Supreme Military Court was not a 'court' within the meaning of Article 5(1) (a) or of Article 5(4).[1] Thus, some of its members were acting under higher authority, and its sittings were held in camera.

It seems clear, and was not disputed by the Dutch Government, that the proceedings did not comply with Article 6(1). It may be that they should be regarded as not having involved the determination of a criminal charge.[2] But, if that is so, then it is difficult to see under what head of Article 5 detention is allowed. The reliance of the Supreme Military Court on Article 5(1) (b) seems clearly misplaced, as will be seen below.

Appeals If a person appeals against his conviction, a difficulty arises as to whether his detention is authorized under Article 5(1) (a) or whether it should be regarded as detention on remand under Article 5(1) (c) and therefore taken into account under Article 5(3). In Austrian and German law,[3] detention pending appeal is considered as detention on remand and does not constitute detention following conviction until the conviction acquires the force of *res judicata*. The Court has held that the detention of a person convicted at first instance falls under Article 5(1) (a), and that the period to be taken into consideration in applying Article 5(3) ends with the delivery of the judgment that terminates the trial in the court of first instance.[4]

If an appeal against conviction is successful, the quashing of the conviction does not of course in any event render unlawful the previous detention; and the same applies to acquittal following a re-trial.[5]

(b) *the lawful arrest or detention of a person for non-compliance with the lawful order of a court or in order to secure the fulfilment of any obligation prescribed by law*

This provision must be viewed in the context of the provisions

---

[1] At 77.   [2] See below, p. 89.
[3] See Golsong, op. cit. p. 46 n. 1 at 57.
[4] The Wemhoff case, paras. 6 to 9 of 'The Law'; see below, p. 68.
[5] 3245/67, *Yearbook* 12, 206 at 236 (release following a re-trial).

of Article 5(1) as a whole, and of the object of Article 5(1) as being to list exhaustively the cases in which a person may be arrested or detained. Detention for the purposes of the criminal law is covered by Article 5(1) (a) and (c). The detention of special classes of persons—minors, vagrants, etc.—which may or may not come under the criminal law, is covered by Article 5(1) (d) and (e). Article 5(1) (b) lists the sole conditions authorizing what might be described as 'civil detention' generally. The other categories of arrest and detention are generally recognized and accepted, and what is important there is the safeguards afforded by procedural and substantive law. In the case of civil detention, however, greater importance attaches to the definition of the grounds for such detention.

The first limb of paragraph (1)(b) authorizes detention, *inter alia*, for failure to comply with an injunction, or with a custody or maintenance order. The second limb authorizes detention, *inter alia*, for failure to comply with an obligation to make an affidavit.[1] In the latter case, however, the detention must be imposed in order to secure the fulfilment of the obligation, and not merely for non-compliance. Thus, if a person has failed to perform some legal obligation, not carrying a penal sanction, he cannot be detained if performance is no longer possible, or if the detention prevents him from carrying it out. He can only be detained if that course is likely to lead to the performance of the obligation. So a person could not be imprisoned for debt if he needed to earn a living in order to repay the debt.

Subject to this, it would seem that imprisonment for debt might conceivably be justified by either limb of Article 5(1) (b), but a restriction on detention in such cases is introduced by Article 1 of the Fourth Protocol, which provides that 'No one shall be deprived of his liberty merely on the ground of inability to fulfil a contractual obligation.'

In the Lawless Case the Irish Government argued before the Commission (but not before the Court) that preventive detention in the sense of detention to prevent the possible commission of an offence might be legitimate under Article 5(1) (b) as being 'to secure the fulfilment of an obligation prescribed by law'. The Commission considered, however, that this provision does not allow arrest or detention for the prevention of offences against

[1] 5025/71, *Yearbook* 14, 692 at 694.

public order or against the security of the State; so wide an interpretation would undermine the whole basis of Article 5. The obligation prescribed by law must be specific.[1]

It might be possible to go further and argue that preventive detention is not authorized by paragraph (1) (b) because this provision only covers cases where there has already been a failure to perform an obligation. It is intended to allow for certain forms of 'civil' detention to enforce an obligation, as opposed to criminal punishment under paragraph (1) (a). It cannot therefore authorize, in any circumstances, detention in anticipation of a breach. This is allowed only under paragraph (1) (c), and is consequently subject to the safeguards of paragraph (3).

(c) *the lawful arrest or detention of a person effected for the purpose of bringing him before the competent legal authority on reasonable suspicion of having committed an offence or when it is reasonably considered necessary to prevent his committing an offence or fleeing after having done so*

Again, 'lawful' refers to domestic law. The Commission has held[2] that detention pending trial is 'lawful' under this paragraph if it is the subject of court proceedings and if the judicial authorities take their decision on the basis of domestic law; the Commission has no power to examine whether, in the course of proceedings before the domestic courts, municipal law is correctly interpreted and applied by the judicial authorities, unless exceptionally they acted in bad faith in interpreting and applying the law, in which case detention would not be lawful under this paragraph.

Apart from the requirement of lawfulness, there are two tests as to whether arrest or detention can be justified under this head. First, in every case,[3] the arrest or detention must be effected, in the terms of paragraph (1) (c), for the purpose of bringing the person before the competent legal authority.

This purpose may be, in the usual case of a person arrested on suspicion of having committed an offence, to bring him before the 'competent legal authority' to decide, depending on the system of criminal procedure in operation, whether criminal charges

---

[1] See the Report of the Commission in the Lawless Case, 'Publications of the Court', Series B, p. 64.
[2] 2621/65, *Yearbook* 9, 474 at 478 f.
[3] Lawless Case, Judgment, paras. 13 and 14.

should be brought, and if so whether the accused should be remanded in custody or should be provisionally released. Under Continental criminal procedure, based on the 'inquisitorial' system, the accused will be brought before the investigating judge (*juge d'instruction*), who will from the outset supervise the investigation of the case, and will subsequently decide what charges, if any, should be brought. Under English criminal procedure, based on the 'accusatorial' system, it is for the police or the prosecuting authorities to investigate the case and bring the charges, the role of the magistrates being limited at this stage to deciding whether the accused should be released, if necessary on bail, and to considering subsequently, in the case of serious crimes, whether there is a sufficient case to go to trial. (For the sake of convenience, a person detained under paragraph (1) (c) will be referred to as the accused, although it will be understood that the protection of Article 5 extends from the moment of arrest, while the person arrested may only be charged much later, if at all. Similarly, detention under paragraph (1) (c) and under paragraph (3) will be referred to as detention on remand or detention pending trial although those terms, too, may be anticipatory.)

For arrest, or detention on remand, to be permissible under paragraph (1) (c), it is not sufficient that it has the purpose specified above. In addition, it must be effected 'on reasonable suspicion of [a person] having committed an offence or when it is reasonably considered necessary to prevent his committing an offence or fleeing after having done so'. Unfortunately, the drafting of this part of the clause is somewhat confused, because it deals at the same time with the conditions permitting arrest and the conditions permitting continuing detention. In interpreting the provision, however, it is necessary to distinguish the two. Presumably the intended meaning is that a person may be *arrested* only when he is suspected of having committed an offence, or if he is about to do so; and that, once arrested, he may be *detained* only if there is a danger of his absconding, or, in exceptional circumstances, to prevent his committing further offences.[1] Clearly, for continuing detention on remand to be permissible, there must be a continuing suspicion; for if it becomes apparent that the grounds of suspicion no longer exist, the accused must be released at once. But such continuing suspicion, while necessary, cannot be

[1] See the Matznetter Case, para. 9 of 'The Law', and below, p. 66.

sufficient to justify continuing detention; this is clearly implied by paragraph (3).[1] Because of the close connection between paragraph (1) (c) and paragraph (3), this subject will be discussed further below.[2]

A person may be arrested, therefore, under paragraph (1) (c) only if there is reasonable suspicion that he has committed an offence or when it is reasonably considered necessary to prevent his doing so. In addition, such arrest must be lawful: that is, it must also comply with the conditions laid down by domestic law, which are generally more strict than those laid down by paragraph (1) (c) itself.[3]

Internment without trial   It is clear that Article 5, and in particular paragraph (1) (c) read together with paragraph (3), preclude internment without trial. According to the Court's judgment in the Lawless case,[4] the arrest or detention of a person under Article 5(1) (c) may be effected only for the purpose of bringing him before the competent legal authority; and a person so arrested or detained will be entitled to the protection of Article 5(3). In that case the Court held that the detention of Lawless, which would otherwise have been in breach of the Convention, was covered by the Irish Government's derogation under Article 15. In the Greek Case, however, the Commission was of the opinion that Article 15, even if it were applicable, could not justify the measures taken by the Greek Government. Both administrative detention of persons considered dangerous to public order and security, and the use of house arrest, as practised by the Government, fell outside any of the categories of deprivation of liberty permitted by Article 5; nor had the requirements of Article 5(4) been observed.[5]

In the Irish case,[6] the Commission declared admissible the allegations relating to internment without trial and detention under the Special Powers Act. Detailed submissions on these questions are contained in the decision on admissibility.[7]

---

[1] See the Stögmuller Case, para. 4 of 'The Law'.
[2] P. 64.
[3] See Golsong, op. cit. p. 46 n. 1 at 43.
[4] See above, p. 51.
[5] *Yearbook* 1969, The Greek Case, pp. 134–5.
[6] See above, p. 25.
[7] *Collection of Decisions* 41, 3.

(d) *the detention of a minor by lawful order for the purpose of educational supervision or his lawful detention for the purpose of bringing him before the competent legal authority*

This clause authorizes, *inter alia*, the exercise of the jurisdiction of juvenile courts in non-criminal cases. Under English law, for example, a court may authorize the detention of a child or young person, even though he has not been found guilty of a criminal offence, if the court is of opinion that he is in need of care or control, and if certain other conditions are satisfied. The court may do so if, for example, his proper development is being avoidably prevented or neglected or his health is being avoidably impaired or neglected or he is being ill-treated; or if he is exposed to moral danger; or if he is beyond the control of his parent or guardian; or again if he is of compulsory school age and is not receiving efficient full-time education suitable to his age, ability, and aptitude.[1] The court may then make a 'care order' committing him to the care of a local authority, or a 'supervision order' placing him under a local authority's supervision.[2] These orders will necessarily constitute a deprivation of liberty under Article 5(1), even if the person affected is not in full-time detention. Conversely, if detention is justified, lesser forms of supervision will *a fortiori* be permissible.

Such orders as these will clearly be 'lawful' orders under paragraph 1 (d). Further, as there is no requirement that the order should be that of a court, the making of such orders by an administrative authority is not excluded. In such cases however the person subject to the order will be entitled under paragraph (4) 'to take proceedings by which the lawfulness of his detention shall be decided speedily by a court and his release ordered if the detention is not lawful.'[3]

The second limb of paragraph (1)(d) allows the minor to be brought before the judicial or administrative authority which is to decide whether or not to order his detention. In each case, the requirement of lawfulness must be examined in the light of the Court's judgment in the Vagrancy cases.[4]

Since paragraph (1) (d) gives the national authorities very wide powers over minors, it is important to ask at what age a person

[1] Children and Young Persons Act 1969, s. 1(2).
[2] Children and Young Persons Act 1969, ss. 1(3), 20 and 11.
[3] See below, p. 72.   [4] See below, p. 56.

ceases to be a minor. This question is presumably to be answered, within reasonable limits, by national law. The Council of Europe has adopted a resolution recommending Member States in principle to reduce the age of majority from twenty-one to eighteen.[1]

(e) *the lawful detention of persons for the prevention of the spreading of infectious diseases, of persons of unsound mind, alcoholics or drug addicts or vagrants*

The leading authority on this provision is the judgment of the Court in the 'Vagrancy Cases' in 1971.[2] Like other leading cases under the Convention, these cases raised fundamental questions about the nature of society and the relations between the individual and the State. Does a person have the right, in an industrialized society and a Welfare State, to live as a tramp or as a hippie? If he has no visible means of support, can he be locked up and detained for an indefinite period, even though he has committed no crime? The judgment of the Court contains pronouncements on a number of fundamental issues under the Convention. Some of these will be discussed elsewhere;[3] so far as Article 5(1) (e) is concerned, it may be assumed that the principles stated by the Court in relation to vagrancy apply equally to the other categories mentioned in this clause.

These cases concerned three applicants, De Wilde, Ooms and Versyp, detained in vagrancy centres in Belgium by order of a magistrate under Belgian legislation then in force. Their principal complaint was that they had no possibility of obtaining a court decision as to the lawfulness of their detention, as provided for by Article 5(4).

The applicants also alleged, however, that their initial detention was unlawful, and the Court's finding on this question is of great importance. The Commission considered that the requirement that the detention should be 'lawful' meant it had no competence to examine the complaints unless they disclosed some evidence of arbitrary action on the part of the national authorities. It was accordingly of the opinion that there was no violation of this provision. This reasoning reflected the customary practice of the

---

[1] Resolution CM (72) 29 of the Committee of Ministers of the Council of Europe.
[2] 'Publications of the Court', Series A.
[3] Below, pp. 57, 72.

Commission in dealing with such complaints; in particular, many applications from persons detained as being of unsound mind had been rejected as inadmissible on similar grounds.[1] Thus in the Vagrancy Cases the Commission stated in its Report:[2]

With respect to this Article which refers to the provisions of municipal law the Commission finds that the vagrants were dealt with in accordance with the procedure prescribed by law.
It is not for the Commission to decide whether the municipal law was correctly applied by the competent authorities in the present case, provided that an examination of the proceedings does not show that the authorities acted arbitrarily.

The Court, in its turn, also found that there was no violation of this provision, but its reasoning was quite different. It first examined the definition of 'vagrants' in Belgian law, namely that 'vagrants are persons who have no fixed abode, no means of subsistence and no regular trade or profession'. It found that that definition 'does not appear to be in any way irreconcilable with the usual meaning of the term "vagrant" ', and that a person who is a vagrant under the terms of that legislation in principle falls within the exception provided for in Article 5(1) (e). The Court then went on to show that, on the facts before the magistrates, the applicants did come within this definition of vagrants.[3] The Court thus not only examined the compatibility of the domestic law with the Convention, but also decided, in effect, that it had been correctly interpreted and applied. It did, it is true, echo the customary language of the Commission in stating that it had 'not found either irregularity or arbitrariness in the placing of the three applicants at the disposal of the Government'.[4] But it reached this conclusion by a process of reasoning which the Commission had always avoided.

It may be thought that the Court's interpretation goes too far. A very high proportion of applications to the Commission comes from persons in detention, any one of whom might be, for example, of unsound mind. Is it possible, it may be asked, for the Commission to control the interpretation and application of domes-

---

[1] See, e.g. 3151/67, *Collection of Decisions* 27, 128.
[2] 'Publications of the Court', Series B, page 97.
[3] 'Judgment of the Court', Series A, para. 68.
[4] Para. 70.

tic law in all these cases, and so to decide whether a person is in fact an alcoholic, a drug addict, or mentally ill? The practical difficulties alone might seem to exclude this interpretation.

On further analysis, however, this argument is not conclusive. First, it is obviously correct to say, as the Court implied, that the national law must be examined for its compatibility with the Convention. A national law could not, to take an extreme case, authorize the detention of persons as being of unsound mind solely on the ground that they expressed opinions hostile to the Government. Nor does this requirement impose any great practical difficulties. It is simply a matter of ensuring that the definitions provided by national law are consistent with the usual meaning of the term in the Member States of the Council of Europe. So far as the interpretation and application of national law is concerned, it is true, of course, that many applications to the Commission come from persons who are apparently mentally disordered. But many of these applicants are at liberty, and not all of those who are detained complain of their detention. In cases of extreme mental derangement, a complaint of unlawful detention might in any event be manifestly ill-founded. Where, however, there is a serious complaint of unlawful detention, it must be the duty of the Commission to obtain the observations of the respondent Government and ultimately to decide for itself, if necessary, on the merits of the case. Any other approach would undermine the effective protection of Article 5.

A further fundamental issue raised in the Vagrancy Cases was whether the voluntary acts of the applicants affected their rights under the Convention. The Belgian Government stated that the applicants had initially reported voluntarily to the police, and that their admission to the vagrancy institutions had been the result of an express or implicit request, express in two cases and implicit in the third. The Government argued that they could not therefore be regarded as having been 'deprived of liberty' within the meaning of Article 5.

The Court rejected this argument. It held that:[1]

. . . the right to liberty is too important in a 'democratic society' within the meaning of the Convention for a person to lose the benefit of the protection of the Convention for the single reason that he gives himself up to be taken into detention. Detention might violate Article 5

[1] Para. 65.

57

even although the person concerned might have agreed to it. When the matter is one which concerns *ordre public* within the Council of Europe, a scrupulous supervision by the organs of the Convention of all measures capable of violating the rights and freedoms which it guarantees is necessary in every case.

There is no provision in Article 5 governing the length of the detention authorized under paragraph (1) (e). In the Vagrancy Cases, two of the applicants had been placed at the disposal of the Government for two years (they were both released earlier), while the third was placed at the disposal of the Government for an indefinite period (which under Belgian law could not exceed one year). Persons detained as being mentally unsound are normally detained for an indefinite period, although often with a right to periodical review.[1]

It will be observed that, as in the case of detention of minors under paragraph (1) (d), there is no requirement that the detention should be imposed by a court; it may be ordered by an administrative authority. It is true that such an order will be subject to judicial control under paragraph (4); but this control appears, from the wording of that paragraph, to relate only to the initial detention.

To commit a person to detention for an indefinite period with no fixed maximum, or for a very long period, may involve a serious infringement of the right to personal liberty. The solution to this problem under the Convention may be as follows. Detention of a person which was initially lawful, because for example he was of unsound mind, may subsequently become unlawful if his condition improves. In that event, even if a previous application has been rejected, he may make a fresh application. This application must not be 'substantially the same' as his previous one, or it will be inadmissible under Article 27(1) (b); but if he or his representatives can substantiate any new grounds for showing that he ought now to be released, his application will be admissible. The same considerations apply to the other conditions mentioned in Article 5(1) (e), with the sole exception of vagrancy, namely infectious diseases, alcoholism, and drug addiction. In all these cases, whatever may be the position under domestic law, there is in effect under the Convention a right to a periodical review. The case of vagrancy is exceptional because here a person is detained

[1] See 2518/65, *Yearbook* 8, 370; cf. 4625/70, *Collection of Decisions* 40, 21.

for his previous rather than for his present condition. In this case, unless a general limit to the length of detention can be inferred from the practice of the contracting States, the only control in the Convention is that it must not be so lengthy as to constitute inhuman or degrading treatment under Article 3.

(f) *the lawful arrest or detention of a person to prevent his effecting an unauthorized entry into the country or of a person against whom action is being taken with a view to deportation or extradition*

Subject to certain other provisions of the Convention, in particular Article 3 and Article 8, and of the Fourth Protocol,[1] there is no right under the Convention to enter or remain in a particular country, and no protection against deportation or extradition. However, Article 5 provides certain procedural guarantees, which go beyond the mere requirement of 'lawfulness'.

In the first place it would seem, although this has not yet been established by the case-law,[2] that the period of detention before a person is expelled must be long enough to enable him to challenge the lawfulness of his detention before the national courts under paragraph (4). In this way, he may be able to obtain a review of his expulsion on the merits. Further, if he makes an application to the Commission, it would seem that the respondent Government should take no irrevocable step until his application has received at least a preliminary examination;[3] for the Government to do so might constitute a hindrance of the 'effective exercise' of the right of petition under Article 25(1).

On the other hand, the period of detention must not be unduly prolonged. This follows from Article 18 of the Convention, which provides that: 'The restrictions permitted under this Convention to the said rights and freedoms shall not be applied for any purpose other than those for which they have been prescribed.' As the prescribed purpose is clearly stated in Article 5(1) (f), detention may not be prolonged for any other purpose; for example, persons entering a country illegally must not be detained for long periods merely to discourage other potential immigrants. Of course, regard must be had to the applicant's own conduct in

---

[1] See above, p. 31, below, p. 129, and below, p. 182.
[2] The issue was raised in the Amekrane case; see above, p. 32.
[3] As in cases under Article 3; see above, p. 32.

considering the period of his detention, as he may have good reason for prolonging it himself.[1]

Finally, the condition of 'lawfulness' must again be interpreted, not merely as excluding any arbitrary action on the part of the authorities, but as requiring, more specifically, that the arrest and detention must comply with all the conditions, both of substance and of procedure, laid down by domestic law.[2]

II THE RIGHTS OF A PERSON ARRESTED OR DETAINED

Article 5(1) enumerates the conditions authorizing arrest or detention. This, however, does not exhaust the protection accorded by Article 5, which goes on to provide further guarantees to persons arrested or detained, whether lawfully or not.

The guarantees provided by paragraphs (2) to (4) are independent of paragraph (1) in the sense that even if the detention is lawful under paragraph (1), the provisions of paragraphs (2) to (4) must be observed.

Thus by paragraph (2), everyone who is arrested must be informed promptly, in a language which he understands, of the reasons for his arrest and of any charge against him. This applies, of course, whether or not the arrest is authorized under paragraph (1) (b) or (c). An arrest which satisfies the conditions of paragraph (1) will none the less be unlawful if it does not comply with paragraph (2).

Paragraph (3) provides guarantees for persons arrested or detained in accordance with the provisions of paragraph (1) (c). Persons lawfully detained on remand are entitled to trial within a reasonable time and, in certain circumstances, to release pending trial.

Under paragraph (4), anyone deprived of his liberty by arrest or detention is entitled to take proceedings by which the lawfulness of his detention shall be decided speedily by a court and his release ordered if the detention is not lawful. In the Vagrancy Cases, the Court held that, even where detention was lawful under Article 5(1), there could still be a violation of paragraph (4).[3]

Finally, Article 5(5) provides that 'Everyone who has been the victim of arrest or detention in contravention of the provisions of

---

[1] See 1983/63, *Yearbook* 9, 286.
[2] See above, pp. 46 and 56.
[3] Para. 73.

this Article shall have an enforceable right to compensation.' Thus there is a right to compensation even if the deprivation of liberty is authorized by paragraph (1), wherever there is a breach of the other provisions of Article 5.

The provisions of paragraphs (2) to (5) will now be considered in turn.

Article 5(2)

The rationale of Article 5(2), which provides that everyone who is arrested shall be informed promptly, in a language which he understands, of the reasons for his arrest and of any charge against him, is evident. A person is *prima facie* entitled to his freedom and is only required to submit to restraints on his freedom if he knows in substance the reason why it is claimed that this restraint should be imposed.[1] The text may be compared with Article 6(3) (a), which provides that everyone charged with a criminal offence must be informed promptly, in a language which he understands and in detail, of the nature and cause of the accusation against him. It is clear that the information to which a person is entitled concerning the charges made against him is more specific and more detailed in connection with his right to a fair trial under Article 6 than in connection with his right to liberty and security of person under Article 5. Such detailed information is necessary to enable him to prepare his defence. For the purposes of Article 5(2), on the other hand, it is sufficient if he is informed in general terms of the reasons for his arrest and of any charge against him.[2]

The relevant principles have been clearly stated in the leading case under English law.[3]

If a policeman arrests without warrant . . . he must in ordinary circumstances inform the person arrested of the true ground of arrest. He is not entitled to keep the reason to himself or to give a reason which is not the true reason. In other words a citizen is entitled to know on what charge or on suspicion of what crime he is seized . . . The requirement that the person arrested should be informed does not mean that technical or precise language need be used . . .

Similarly, in the view of the Commission, Article 5(2) does not

---

[1] See *Christie* v. *Leachinsky* [1947] A.C. 573 at 587–8.
[2] 343/57, *Yearbook* 2, 412 at 462.
[3] See *Christie* v. *Leachinsky* [1947] A.C. 573, at 588.

require that the information be given in a particular form[1] or in writing,[2] or that the reasons be set out in the text of the decision authorizing detention.[3]

More doubtful is the Commission's decision that an applicant who had been interrogated in detail by the investigating judge and had been confronted with his co-accused must on those grounds have been fully aware of the reasons for his arrest and the nature of the charges against him.[4]

The requirement that the information should be given 'in a language which he understands' may create difficulties, particularly in view of the numbers of migrant workers in Europe, and in the absence of a multilingual police force. However, the Commission has held that this requirement is satisfied if, immediately after his arrest, a person is interrogated by the investigating judge in his mother tongue.[5]

Does the expression 'informed in a language which he understands' require also that he should in fact understand the charge, that it should be explained if necessary at a level within his comprehension? The text speaks of *a* language (*une langue*). But having regard to the purpose of the provision, the answer should be affirmative. If this interpretation goes too far, then it would seem that the information should at least be given in language which would be understood by a person of average intelligence.

Article 5(3)

Article 5(3), as stated above, guarantees certain rights to persons arrested or detained in accordance with the provisions of Article 5(1) (c). The first part of Article 5(3) is concerned with rights immediately on arrest; the second part deals with detention on remand and will be considered below under that head.

The right on arrest is to be brought promptly before a judge or other officer authorized by law to exercise judicial power. Generally this provision appears to be well respected in the Contracting States, and it has raised few problems. In the Lawless Case an Irish law infringing this right was held to be covered by the Irish Government's derogation under Article 15.[6] In an application

---

[1] 2621/65, *Yearbook* 9, 474 at 480; 4220/69, *Yearbook* 14, 250 at 276.
[2] 1211/61, *Yearbook* 5, 224 at 228.   [3] See n. 1.
[4] 1936/63, *Yearbook* 7, 224 at 244.
[5] 2689/65, *Yearbook* 10, 238 at 270.
[6] See below, p. 205.

against the Netherlands,[1] the Commission, relying on the concept of 'margin of appreciation'[2] which appears particularly inappropriate in this context, held that a delay of four days did not go beyond the requirements of the Convention. It considered the legal provisions in force in the Member States, where it appears that the maximum period rarely exceeds forty-eight hours.[3]

Detention on remand

Article 5(3) next provides that 'Everyone arrested or detained in accordance with the provisions of paragraph (1) (c) of this Article . . . shall be entitled to trial within a reasonable time or to release pending trial . . .'

The interpretation of this provision has given rise to a substantial and complex body of case-law and requires somewhat extended treatment. It should be added that most of the cases have arisen under the Continental system of criminal procedure which appears to involve very much longer investigations than are generally found in England.[4]

The discussion here will be under three heads. First, what are the rights guaranteed by this provision? Second, what period of time is to be taken into consideration in deciding whether a person detained on remand has been brought to trial within a reasonable time? Third, by what criteria is the 'reasonableness' of the time to be assessed?

The rights guaranteed

In approaching this provision, it is essential at the outset to distinguish two closely related but separate ideas. On the one hand, there is the question whether the reasons which may have justified the initial arrest or detention under paragraph (1) (c) still exist. On the other hand, there is the question whether a person whose detention is still justified, in the sense that there are still good reasons for not releasing him, may none the less have been detained too long because his trial has been too long delayed. In either case, the person concerned may have been detained beyond a reasonable time, contrary to Article 5(3).

[1] 2894/66, *Yearbook* 9, 564.   [2] See below, p. 201.
[3] See Fawcett, p. 93, n. 4; cf. 4960/71, *Collection of Decisions* 42, 49.
[4] See Harris, 'Recent cases on pre-trial detention and delay in criminal proceedings in the European Court of Human Rights', *British Year Book of International Law*, 1970, 87.

So far as the *grounds* of detention are concerned, a literal interpretation of Article 5(1) (c) and Article 5(3) would seem to authorize indefinite detention on remand merely on the ground that justified initial arrest, i.e. in the usual case, suspicion of having committed an offence. Further, the only limitation on the *period* of such detention would be the requirement that the detained person be brought to trial 'within a reasonable time'.

Such an interpretation is unacceptable and has rightly been rejected by the Court in a succession of cases.[1] The Court has stated, in effect, that the continuing detention must be justified, so long as it lasts, by adequate *grounds*; and that, independently of those grounds, its *period* must also not exceed a reasonable time. The Court expressed the matter in the following way in the Stögmuller Case:[2]

It is true that paragraph (1) (c) authorises arrest or detention for the purpose of bringing 'before the competent legal authority' on the mere grounds of the existence of 'reasonable suspicion' that the person arrested 'has committed an offence' and it is clear that the persistence of such suspicions is a condition *sine qua non* for the validity of the continued detention of the person concerned, without it being necessary to go into the point whether detention maintained in spite of the disappearance of the suspicions on which the arrest was grounded violates Article 5, paragraph (1), or Article 5, paragraph (3), or these two provisions read together.

Article 5, paragraph (3), clearly implies, however, that the persistence of suspicion does not suffice to justify, after a certain lapse of time, the prolongation of the detention. That paragraph stipulates that the detention must not exceed a reasonable time.

But Article 5(3) certainly does not stipulate expressly that detention must not exceed a reasonable time. It appears to say only that the person detained is entitled to trial within a reasonable time *or* to release pending trial. What is a reasonable time for bringing a person to trial is not at all the same as a reasonable time for keeping him in detention. How then has the Court reached the conclusion that 'the purpose of the provision under consideration is essentially to require his provisional release once his continuing deten-

[1] See the Neumeister, Wemhoff, Stögmuller, Matznetter, and Ringeisen Cases. The periods of detention were respectively 26 months, 3 years, 24 months, 26 months, and 29 months.

[2] Para. 4 of 'The Law'.

tion ceases to be reasonable'?[1] (This of course is quite apart from its purpose, in relation to a person whose detention continues to be justified, of ensuring that he is brought to trial within a reasonable time.)

The reasoning of the Court is to be found in the Neumeister and Wemhoff Cases. In the Neumeister Case the Court stated:[2]

> The Court is of opinion that this provision cannot be understood as giving the judicial authorities a choice between either bringing the accused to trial within a reasonable time or granting him provisional release even subject to guarantees. The reasonableness of the time spent by an accused person in detention up to the beginning of the trial must be assessed in relation to the very fact of his detention. Until conviction he must be presumed innocent, and the purpose of the provision under consideration is essentially to require his provisional release once his continuing detention ceases to be reasonable.

The Court explains in the Wemhoff Case[3] its opinion that this provision cannot be understood as giving the judicial authorities a choice:

> The Court is quite certain that such an interpretation would not conform to the intention of the High Contracting Parties. It is inconceivable that they should have intended to permit their judicial authorities, at the price of release of the accused, to protract proceedings beyond a reasonable time. This would, moreover, be flatly contrary to the provision in Article 6(1) cited above.

The reasoning is not entirely satisfactory, since there is no harm in construing one provision of the Convention in a way which might authorize an unacceptable practice, if that practice is prohibited by another provision. The Court is nevertheless clearly right in holding that the use of the word 'or' does not give the authorities a choice.

This does not mean that 'or' should have been 'and'. Article 5(3) does not impose two concurrent obligations, both to bring the accused to trial within a reasonable time and to release him pending trial. If he is provisionally released, Article 5, which is concerned only with the rights of detained persons, ceases to

---

[1] Neumeister Case, para. 4 of 'The Law'.
[2] Ibid. [3] Para. 5 of 'The Law'.

apply, and there is thenceforth no obligation under Article 5 to bring him to trial within a reasonable time, though the proceedings will of course continue to be subject to Article 6.

It is clear from the structure of Articles 5 and 6 that Article 5(3) applies only to persons still in detention awaiting trial, and has no application to persons provisionally released, unless they are subsequently further detained. Despite the reference to 'arrested or detained' it is evident from the very wording of the provisions that the guarantees of Article 5(3), and indeed of Article 5(4), apply only in the case of continuing detention.

The conclusion therefore must be that a person detained on remand has the right not to be detained beyond a reasonable time; and that this involves (a) the right to be released if there cease to be adequate grounds for his detention; (b) if he is not released, the right to be brought to trial within a reasonable time.

The right to be released

What grounds are adequate, under Article 5(3), to justify continuing detention? Reference must be made again to the provisions of paragraph (1) (c). We have already seen that continuing suspicion that the detained person has committed the offence does not suffice;[1] this, indeed, would justify detention to the date of trial in every case. Continuing suspicion is a necessary, but not a sufficient, condition. Are the other grounds mentioned in Article 5(1) (c) exhaustive, that is, may a person be detained on remand only 'when it is reasonably considered necessary to prevent his committing an offence or fleeing after having done so'? The usual reason is of course the latter, to prevent *the risk of absconding*. But the risk must be substantiated in each case, and the decisions of the national authorities are subject to the control of the Commission and the Court, which have held in a number of cases that the risk of absconding did not justify detention at the outset, or could no longer do so after a certain date in the proceedings.[2] In any event, where the danger of absconding can be avoided by bail or other guarantees, the accused must be released.[3]

---

[1] See above, pp. 52 and 64; the Stögmuller Case, para. 4 of 'The Law'.

[2] See, e.g. the Neumeister Case, para. 9 *et seq.*, of 'The Law'; the Matznetter Case, para. 11 of 'The Law' (but detention justified by danger of repetition of offences); and *Vampel* v. *Austria*, p. 69, below.

[3] See the Wemhoff Case, para. 15 of 'The Law' and p. 71, below.

The risk of a further offence was held by the Court in the Matznetter Case to be a reason compatible with Article 5(3) 'in the special circumstances of the case'.[1] But, if it was capable of justifying detention, the question had still to be answered whether it did in fact. The Court held, in that case, that it justified detention, but in the Ringeisen Case that it did not.[2]

Other grounds which have been accepted by the Court as in principle capable of justifying detention are the risk of suppression of evidence[3] and of collusion.[4] As these do not necessarily constitute criminal offences in the law of the Contracting States, it would seem that the grounds stated in paragraph (1) (c), the risk of absconding and the risk of a further offence, are not exhaustive, and no rigid set of criteria is applicable under paragraph (3). The facts of each case must be examined to see whether, in the light of the reasons given by the national authorities, detention was unduly prolonged.

Thus the Commission and the Court must review and assess the reasons given by the national authorities for refusing release. 'It is for the national judicial authorities to seek all the facts arguing for or against the existence of a genuine requirement of public interest justifying a departure from the rule of respect for individual liberty;'[5] and it is essentially on the basis of the reasons given in the decisions on the applications for release pending trial that the issue of a violation of Article 5(3) must be determined.[6]

In reviewing and assessing the reasons given by the national authorities, the Commission and the Court must first consider whether those reasons are compatible with Article 5(3) in the sense that they are in principle capable of justifying detention on remand; and secondly, they must consider whether continued detention was actually justified on the facts of the particular case.[7]

The right to trial within a reasonable time

For the reasons stated above, this right arises under Article 5 only

---

[1] Para. 9 of 'The Law'.   [2] Para. 107.

[3] The Wemhoff Case, paras. 13 & 14 of 'The Law'.

[4] The Ringeisen Case, para. 106.

[5] The Neumeister Case, para. 5 of 'The Law'.

[6] Ibid.; cf. Wemhoff Case, para. 12 of 'The Law'; Stögmuller Case, para. 3 of 'The Law'; Matznetter Case, para. 3 of 'The Law'; and Ringeisen Case, para. 104. See also 3637/68, *Collection of Decisions*, 31, 51 at 66 *et seq.*

[7] For this assessment see below, p. 70.

in the case of persons who are detained until trial. If a person is released at any stage before his trial, the situation is governed by Article 6(1).

The questions to be considered here are, first, what period of time is to be taken into consideration in deciding whether a person detained on remand has been brought to trial within a reasonable time; and secondly, by what criteria the 'reasonableness' of the time is to be assessed.

The period to be considered

The period to be taken into consideration in applying Article 5(3) begins, necessarily, with arrest or detention. The Court held in the Wemhoff case that it ends with the delivery of the judgment that terminates the trial in the court of first instance,[1] and that it does not extend to the date on which conviction becomes final, that is, after appeal or on expiry of the time-limit for appeal. The reason which the Court found decisive in favour of this interpretation was that a person convicted at first instance is in the position provided for by Article 5(1) (a), which authorizes deprivation of liberty 'after conviction'. This last phrase cannot be interpreted as being restricted to the case of a final conviction, for this would exclude the arrest immediately on conviction of all those who appear for trial while still at liberty.

In the Rosenbaum Case the Commission followed the Court and took as the end of the period the date of the applicant's conviction by the court of first instance.[2] In a later decision,[3] however, the Commission departed from this reasoning; having referred to the provisions of the German Code of Criminal Procedure whereby the execution of a penalty cannot commence until the conviction acquires the force of *res judicata*, the Commission held that detention during cassation proceedings should not be considered as detention after conviction under Article 5(1) (a) but as detention on remand under Article 5(1) (c). The Commission was not concerned in this case with the length of detention on remand but it is clear that the period to be considered would extend on this view beyond conviction at first instance.

[1] The Wemhoff case, paras. 6 to 9 of 'The Law'.
[2] 3376/67, *Collection of Decisions* 29, 31; cf. 3843/68, *Collection of Decisions* 32, 30 at 35.
[3] 3911/69, *Collection of Decisions* 30, 76.

In the Ringeisen Case the Commission requested the Court to review its decision in the Wemhoff Case on this point, or at least to interpret it in such a way that detention after conviction might be considered as remaining subject to Article 5(3) until the conviction becomes final in cases where the national law treats it up to that time as detention on remand. Ringeisen had been detained on two separate charges and separate proceedings were pending in each. His detention after conviction in one case was also covered by remand in custody in the other case. In the circumstances the Court did not consider it necessary to pronounce on the issues raised by the Commission; it held that its finding on Article 5(3) covered the whole period of Ringeisen's detention.[1]

The issue was of some practical importance in Austrian procedure. An applicant who was alleged to have made a suicide pact with his mistress, shot her and then himself.[2] Neither was killed by the shooting, but she was suffocated by exhaust fumes which he introduced into his car, and he was totally paralysed. He was subsequently convicted of murder, and complained, *inter alia*, of the length of his detention on remand. It was common ground between the parties that the usual reasons for detention on remand did not exist in the applicant's case: he was totally paralysed and consequently there was no risk of his absconding or committing further offences; he had fully confessed to the offence and there were no witnesses of the incident, so that there was no risk of collusion. The sole ground for the applicant's detention was the existence of Article 180 of the Austrian Code of Penal Procedure which made detention on remand obligatory in cases where the person concerned was charged with a crime for which the law provided a minimum penalty of ten years' imprisonment.

Under the Austrian Code of Criminal Procedure, detention pending appeal is considered as detention on remand, and there was no provision for a person detained on remand to be released on the ground that he was unfit for detention; so the applicant could not be released pending appeal. After his conviction was upheld, however, he was released as being unfit for detention by reason of his paralysis and his need for continuous medical care. It would have been difficult to find in this case that detention pending appeal was not detention on remand, when it was precisely because it had this character that the applicant had to

---

[1] Para. 109.   [2] 4465/70, *Yearbook* 14, 476.

remain in prison for a further eight months between trial and appeal.

The proceedings before the Commission were suspended after the Austrian Code of Criminal Procedure was amended so as to abolish obligatory detention on remand in such circumstances.[1]

It remains uncertain, therefore, whether the protection of Article 5(3) extends to detention pending appeal.

Assessment of what is reasonable

Just as the duration of the period to be considered, for the purposes of Article 5(3), is different from that to be considered under Article 6(1), so the assessment of what period is 'reasonable' differs in the two cases. 'Article 5, which begins with an affirmation of the right of everyone to liberty and security of person, goes on to specify the situations and conditions in which derogations from this principle may be made, in particular with a view to the maintenance of public order, which requires that offences shall be punished. *It is thus mainly in the light of the fact of the detention* of the person being prosecuted that national courts, possibly followed by the European Court, must determine whether the time that has elapsed, for whatever reason, before judgment is passed on the accused has at some stage exceeded a reasonable limit, that is to say imposed a greater sacrifice than could, in the circumstances of the case, reasonably be expected of a person presumed to be innocent.'[2]

Consequently, Article 5(3) requires that there must be 'special diligence' in bringing the case to trial if the accused is detained.[3] He is entitled to have his case given priority and conducted with particular expedition.[4]

Thus the standard imposed by Article 5(3) is higher than that imposed by Article 6(1). By what method can it be decided whether the standard has been achieved?

In the earlier cases, the Commission elaborated a list of criteria, including the complexity of the case, the conduct of the accused, and the conduct of the judicial authorities, to be taken into account in deciding whether detention on remand exceeded a

---

[1] Stock-taking note, DH(73) 8, p. 34.
[2] Wemhoff Case, para. 5 of 'The Law'. (Italics supplied.)
[3] Stögmuller Case, para. 5 of 'The Law'.
[4] Wemhoff Case, para. 17 of 'The Law'.

reasonable time.[1] The Court, however, rejected this approach, and considered that the essential question was whether the reasons given by the national authorities to justify continued detention were relevant and sufficient to show that it was not unreasonably prolonged.[2] It seems, however, that the Commission and the Court have not completely maintained the distinction between the grounds justifying detention and the right to trial within a reasonable time. In the former case, it is appropriate to suggest that they must review and assess the reasons given by the national authorities for refusing release.[3] In the latter case, however, which we are now considering, the question is whether the authorities were sufficiently expeditious in bringing the case to trial. Here the Commission and the Court must consider, it would seem, quite different factors, such as the reasons for the delay, the complexity of the case, and whether the accused himself contributed to the delay. Here the criteria proposed by the Commission may after all be relevant; and these factors have in fact been taken into consideration by the Court.

Bail[4]

Finally, Article 5(3) recognizes that 'Release may be conditioned by guarantees to appear for trial'. According to the Court, these words 'show that, when the only remaining reason for continued detention is the fear that the accused will abscond and thereby subsequently avoid appearing for trial, his release pending trial must be ordered if it is possible to obtain from him guarantees that will ensure such appearance'.[5]

It follows from this principle that in those countries which have the system of bail or other financial sureties, the amount of such sureties must not be excessive, and must be fixed by reference to the purpose for which they are imposed, namely to secure that the accused appears for trial.[6] It must never be fixed exclusively by

[1] See, e.g. Report of the Commission in the Matznetter Case, Publications of the Court, Series B, p. 25 et seq.

[2] Wemhoff Case, para. 12 of 'The Law'.

[3] See above, p. 67.

[4] See Daintith and Wilkinson, 'Bail and the Convention: British reflections on the Wemhoff and Neumeister cases', American Journal of Comparative Law, 1970, 326.

[5] Wemhoff Case, para. 15 of 'The Law'.

[6] Neumeister Case paras. 13 and 14 of 'The Law'; cf. 4225/69, Yearbook 13, 864 at 884.

reference to the seriousness of the charge. If the accused cannot be released because the guarantees demanded are excessive, his detention will be unlawful under Article 5(3). Detention is not authorized solely on the ground that the guarantees demanded cannot be provided; it is authorized only if the guarantees demanded are necessary to secure his appearance but no greater than necessary. The question in each case is: having regard to the person concerned, his means, and his relation to the sureties, if any, is there a sufficient deterrent to dispel any inclination on his part to abscond?[1] It is imporrtant to recall, in this connection, that the authorities do not have a choice between bringing the accused to trial within a reasonable time and releasing him on bail.[2] Release, if necessary on bail, will often be obligatory.

Article 5(4)

Article 5(4) provides that: 'Everyone who is deprived of his liberty by arrest or detention shall be entitled to take proceedings by which the lawfulness of his detention shall be decided speedily by a court and his release ordered if the detention is not lawful.'

In contrast with paragraph (3), paragraph (4) covers, *prima facie*, all forms of arrest and detention. There is a right to judicial control of the legality of the deprivation of liberty, that is, of whether it is lawful under one of the conditions listed exhaustively under paragraph (1).

The Court has held that this provision does not apply, however, where detention has been ordered by a court following proper judicial procedure. The purpose of paragraph (4) is to guarantee the right of persons arrested or detained to judicial supervision; when the decision depriving a person of his liberty is taken by an administrative body, there is a right of recourse to a court, but if the decision is taken by a court following proper judicial procedure, and respecting the fundamental procedural guarantees, the supervision required by paragraph (4) is incorporated in the decision and there is no requirement for a second judicial authority to review the decision.[3]

The terms of paragraph (4) are open to either interpretation, and the issue is a difficult one. The Court's interpretation is open to the objection that the expression 'Everyone who is deprived of

---

[1] Ibid.   [2] See above, p. 65.
[3] The Vagrancy Cases, para. 76.

his liberty by arrest or detention' is very wide and makes no reference to a distinction between detention by judicial and by administrative process. It could also be argued that, given the possibility of two interpretations which are equally defensible, that interpretation which more effectively secures the protection of human rights should be preferred to the more restrictive interpretation.[1] The Court relied on the analogy of 'conviction by a competent court' under paragraph (1) (a), and it is true that in this case the right to judicial review of the lawfulness of detention is not universally recognized and the Convention itself does not guarantee any right of appeal.[2] But under English law an action for *habeas corpus*, for example, will lie even where a person is serving a prison sentence on conviction of an offence. In any event, the Court's interpretation seems to have been unnecessary for its decision, since it held that the proceedings in issue did not comply with the requirements of Article 5.[3]

It would seem, too, that what constitutes a 'court', and what procedural guarantees are implied by the use of that term in Article 5(4), must depend upon the circumstances of the case. It had already been held in the Neumeister case that the term 'court' in paragraph (4) implies only that the authority called upon to decide '. . . must be independent both of the executive and of the parties to the case; it in no way relates to the procedure to be followed'.[4] The Chamber accordingly held that proceedings under paragraph (4) to challenge detention on remand under paragraph (1) (c) do not require the application of the principle of 'equality of arms'.[5]

The Commission subsequently expressed the view that different considerations apply to proceedings relating to the release of persons detained as being of unsound mind, since in such cases different investigations were required, and there was generally less need for speed. It might be necessary, therefore, that such proceedings should be accompanied by certain guarantees, in other words that certain elements of the notion of 'fair hearing' (a reference to Article 6(1)) are applicable.[6]

In the Vagrancy Cases,[7] the plenary Court recognized that

[1] See above, p. 17.   [2] See below, p. 84.   [3] See below, p. 74.
[4] Para. 24 of 'The Law'.   [5] For this principle, see below, p. 99.
[6] 3151/67, *Collection of Decisions* 27, 128 at 135; cf. 4625/70, *Collection of Decisions* 40, 2.
[7] See above, p. 55.

the principle stated in the Neumeister Case might not apply in a different context, even in another situation also governed by paragraph (4).[1] It held that although the procedure followed by the magistrate in the Vagrancy Cases had certain judicial features, these were 'not sufficient to give the magistrate the character of a "court" within the meaning of paragraph (4) when due account is taken of the seriousness of what is at stake, namely a long deprivation of liberty attended by various shameful consequences.'[2] Hence the Court found that that procedure was in breach of Article 5(4).

In execution of the Court's judgment, the Belgian Government shortly afterwards amended its legislation on vagrancy so as to give persons detained as vagrants the right of appeal to a court of law. By a transitional provision, this remedy was also made available to persons detained at the time when the new law entered into force.

In conclusion, therefore, it seems that what constitutes a court, and what procedures are necessary, under Article 5(4), depends in each case on the particular circumstances and on the consequences of the decision in question. In every case it will be helpful to compare the requirements of Article 5(4) with the scope and content of the procedural safeguards guaranteed under Article 6(1), as interpreted by the judgment of the Court in the Ringeisen case.[3]

Article 5(5)

Article 5(5) provides that: 'Everyone who has been the victim of arrest or detention in contravention of the provisions of this Article shall have an enforceable right to compensation.'

It is not clear why special provision is made for compensation for a breach of Article 5(1) to (4), when there is no such special provision in relation to the other rights guaranteed by the Convention, and when there is a general provision under Article 13 for an effective remedy for any violation. A possible explanation is that, if there were no express provision for financial compensation, release from unlawful detention, which it is the object of paragraphs (3) and (4) to secure, might have been considered an adequate remedy.

The Commission and the Court have given little guidance in

---

[1] Para. 78.   [2] Para. 79.   [3] See below, p. 79.

the interpretation of Article 5(5). The view expressed by the Commission in one case, that even an applicant who claims to have been unlawfully detained for several years must show damage before he can claim compensation, seems very dubious.[1] In the Wemhoff Case, although the Commission considered that there had been a violation of Article 5(3), it was unanimously of the opinion that it could not consider the applicant's claim under Article 5(5) before: (1) the competent organ, namely the Court or Committee of Ministers, had given a decision on the question whether Article 5(3) had been violated; and (2) the applicant had had an opportunity, with respect to his claim for compensation, to exhaust domestic remedies in accordance with Article 26.[2] The Commission's interpretation must be regarded as very doubtful. Once a breach of the Convention has been established by the Court or the Committee of Ministers, an applicant who has suffered damage is in any event entitled to compensation from the respondent Government, and if this were the only purpose of Article 5(5) that provision would be superfluous. Its object must therefore be to give a person unlawfully arrested or detained the right to damages under national law. The Court held that there had been no breach of Article 5(3) and did not deal with paragraph (5).

Where, however, the Court finds that an applicant has been unlawfully deprived of his liberty, he has an alternative method of claiming compensation. On the Court's interpretation of Article 50 of the Convention, the applicant, if he has been unable to obtain compensation from the Government, can apply directly to Strasbourg, without making a fresh application to the Commission under Article 25, and without any requirement as to the exhaustion of domestic remedies.[3]

Conclusions

Some general conclusions may be drawn from this examination of Article 5 of the Convention. Protection against arbitrary arrest and detention is clearly the central feature of any system of guarantees of the liberty of the individual. Article 5 contains a remarkable attempt to specify exhaustively the conditions authorizing

[1] 2932/66, *Collection of Decisions* 31, 8 at 15.
[2] Opinion, para. 76.
[3] See below, p. 265.

arrest and detention, and to provide for appropriate procedural guarantees. It must be recognized, however, that the drafting of the Article is not always satisfactory and often too compressed. Difficulties have inevitably arisen in confronting its provisions with the very detailed, and also very diverse regulation of the matter in the substantive and procedural law of the Contracting States. To some extent the defects of drafting have been remedied by the substantive body of case-law developed by the Commission and the Court. Even so, however, some of the terms contained in Article 5 have been unduly neglected. In particular, the requirement of lawfulness has not been given full weight in the Commission's decisions; the Court's judgment on the interpretation of Article 5(1) (e) must be given full effect in relation to the other provisions of Article 5. Finally, little effect has been given to some of the guarantees laid down by the Article, especially under paragraph (5).

Further, it is doubtful whether the provisions of Article 5 have had much impact on the day-to-day administration of criminal justice in the Contracting States. The operation of the system of bail in England,[1] of the institutions of *garde à vue* and *détention préventive* in France,[2] and the length of periods of detention on remand in other States, do not seem to have been much affected by adherence to the Convention. It is true that both in Austria and in the Federal Republic of Germany, reforms of criminal procedure have been introduced, in part in response to the requirements of the Convention, intended to limit to six months, apart from exceptional cases, the period of detention on remand, and other more limited reforms have been made.[3] But Article 5, as has been seen, embodies a minimum level of protection. It is doubtful whether in many countries even this minimum level is attained in a high proportion of cases.

ARTICLE 6

The right to a fair trial

Article 6, which guarantees the right to a fair trial, occupies a

[1] See Daintith and Wilkinson, op. cit. p. 71 n. 4.
[2] See G. Levasseur, 'La Convention et la procédure pénale française . . .', *Revue des Droits de l'Homme*, 1970, 595.
[3] See above, p. 69.

central place in the system of the Convention. The importance, for the protection of the liberty of the individual, of a fair trial in criminal cases does not require elaboration. Further, the protection against unlawful detention in Article 5 would lose its effectiveness if persons 'detained after conviction' under Article 5(1) (a) could be convicted without the safeguards of a fair trial.[1]

A fair trial, in civil and criminal cases alike, is a basic element of the notion of the rule of law, part of the common heritage, according to the Preamble, of the Contracting States.

The structure of Article 6 is straightforward. The right to a fair trial is stated in paragraph (1), and applies equally to civil and criminal proceedings. Paragraphs (2) and (3) enumerate certain specific procedural guarantees, which are confined to criminal proceedings. These guarantees do not, however, exhaust the notion of a fair trial. Thus a trial may not conform to the standard of a fair trial under paragraph (1) even if all the rights guaranteed by paragraphs (2) and (3) have been respected.[2]

The first sentence of Article 6(1) provides that 'In the determination of his civil rights and obligations or of any criminal charge against him, everyone is entitled to a fair and public hearing within a reasonable time by an independent and impartial tribunal established by law.'[3] The second sentence specifies the exceptions to the principle that the trial must be public. Otherwise there are no exceptions whatsoever to any of the rights guaranteed by Article 6, subject only to the possibility of derogation under Article 15 in time of war or a state of emergency.[4]

Before considering the detailed rights guaranteed by Article 6(1), it is necessary to examine in some detail the general scope of that provision. To what proceedings does it apply? The expressions

[1] See above, p. 48.

[2] The Pfunders Case (*Austria* v. *Italy*), Report of the Commission, *Yearbook* 6, 740 at 790 f.; see below, p. 114.

[3] The French text reads: 'Toute personne a droit à ce que sa cause soit entendue équitablement, publiquement et dans un délai raisonnable, par un tribunal indépendant et impartial, établi par la loi, qui décidera, soit des contestations sur ses droits et obligations de caractère civil, soit du bien-fondé de toute accusation en matière pénale dirigée contre elle.' The differences of syntax and structure between the two texts have increased the difficulties of interpretation. See Golsong, 'International Treaty Provisions on the Protection of the Individual against the Executive by Domestic Courts', in *Judicial Protection against the Executive*, Cologne, New York, 1971, Volume 3, 245.

[4] See below, p. 204. For the effect of Article 17 in relation to Article 6, see below, p. 211.

'civil rights and obligations' and 'criminal charge' have been the subject of some controversy which has not yet been fully resolved.

Civil rights and obligations

It is evident that 'determination of civil rights and obligations' covers ordinary civil litigation between private individuals. The basic problem in defining this term is to know whether it is intended to cover also certain rights which, under some systems of law, fall under administrative law rather than under private law. If, for example, a public authority expropriates my land, do I have the right to a court hearing? Naturally enough, the issue has often arisen before the Commission, but it has almost always happened that the application was rejected on some other ground, without the issue being resolved.[1]

Thus, in one application from the United Kingdom, where an order was made for the compulsory acquisition of three houses owned by the applicant, he argued that he had been denied the right to a fair and public hearing under Article 6(1). The United Kingdom Government submitted that the exercise by the local authority, and by the Minister, of their powers under the relevant legislation were acts of public administration, governed by public law, and, accordingly, that the decisions complained of did not involve the determination of any civil rights within the meaning of Article 6(1). In the event, the Commission left the question open and rejected the application for non-exhaustion of domestic remedies.[2]

The Commission has, however, consistently stated that the question cannot be answered by reference to the categories of domestic law; it is immaterial whether the claim in issue is characterized by that law as falling under civil law or not. Thus, it has frequently said that the term 'civil rights and obligations' employed in Article 6(1) cannot be construed as a mere reference to the domestic law of the State concerned, but relates to an autonomous concept which must be interpreted independently of the rights existing in the domestic law, although the general principles of the domestic law of the Contracting Parties must necessarily be taken into consideration in any such interpretation.[3]

---

[1] See, e.g. 3332/67, *Collection of Decisions* 34, 1, and 4430/70, *Collection of Decisions* 37, 112 (claims for compensation determined by the Foreign Office with no judicial remedy). See Golsong, op. cit. p. 77 n. 3.

[2] 3651/68, *Yearbook* 13, 476.   [3] 1931/63, *Yearbook* 7, 212 at 222.

Thus, a right may be a 'civil right' under Article 6(1) even though, under the domestic law of the State concerned, it falls under public and not under private law.[1] Conversely, a claim against the State for compensation, for example, may be outside the scope of that provision, even though under domestic law it is dealt with by the civil courts.[2]

In the Ringeisen Case, the question could no longer be left open. In addition to the criminal proceedings against the applicant which have already been referred to, the Commission had to consider whether 'civil rights' were involved in an application by Ringeisen for approval of the transfer to him, from a private person, of certain plots of land in Austria. He alleged that the Regional Real Property Transactions Commission which had heard his appeal against the decision of the District Commission, was biased, and consequently that it was not an impartial tribunal as required by Article 6(1).

On the meaning of 'civil rights and obligations' the majority of the Commission was of the opinion that the term 'must be interpreted restrictively so as to comprise such legal relationships only as are typical of relations between private individuals, to the exclusion of such legal relations in which the citizen is confronted with those who exercise public authority'.[3] The reasoning in support of this opinion is sufficiently important to be quoted *in extenso*:

Although the exact delimitation may give rise to doubt in certain border-line cases, a distinction based on this general criterion corresponds to the actual legal situation in most, if not all, contracting states. It is characteristic of the modern European State that the rights and obligations of the individual in many respects are not determined exhaustively by abstract rules of law, but depend upon the determination by administrative decision in each specific case. The use of land is one important field. Very rarely has the owner an unlimited right to use the land as he pleases. If he wants to convert it from one use to another, if he wants to build on his land or to demolish a house, or if he wants to divide the land or the site he owns, his right to do so may be subject to a permission by a public authority. Such permission may in some circumstances be granted him as of right, but in other circumstances the public authority may exercise a certain measure of administrative discretion.

---

[1] See the Ringeisen Case, below.
[2] 4618/70, *Collection of Decisions* 40, 11.
[3] Report of the Commission in the Ringeisen Case, para. 142.

The contractual rights and obligations of private individuals may likewise be subject to public control and approval in each particular case. Import and export licences are still an important element in the regulation of international trade. The exercise of certain trades or professions may also be subject to approval by a public authority.

Even interference with private property, such as expropriation of land for public use, demolition orders in case of slum clearance, orders relating to urban development etc. is decided by administrative bodies or authorities.

These examples, to which numerous others could be added, seem to indicate that it it is a normal feature of contemporary administrative law that the rights and obligations of the citizen, even in matters which relate very closely to his private property or his private activities, are determined by some public authority which does not fulfil the conditions laid down in Article 6, paragraph (1) with respect to independent and impartial tribunals.

It is true that there is in all countries a legitimate concern to protect the citizen against arbitrary administrative action. This concern may result in the adoption of legislative or other rules concerning administrative procedure. It may result in the introduction of judicial review of administrative action, and the states members of the Council of Europe have for historical and other reasons adopted widely divergent systems of such judicial review. One common feature, however, seems to be that there are certain elements of administrative discretion which cannot be reviewed by the judge. If the administrative authority has acted properly and within the limits of the law, the judge can very rarely, if ever, decide whether or not the administrative decision was well founded in substance. To that extent, there is no possibility of bringing the case before an independent and impartial tribunal, even if there is dispute ('contestation') between the citizen and the public authority.

Consequently, it would seem to be incompatible with the intentions of the contracting parties to adopt an extensive interpretation of the term 'civil rights and obligations'.

The Commission accordingly considered that Article 6(1) was not applicable.

A minority of the Commission expressed a different opinion,[1] according to which Article 6(1) applied also to interferences by public authorities with the rights and obligations flowing from domestic law. The minority argued that the term 'civil rights and obligations' would lose its autonomous character if it were con-

[1] Para. 143.

fined, as in certain Continental legal systems, to private law. Secondly, the minority considered that it would be anomalous if a Convention envisaging the protection of the individual against the State did not grant the individual any right to a judicial remedy or any right to a fair trial in the case of an arbitrary interference by public authorities with the rights granted by domestic law. Finally it was argued, following the opinion of the Court in the Wemhoff Case,[1] that where there was a disparity between the French and English text of the Convention it was 'necessary to seek the interpretation that is most appropriate in order to realize the aim and achieve the object of the treaty, not that which would restrict to the greatest possible degree the obligations undertaken by the Parties'.

The minority of the Commission concluded that Article 6(1) was applicable, and that in the present case it had been violated.

Both the majority and the minority view were further developed in the hearings before the Court. The Court held that Article 6(1) was applicable, although it had not been violated in the present case because, in so far as Ringeisen had alleged bias, that charge had not been made out. As to the interpretation of Article 6(1) it held as follows:[2]

For Article 6, paragraph (1), to be applicable to a case ('contestation') it is not necessary that both parties to the proceedings should be private persons, which is the view of the majority of the Commission and of the Government. The wording of Article 6, paragraph (1), is far wider; the French expression 'contestations sur (des) droits et obligations de caractère civil' covers all proceedings the result of which is decisive for private rights and obligations. The English text, 'determination of . . . civil rights and obligations', confirms this interpretation.

The character of the legislation which governs how the matter is to be determined (civil, commercial, administrative law, etc.) and that of the authority which is invested with jurisdiction in the matter (ordinary court, administrative body, etc) are therefore of little consequence.

In the present case, when Ringeisen purchased property from the Roth couple, he had a right to have the contract for sale which they had made with him approved if he fulfilled, as he claimed to do, the conditions laid down in the Act. Although it was applying rules of administrative law, the Regional Commission's decision was to be decisive

---

[1] Para. 8 of 'The Law'.
[2] Para. 94.

for the relations in civil law ('de caractère civil') between Ringeisen and the Roth couple. This is enough to make it necessary for the Court to decide whether or not the proceedings in the case complied with the requirements of Article 6, paragraph (1), of the Convention.

The difficulties which may result from this interpretation will be apparent from the reasoning of the majority of the Commission quoted above.

It does not, of course, follow from the Court's decision, however, that all decisions of public authorities which affect a person's legal situation are subject to the guarantees of Article 6(1) and require the availability of judicial review. Such an interpretation would be far too sweeping and totally out of line with the administrative law of many Convention States. It was a special feature of the Ringeisen Case that there was a pre-existing relationship under civil law between private individuals, which was directly 'determined' by the acts of the public authorities. Seen in this light, the Court's judgment does not have the dire consequences for public administration which have sometimes been attributed to it. Nor does it necessarily invalidate previous decisions of the Commission that certain claims fall outside the protection of Article 6(1), such as claims to be admitted to the public service,[1] certain proceedings regarding taxation[2] or social security contributions,[3] and proceedings concerning applications for release from detention.[4] Applications for release from detention on remand are clearly outside the scope of Article 6(1).[5]

Perhaps, however, the case-law of the Commission is modified by the Court's judgment in the Ringeisen Case to the extent that proceedings of the kinds referred to are *in principle* outside the scope of Article 6(1), but that they may be brought within the scope of this provision if the proceedings are liable to affect pre-existing relations under civil law between private individuals. Where this is so, then it is no longer correct to say that 'the right to have a purely administrative decision based upon proceedings comparable to those prescribed by Article 6 for proceedings in

[1] 1931/63, *Yearbook* 7, 212; 3937/69, *Collection of Decisions* 32, 61.
[2] 1094/64, etc., *Yearbook* 9, 268.
[3] 2248/64, *Yearbook* 10, 170.
[4] 606/59, *Yearbook* 4, 340 (application to be released on probation); 1760/63, *Yearbook* 9, 166 (application for conditional release).
[5] 'Judgment of the Court', the Neumeister Case, para. 23 of 'The Law'; for proceedings after conviction see below, p. 89.

court is not as such included among the rights and freedoms guaranteed by the Convention.'[1]

Where, however, the administrative decision does not affect any legal relationship between private individuals, Article 6(1) does not apply. Thus, applying the Court's ruling in the Ringeisen case, the Commission held that, in such a case, there is no right to a fair hearing in proceedings to set aside a decision of the planning authorities.[2] Similarly, Article 6(1) does not apply to proceedings on a claim for a pension.[3]

Criminal charge

Article 6(1) applies to proceedings involving the determination of a 'criminal charge'. Paragraphs (2) and (3) apply to 'Everyone charged with a criminal offence'. The scope of paragraph (1) in so far as it relates to criminal proceedings appears therefore very similar to, if not identical with, the scope of paragraphs (2) and (3).

The protection of Article 6 therefore starts from the time when a person is charged with a criminal offence. This is not, however, necessarily the moment when formal charges are first made against a person suspected of having committed an offence. For, in the first place, the protection of Article 6 does not depend on the particular features of the system of criminal investigation and prosecution, which may and do vary considerably between the Contracting Parties. Like 'civil rights and obligations'[4], the term 'charge' cannot be construed in the terms of the domestic law of any of the Contracting States but must be interpreted independently.[5] The extent of the obligations imposed by Article 6 must be uniform; here as elsewhere a European standard must be developed.[6]

Secondly, the object of Article 6 is to protect a person throughout the criminal process. Formal charges, however, may be brought at various stages in the course of the investigation. Consequently, it is necessary to find a criterion for the opening of criminal pro-

[1] 1329/62, *Yearbook* 5, 200 at 208.
[2] 5428/72, *Collection of Decisions* 44, 49.
[3] 3959/69, *Collection of Decisions* 35, 109; 5713/72, *Collection of Decisions* 44, 77.
[4] See above, p. 78.
[5] Opinion of the Commisssion in the Soltikow case, para. 26, *Yearbook* 14, 868 at 870, and in the Huber case, para. 65.
[6] See abovd, p. 19.

ceedings which is independent of the actual development of the procedure in a specific case.

In accordance with these principles, the Commission has held that the mere interrogation of a person may not be sufficient to hold that he is faced with a criminal charge.[1] The criteria for deciding whether the protection of Article 6 has started to operate are considered further below.[2]

Article 6(1) applies not only to the proceedings before the court of first instance, but also to proceedings before appeal courts, and even to proceedings in cassation, i.e. where the higher court has the power to quash the decision of the lower court but not to substitute its own decision. The justification of a wide interpretation of Article 6(1) was given by the Court in the Delcourt Case, holding that it was applicable to proceedings before the Belgian Court of Cassation.[3] The Court argued that 'In a democratic society within the meaning of the Convention, the right to a fair administration of justice holds such a prominent place that a restrictive interpretation of Article 6(1) would not correspond to the aim and the purpose of that provision.'[4]

Although the judgment of the Court of Cassation could only confirm or quash a decision, and not reverse or replace it, it could not be said that the court did not determine a criminal charge. The Government had argued that the Court of Cassation does not deal with the merits of cases submitted to it; accordingly there was not, strictly speaking, a prosecution or a defence before the Court.

This argument was rejected; 'a criminal charge is not really "determined" as long as the verdict of acquittal or conviction has not become final. Criminal proceedings form an entity and must, in the ordinary way, terminate in an enforceable decision. Proceedings in cassation are one special stage of the criminal proceedings and their consequences may prove decisive for the accused. It would therefore be hard to imagine that proceedings in cassation fall outside the scope of Article 6(1).'

The judgment continues: 'Article 6(1) of the Convention does not, it is true, compel the contracting States to set up courts of appeal or of cassation. Nevertheless, a State which does institute such courts is required to ensure that persons amenable to the law

[1] 4483/70, *Collection of Decisions* 38, 77, and Opinion of the Commission in the Huber case, para. 69.
[2] P. 107.　　　[3] See below, p. 100.　　　[4] Para. 25.

84

shall enjoy before these courts the fundamental guarantees contained in Article 6.'[1]

The principle that Article 6 applies also to criminal appeals is perhaps more evident to the Continental than to the English lawyer Under the criminal procedure of some Continental countries, if a person is convicted of a criminal offence, that conviction does not acquire the force of *res judicata* until either the conviction is affirmed on appeal or the time for appealing has expired. He is still regarded as a person 'charged with a criminal offence' and the guarantees of Article 6 therefore apply equally to the appeal proceedings. This reasoning may not strictly apply under English criminal law, but is clear that the protection given by the provision cannot vary from one State to another according to the special features of domestic law. Again, the concept of 'criminal charge' must be treated as an autonomous concept in the same way as the concept of civil rights and obligations.[2]

The Commission has considered the question whether the rights guaranteed under Article 6 apply, not in the appeal itself, but in proceedings on an application for leave to appeal. In many countries, as in England, there is provision for a filtering process the object of which is to prevent appeals from being examined *in extenso* when there appears to be no prospect of their succeeding.

In England, applications for leave to appeal are normally examined by a single judge in chambers, that is, in private, and in the absence of the accused. The Commission considers that such proceedings do fall within Article 6.[3] It has held that the principle of equality of the parties[4] is respected in such cases because neither the accused nor the prosecution is present or represented.[5] It is true that the proceedings are not held in public, but as the accused has the right of appeal to the full Court against the decision of the single judge, this defect can be remedied on appeal. The Commission's reasoning may be questioned: what should be a remedy for an isolated infringement can hardly remedy a defect inherent in the system. But in the context of this procedure, these doubts are perhaps misplaced. Of course it would be wholly unsatisfactory if the trial at first instance were conducted in the same manner, with the guarantees of Article 6(1) available only on appeal; but the

---

[1] Para. 25.   [2] See above, p. 83.
[3] 3075/67, *Yearbook* 11, 466.   [4] See below, p. 99.
[5] See note 3, above.

application for leave to appeal can reasonably be regarded as merely a step in the process of appeal.[1]

Different considerations apply to German appeals to the Federal Constitutional Court. Here a chamber of three judges subjects appeals to a preliminary examination which the Commission has held to be outside the scope of Article 6 on the ground that the function of the Chamber is not to hear the case but solely to decide whether the formal requirements for lodging a constitutional appeal have been fulfilled.[2] This view of the function of the Chamber, however, is not easy to justify, since it also has the power to reject a constitutional appeal as being manifestly ill-founded; here it is concerned at the stage of admissibility, like the Commission itself,[3] with the merits of the case.

The Commission has also been called upon to consider the question whether, under the English system of probation, the provisions of Article 6(1) apply to the proceedings where a probationer is brought before the court on the ground that he has failed to comply with a condition of the probation order. The Commission had already decided that Article 6 does not in general apply to a case where the person concerned is no longer on trial but has already been convicted: for example, under the Continental equivalent of the probation system, where a person is conditionally released from the remainder of his sentence. Thus where an applicant conditionally released from sentence was subsequently convicted of another offence, and the Austrian court consequently revoked his conditional release, the Commission held that Article 6 did not apply to these proceedings.[4]

It was therefore arguable that, under the English system, since the probationer in breach of a probation order is no longer on trial but has already been convicted, the proceedings do not constitute the determination of a criminal charge. In the case before the Commission, the applicant had been put on probation with a condition that he should reside at a certain hospital or any place directed by a certain doctor for a period not exceeding twelve months, and receive treatment from him. The applicant contended that the probation order was invalid on the ground that he was told it was not legally enforceable. He complained that he was

---

[1] 3168/67, not published; cf. 4133/69, *Yearbook* 13, 780 at 786–7.
[2] 436/58, *Yearbook* 2, 386.   [3] See below, p. 243.
[4] 1140/61, *Collection of Decisions* 8, p. 57.

charged with failing to comply with a condition of a probation order, namely leaving the hospital without the doctor's permission, and that when he appeared before Quarter Sessions he was not allowed to plead, but was told that he was appearing for sentence only. He was sentenced to four years' imprisonment.

On his complaint that the probation order was invalid because it was not legally enforceable, the Commission held that the question whether or not such a condition was legally enforceable had no bearing on the validity of a probation order, the essential object of which is to seek the voluntary compliance of the probationer. With regard to the proceedings before Quarter Sessions, the Commission observed that the applicant's failure to comply with the condition of the probation order empowered the court to pass sentence on him for the original offence. The applicant was not, therefore, being charged, as he thought, with failing to comply with a condition of the probation order, and was not, strictly speaking, appearing on a charge at all, since he was liable to sentence for an offence of which he had been finally convicted. The Commission held, nevertheless, that the provisions of Article 6(1) did apply to the determination of the question whether or not the applicant had failed to comply with the condition under the probation order; for 'a finding on this issue, since it could and did in the present case lead to the imposition of a sentence, was in substance the determination of a criminal charge within the meaning of Article 6(1).'[1]

The Commission thus distinguished the present case from the Continental system of conditional release on the ground that under that system the applicant has already been sentenced at the time of his original conviction and the result of the proceedings is at most to restore the original sentence. Under the English system, however, the question of a breach of the probation order is a preliminary question to that of sentence, and the whole of this process may therefore be regarded as together constituting the determination of a criminal charge.

The situation may be different when the court is concerned, not with the question of liability to sentence, but with the determination of sentence. Here the accused has already been convicted (whether or not the conviction is final) and the proceedings are concerned exclusively with the question of sentence. This situation

---

[1] 4036/69, *Collection of Decisions* 32, 73.

may arise if a person appeals not against conviction but only against sentence; or under English law, if a person pleads guilty to an offence.

The Commission has stated that complaints concerning proceedings on sentence could raise issues under Article 6.

This view was implicit in the decision to declare admissible the Pataki and Dunshirn cases.[1] Here the Commission examined on the merits complaints which related solely to proceedings on sentence before the Austrian appeal court.

It is true that, in the Nielsen case, the Commission expressed the opinion that 'in the circumstances of the present case the provisions of Article 6 of the Convention relate to the establishment of the guilt of the accused person and do not concern the determination of the actual penalty to be inflicted upon the convicted person within the range of the penalties authorized by the relevant penal law.'[2] This view, however, was expressed in the context of the applicability of Article 6 with respect to the decision of the Special Court of Revision not to order the reopening of the case; at this stage the question of sentence did not arise.

In an English case, where the accused had pleaded guilty and therefore there was no trial in the accepted sense on the question of conviction,[3] he complained that, in the proceedings on sentence, he was not properly represented, was not allowed to say anything in his own defence, and was not allowed to examine witnesses.

The Commission, while rejecting the applicant's complaints as manifestly ill-founded, stated that the determination of a criminal charge, within the meaning of Article 6(1), includes not only the determination of the guilt or innocence of the accused, but also in principle the determination of his sentence.[4]

Thus, the defendant should have the opportunity of being represented where the prosecution gives evidence in relation to sentence. The Commission observed that questions of sentence may be closely related to questions of guilt and innocence, and that in the criminal procedure of many States Parties to the Convention they cannot be separated at this stage of the proceedings.

---

[1] See below, p. 99.   [2] *Yearbook* 4, 490 at 586.

[3] For the compatibility of this system with Article 6, see p. 97, below.

[4] 4623/70, *Collection of Decisions* 39, 66; cf. 5076/71, *Collection of Decisions* 40, 64; 4834/71, *Collection of Decisions* 44, 124.

Again, the underlying principle is that the protection afforded by Article 6 should have the same extent in all contracting States. And, if the proceedings on sentence are separable from those leading to conviction, it is just as important that this protection should apply to the former as to the latter.

On the other hand, it is clear that proceedings after conviction and sentence have become final fall outside Article 6. Thus it does not cover an application by a convicted prisoner for release on probation or parole,[1] or for a new trial,[2] or for review of his sentence after the decision has become *res judicata*.[3] Nor does Article 6(1) apply on an application for provisional release pending trial.[4]

The position is uncertain where disciplinary action is taken outside the criminal courts. In an early decision, the Commission held that a civil servant convicted under the Civil Service criminal code, and sentenced to a fine of one-fifth of his yearly pension, could not claim the protection of Article 6.[5] This decision has been followed in certain later cases.[6] The principle cannot be extended too far. If the sanction imposed is merely a censure,[7] the guarantees of judicial process may be unnecessary. If, however, a person is in effect prosecuted outside the ordinary courts, and is liable to sanctions as severe as those which may be imposed by the criminal courts, the protection of Article 6 becomes even more necessary than under the normal judicial system.

If that principle is accepted as applying to civilians, does it apply also, at least outside time of war, to the armed forces? The issue has been raised in relation to military discipline by applications by five Dutch soldiers.[8] The applicants, who had been sentenced for certain offences, complained, *inter alia*, that the proceedings before the military authorities, including the Supreme Military Court, did not satisfy the requirements of Article 6 of the Convention.

---

[1] 606/59, *Yearbook* 4, 340; 1760/63, *Yearbook* 9, 166; 4133/69, *Yearbook* 13, 780 at 790–1.

[2] 864/60, *Collection of Decisions* 9, 17; cf. 4429/70, *Collection of Decisions* 37, 109.

[3] 1237/61, *Yearbook* 5, 96 at 102.

[4] Neumeister, paras. 22 and 23 of 'The Law'; Matznetter, para. 13 of 'The Law'.

[5] 734/60, *Collection of Decisions* 6, 29.

[6] See 4121/69, *Yearbook* 13, 772, and cases cited at 778.

[7] As in 4274/69, *Yearbook* 13, 888, where Article 6 was not invoked.

[8] 5100/71, etc., *Collection of Decisions* 42, 61; see above, p. 48.

The complaints were declared admissible and proceedings are still pending. It is significant that a reservation made by France to Articles 5 and 6 provides that those Articles shall not hinder the application of certain provisions of French law governing the system of discipline in the armed forces.

Having discussed the scope of Article 6, we may now examine the substance of the rights guaranteed under that Article. Under paragraph (1) they are broadly the same in civil and in criminal proceedings, that is, in essence, the right to a fair trial within a reasonable time. However, in one fundamental respect, the analogy cannot be maintained. The question is whether Article 6(1) not only provides for certain procedural safeguards in the course of court proceedings but also guarantees, in relation to civil rights and obligations, the right to institute proceedings. The question does not arise in criminal cases, for here the right is simply to have a criminal charge determined, that is, to have the charge, once preferred, finally disposed of by the courts. That is the substantive right in criminal cases, which is accompanied by the procedural guarantees of fair trial, reasonable time, and so on. But in these cases criminal proceedings have *ex hypothesi* already been commenced.[1] The question is whether, in civil cases, there is a substantive right of access to the courts.

Right of access to the courts

The first case in which the Commission had to consider the issue expressly was the case of Knechtl against the United Kingdom.[2]

The applicant, while serving a prison sentence in England, frequently complained of pains in his left leg. He was examined by doctors, including prison doctors and private consultants, and certain forms of treatment were prescribed, but his condition did not improve. Finally, after further examination, his left leg was amputated below the knee. The pathologist's report on the leg which was removed showed that he had been suffering from a rare disease.

The applicant alleged that he lost his leg through the negligence of the prison authorities and of certain doctors. On four occasions

---

[1] For the commencement of proceedings, see p. 107, below.

[2] *Yearbook* 13, 730; cf. Eissen, 'Le "droit à un tribunal" dans la jurisprudence de la Commission', *Miscellanea W. J. Ganshof van der Meersch I*, Brussels 1972, 455.

he petitioned the Home Secretary, as was required by the Prison Rules, with a view to seeking legal advice or legal aid in order to commence legal proceedings to claim damages for negligence. Permission was not granted and finally he was informed that the Home Secretary was not prepared to grant his request to consult a solicitor.

The United Kingdom Government submitted that Article 6(1) does not guarantee any right to initiate proceedings before a court of law but only lays down certain procedural safeguards where proceedings have once been intitiated. It further submitted that, even if Article 6(1) does guarantee the right to bring proceedings, it must be subject to certain limitations in the case of prisoners.[1] It would be difficult to argue, however, that such limitations are an 'inherent feature'[2] of detention, since the restrictions imposed under the English Prison Rules appear to have had no parallel in most other Contracting States.

The Commission declared the application admissible but the case was subsequently settled, the applicant accepting an *ex gratia* payment from the Government. The Government had meanwhile changed the prison practice to provide that if a prisoner had suffered some physical injury or disablement, or impairment of his physical condition, and alleged medical negligence, he should be allowed to consult a solicitor and to give instructions for the institution of proceedings in accordance with the latter's advice without restriction unless there were overriding considerations of security.[3]

The revised practice did not, however, extend to cover the Golder case,[4] which was under consideration at the same time, and which may have enabled the Commission to accept a more restricted modification of the prison practice than would otherwise have been compatible with the 'general interest'.[5] Here the applicant was detained in an English prison where serious disturbances broke out. He was accused by a prison officer of having assaulted him, and wished to bring proceedings for defamation in order to have his record cleared. As the Government was apparnetly not prepared to modify its practice to cover this type of

[1] See below, p. 198, for limitations on the rights of prisoners.
[2] See below, p. 199.
[3] See the Government White Paper, 'Legal Advice to Prisoners', set out in the Appendix to the Commission's Report.
[4] 4451/70, *Yearbook* 14, 416. [5] See below, p. 254.

action, no settlement of the case was possible, and it was subsequently referred to the Court.

The Commission stated in its Report that, having had regard to all the elements of interpretation, including in particular the ordinary meaning of Article 6(1) in the English and French texts, and the objects and purposes of the Convention and of Article 6 itself, it was unanimously of the opinion that Article 6(1) guarantees a right of access to the courts.[1] Indeed the existence of such a right seems to have been the unexpressed but underlying assumption of the Commission's opinion, if not of the judgment of the Court, in the Ringeisen case.

The right of access to the courts may, however, be qualified in certain respects. In one case[2] an applicant had attempted to bring legal proceedings in respect of a speech in the Austrian Parliament which he considered defamatory. The court found the action inadmissible on the ground of parliamentary immunity under the Austrian Constitution; its decision was confirmed by the Court of Appeal. The applicant's complaint was rejected by the Commission on the ground that the principle of parliamentary immunity was a principle of public law generally recognized in States having a parliamentary regime, and above all in States Parties to the Convention. Further, the principle was expressly included in Article 40 of the Statute of the Council of Europe, in relation to the Consultative Assembly. Consequently, the Commission concluded that the provisions of Article 6(1) should be interpreted subject to the exception of parliamentary immunity, and that it was inconceivable that the Parties to the Convention should have intended, in undertaking to recognize the right set out in that Article, to derogate from a fundamental principle of the parliamentary system to be found in most of their constitutions.

While the Commission's decision that the application was incompatible may be correct, the reasoning is not satisfactory. It comes close to recognizing the existence of inherent limitations on the rights guaranteed by the Convention; and this view, for reasons set out below, cannot be accepted. A preferable interpretation of Article 6(1) would be as follows.

Parliamentary immunity, and diplomatic immunity, should not be regarded as limitations on the right of access to the courts, since that right does not require that courts should have unlimited

[1] Para. 73. [2] 3374/67, *Collection of Decisions* 29, 29.

jurisdiction.[1] There are two elements involved in the right of access. The first is that it should be respected by the law in such a way that no one is excluded from the courts. The second is that where there are any necessary limitations imposed by law on the court's jurisdiction, it is the courts themselves which should decide in the event of dispute. The right to a fair hearing is not a right to a final determination on the merits of every case, but the right to a fair hearing 'in the determination' of the case. Immunity from suit must therefore be justified on a ground which does not exclude access to the courts. Thus, in the Golder case, the Commission stated that 'both parliamentary and diplomatic immunity are applicable not by virtue of the person of the plaintiff but by virtue of the person of the defendant. The obstacle is therefore on the other side: not the court, but the defendant, is inaccessible. And it is for the court to apply the corresponding limitation of its jurisdiction.'[2] Similar considerations apply to persons whose access to the courts is restricted; for example, infants, bankrupts, and persons of unsound mind.[3]

The Commission has held that the right to a fair hearing by a court in civil cases may be renounced by means of an arbitration clause. The applicant, of German nationality, was employed by a German school in Spain. His contract of employment, signed at Bonn and countersigned by an official of the Foreign Office, included an arbitration clause providing that an accredited representative of the Federal Republic should arbitrate in any disputes that might arise. The applicant was dismissed from his post, and brought actions before both the German and the Spanish courts, in both cases without success. The Commission, rejecting his complaints against the German authorities under Article 6(1), stated that 'the inclusion of an arbitration clause in an agreement between individuals amounts legally to a renunciation of the rights defined by Article 6(1)', and that 'nothing in the text of that Article nor of any other Article of the Convention explicitly prohibits such renunciation.'[4]

The decision that rights under Article 6(1) may be waived should be treated with caution and certainly has no application

---

[1] Cf. Golder report, para. 93 *et seq.*   [2] Para. 93.

[3] Cf. Golder report, para. 95.

[4] 1197/61, *Yearbook* 5, 88 at 94–6. See Ganshof van der Meersch in *Human Rights in National and International Law*, ed. Robertson, Manchester, 1968, 97 at 131.

to the right to a fair trial in criminal cases.[1] The fact that such a waiver is not explicitly prohibited has not been treated as material in relation to other rights guaranteed by the Convention.[2] The facts of the case, in any event, were not entirely clear, and it is not apparent from the decision that the Commission's opinion concerning the effect of the arbitration clause was entirely in point. In fact both the Spanish and the German courts appear to have dealt with the claims on the merits. At no stage did they disclaim jurisdiction on the ground of the arbitration clause. As the applicant had hearings on the merits, but failed, the ruling on the effect of an arbitration clause is otiose.

The matter is of course of great practical importance. Under English law, an arbitration agreement can never oust the jurisdiction of the courts. In other systems, even if the courts' jurisdiction is ousted, they may still retain a limited jurisdiction. It is doubtful whether a law permitting the complete exclusion of access to the courts by means of an arbitration agreement would be consistent with Article 6(1).

The right to have a criminal charge finally determined involves two elements: first, criminal proceedings, once instituted, must be finally terminated. They cannot be reopened unless fresh charges are brought. Second, proceedings must not be terminated in a way that implies that the accused may be guilty, except if he is convicted by the decision of a competent court. This follows from the presumption of innocence laid down by Article 6(2).

The first issue arose in an application concerning English criminal procedure, the second in a case concerning criminal procedure in the Federal Republic of Germany.

Two applicants, Roy and Alice Fletcher, were convicted, together with a third person, of the murder of a child. They had set fire to a house, knowing it to be occupied, and the child was burned to death. Two charges were brought against Roy Fletcher, one for murder and one for arson, but at the trial he was required to plead only to the first charge, on which he was convicted. At the end of the trial, counsel for the prosecution requested that the second count should remain on the file, and the judge agreed. The Commission considered whether this was consistent with the requirement that a criminal charge should be determined. It was satisfied, however, after obtaining the respondent Government's

[1] See below, p. 97.   [2] See above, pp. 44 and 57.

observations, that it is the established practice in English law that a second indictment left on the file is never proceeded with so long as the conviction on the charge of murder remains undisturbed. Consequently, once the applicant's conviction for murder had been affirmed on appeal, he could no longer be said to be under a criminal charge.[1]

However, there appears to be nothing in the Convention to prevent a person being tried a second time for the same offence. It is curious that, in a Convention which requires that criminal proceedings should be finally determined, there is no provision for the rule that no one may be tried twice for the same offence, or *non bis in idem*. The Commission has held that neither Article 6 nor any other Article of the Convention guarantees, expressly or by implication, the principle *non bis in idem*.[2] More recently, however, it has left open the possibility that the principle may be considered under Article 6(1).[3]

A proposal by the Commission that the principle should be added to the Convention was not accepted. Instead the rule was included in certain other Council of Europe conventions in criminal matters.[4] These conventions, however, apply the rule only in proceedings for the same offence before the courts of different countries.

As mentioned above, criminal proceedings must not be terminated in such a way as to imply that the accused is guilty, unless he is duly convicted. This question arose in a somewhat spectacular fashion in the Soltikow case.[5]

The criminal proceedings in issue were based on two articles published in 1952, on the basis of documentation assembled by Soltikow, a journalist and writer, concerning the events of 1938 leading up to the Nazi 'night of terror', the Kristallnacht, when the Nazis attacked the Jewish community in Germany. The pretext of the Kristallnacht was the murder of a German diplomat in Paris, Ernst vom Rath, by a 17-year-old Jew, Herschel Grynspan. According to the articles published in 1952, Grynspan was not

---

[1] 3034/67, *Collection of Decisions* 25, 76 at 86–7.

[2] 1197/61, *Yearbook* 5, 88.

[3] 4212/69, *Collection of Decisions* 35, 151.

[4] European Convention on the International Validity of Criminal Judgments, E.T.S. No. 70, Article 53, and European Convention on the Transfer of Proceedings in Criminal Matters, E.T.S. No. 73, Articles 35–7.

[5] 2257/64, *Yearbook* 11, 180.

acting as an agent of world Jewry, as the Nazis had claimed, but had had homosexual relations with vom Rath.

Criminal proceedings involving Soltikow, for defamation of the memory of the dead, were started at the instance of vom Rath's brother in 1952, and were not finally terminated until 1964. After immensely thorough investigations, the court, having heard many witnesses in Germany and, by rogatory commissions, abroad, decided in March 1964 to discontinue the proceedings under an amnesty law. At Soltikow's request, however, the proceedings were resumed, as they had to be by law if such a request was made. The court then fixed the date of the trial, at which more than sixty witnesses were to be heard. But when Soltikow requested, before the trial, that additional evidence, mostly from abroad, should be examined, the court cancelled the trial on the ground that in any event, the applicant's guilt and the consequences of his act were insignificant.

Soltikow complained before the Commission *inter alia*, of the length of the criminal proceedings, and also of the fact that, as a result of the termination of the proceedings, he was deprived of his right to a hearing and determination of the criminal charges against him.

Of course, the right to have a criminal charge determined does not preclude the prosecuting authorities, or the investigating authorities under the inquisitorial system, from discontinuing criminal proceedings. What could be inconsistent with Article 6(1) is to discontinue criminal proceedings in such a way as to imply that the accused person is guilty. The applicant in the present case contended, however, that he was entitled to an acquittal, and that he was deprived of this right by the termination of the case as being insignificant. The termination of the case was unwarranted taking into consideration the length and extent of the previous examination as well as the great historical importance of the events involved. Further, the applicant alleged that the court had in effect found him guilty, even if his guilt was said to be minor.

This issue under Article 6(1) was not resolved in this application, as the complaint was rejected by the Commission for non-exhaustion of domestic remedies. The applicant had failed to bring a constitutional appeal against the decision to terminate the proceedings. The complaint concerning the length of the criminal proceedings, which lasted over ten years, was declared admissible but the

Commission ultimately reached the conclusion that there had been no violation of the Convention in this respect, principally on the ground that the proceedings were greatly protracted by the applicant's own conduct.[1]

In a further application, Soltikow complained of other criminal proceedings against him which had also been discontinued on the ground that his guilt was insignificant and the consequences of his action unimportant.[2] He had exhausted domestic remedies in respect of this complaint by bringing a constitutional appeal. However, the Commission observed that, under the provision of the German Code of Criminal Procedure applied in this case, the court had heard the accused before deciding to discontinue the proceedings. That provision was therefore not as such inconsistent with Article 6(1) and had been properly applied. The Commission's decision is questionable since, if Article 6(1) is read together with the presumption of innocence in Article 6(2), it seems clear that criminal proceedings may be ended in a manner unfavourable to the accused only by a final determination of guilt. They should not be discontinued on the basis that the guilt of the accused is insignificant, but, at the most, that his guilt, *if it was to be established*, would in any event be insignificant.

The Commission has examined whether the system under English criminal procedure, whereby an accused may, at the opening or in the course of his trial, plead guilty to a criminal charge, is consistent with Article 6(1) and (2). Under this procedure, if a person pleads guilty, there is no trial in the usual sense. If the judge is satisfied that the accused understands the effect of his plea, his confession is recorded, and the subsequent proceedings are concerned only with the question of his sentence.

It is clear that a person cannot be deemed, by his plea of guilty, to have waived his right to a fair trial. The position may be different in civil proceedings,[3] but in criminal cases the right to a fair trial, like the right to liberty of the person of which it is a constituent part, is too important in a democratic society for it to be waived.[4] In this respect, the right to a fair trial must be distinguished from the right to have a criminal charge determined in a reasonable time. If the delay in the determination of a criminal charge is substantially due to the conduct of the accused, he cannot complain

---

[1] Report, paras. 29 and 30. [2] 4550/70, *Collection of Decisions* 38, 123.
[3] See above, p. 93. [4] See above, p. 57.

of the delay.[1] But the conduct of the accused cannot relieve the court of the responsibility of ensuring a fair trial.

It may be asked, therefore, if this responsibility is adequately discharged if the courts, as in England and certain other countries, are satisfied of a person's guilt merely on the ground that he has pleaded guilty and appears to understand the effect of his plea, or whether they should not proceed *ex officio* to an examination of the case.

When confronted with this issue, however, the Commission stated that, having examined this practice in the context of English criminal procedure and also in other systems among those States Parties where a similar practice is found, it was satisfied that the practice as such was not inconsistent with the requirements of Article 6(1) and (2). In arriving at this conclusion, the Commission had regard to the rules under which the practice operates and in particular to the safeguards which are provided to avoid the possibility of abuse.[2]

The practice might, however, infringe the Convention in a case where improper pressure was put on the accused to plead guilty. The applicant had alleged that pressure was put on him by both the trial judge and his own counsel. But the evidence submitted by the applicant did not satisfy the Commission on this point.[3]

The practice of imposing a summary penalty without a hearing is not contrary to Article 6(1) at any rate if there is a possibility of applying to the court for a normal trial.[4]

Fair hearing

In applying the provisions of Article 6 to criminal proceedings, it is necessary to have regard to the totality of the proceedings by which the criminal responsibility and the sentence of an accused person are determined and not merely to one stage of the proceedings. One particular incident or one particular aspect may have been so prominent or have been of such importance as to be decisive for the general evaluation of the trial as a whole. But even in this contingency, it is on the basis of an evaluation of the trial in its entirety that the answer must be given to the question

---

[1] See below, p. 109.
[2] 5076/71, *Collection of Decisions* 40, 64 at 66–7.
[3] Ibid.   [4] 4260/69, *Collection of Decisions* 35, 155.

whether or not there has been a fair trial.[1] The same principle applies to civil proceedings.[2]

It is not possible, therefore, to state in the abstract the content of the requirement of a fair hearing; this can only be considered in the context of the trial as a whole. It is, however, possible to indicate a number of elements which are of importance in assessing whether this requirement has been fulfilled in a particular case.

Thus, the Commission has repeatedly stated that the principle of *equality of the parties* (égalité des armes; Waffengleichheit— sometimes 'translated' as equality of arms) is an inherent element of a fair hearing under Article 6(1),[3] and this view has been approved by the Court.[4] The principle is also closely related to the requirement of an 'independent and impartial tribunal'.

In the cases of Pataki and Dunshirn,[5] the applicants had complained that, under the Austrian Code of Criminal Procedure, the procedure before the Criminal Court of Appeal violated the right to a fair hearing in that the applicants had no right of representation, whereas the Public Prosecutor was present. The Commission in its report was of the opinion that the 'equality of arms', i.e. the procedural equality of the accused with the prosecutor, was an inherent element of a 'fair hearing' and that the proceedings concerned were not in conformity with the Convention.

However, the Commission then took note of new Austrian legislation which amended the Code of Criminal Procedure and, in *ad hoc* and retroactive form, gave the applicants the possibility of new appeal proceedings under the amended procedure.

The Commission accordingly proposed that no further action should be taken in these cases and subsequently the Committee of Ministers so decided after expressing its satisfaction at the new legislative measures.

A second group of cases against Austria, the Ofner and Hopfinger case,[6] raised a similar problem. Under Austrian procedure a draft of the appeal court's decision was submitted to the Attorney-

---

[1] Opinion of the Commission in the Nielsen Case, *Yearbook* 4, 494 at 582; Opinion of the Commission in the Pfunders Case (*Austria* v. *Italy*), *Yearbook* 6, 740 at 792.

[2] 2804/66, *Collection of Decisions* 27, 61 at 73.

[3] 1169/61, *Yearbook* 6, 520 at 574.

[4] Neumeister Case, para. 22 of 'The Law'.

[5] *Yearbook* 6, 714.   [6] *Yearbook* 6, 676.

General (*Generalprokurator*) for his observations. Here, however, the Commission was of the opinion that there was no violation of the principle of equality of the parties. The Commission appears to have been influenced by various considerations in reaching this opinion. First, the proceedings could not lead to a *reformatio in peius*, that is, the situation of the accused could not be worsened as a result of these proceedings, as his sentence could not be increased. Second, the Attorney-General's position was distinct from that of the Public Prosecutor. Nevertheless, the Commission considered that, if

the Attorney-General had tried to influence the decision to the disadvantage of the accused without the latter being heard, it might have been doubtful whether the principle of equality would have been observed. But this did not happen. What happened was simply that the Attorney-General in one single word (*einverstanden*) expressed his agreement with the report. In these circumstances his intervention cannot reasonably be said to violate the principle of equality.[1]

In the Delcourt Case, a situation comparable with the Pataki and Dunshirn cases was referred to the Court.[2] The applicant, who had been convicted of a number of offences involving fraud and had appealed to the Belgian Court of Cassation, complained that a member of the Procureur général's department attached to the Court of Cassation, having made his submissions in open court, subsequently took part, as provided by Belgian law, in the Court's deliberations. The Court of Human Rights pointed out that the Belgian law did not seem to have any equivalent today in the other Member States of the Council of Europe. Nevertheless it found, after examining the position and functions of the Procureur général's department attached to the Court of Cassation, that there was no violation of Article 6(1). That department was concerned, not with the prosecution of crime, but with the observance by the judges of the law. 'It assists the Court to supervise the lawfulness of the decisions attacked and to ensure the uniformity of judicial precedent.'[3]

Subsequently the Commission applied the same reasoning to the

[1] At 704.
[2] 'Publications of the Court', Series A; *Yearbook* 13, 1100. See further, Velu, *L'Affaire Delcourt*, Brussels, 1972.
[3] Para. 34.

role of the Procureur-Generaal attached to the Dutch Supreme Court (Hoge Raad).[1]

The principle of equality of the parties applies also, of course, to civil cases. The Commission has held that the right to a fair hearing implies that everyone who is a party to civil proceedings shall have a reasonable opportunity of presenting his case to the court under conditions which do not place him under a substantial disadvantage *vis-à-vis* his opponent.[2]

Thus, although the provisions of Article 6(3) (d) relating to the examination of witnesses apply only to criminal proceedings, the refusal of a court to allow a party to a civil action to call a witness or to examine a witness against him might infringe his right to a fair hearing.[3]

Similarly, complaints concerning the refusal of legal aid in either civil or criminal proceedings may on this ground raise an issue under Article 6(1), although the right to legal aid is guaranteed expressly only in criminal cases under Article 6(3) (c).[4] Legal aid in civil cases may also be necessary to secure the right of access to the courts,[5] especially in systems where a party can appear only if represented by a lawyer.

In particular, Article 6(1) imposes an obligation on the court to ensure a fair hearing if the accused, or the parties to civil proceedings, are not properly represented. Hence the Commission has frequently considered whether complaints against a lawyer, even if outside its competence *ratione personae* in so far as they are directed against a private individual,[6] may nevertheless raise the issue of whether the applicant has had a fair hearing.[7]

Appearance in person

Does 'hearing' imply the presence of the parties in person? The Commission has expressed the view that in certain classes of case or in certain sets of circumstances a fair hearing is scarcely conceivable without the presence in person of the party concerned;

---

[1] 3692/68, *Yearbook* 13, 516.
[2] 434/58, *Yearbook* 2, 354 at 370 f.; 2804/66, *Collection of Decisions* 27, 61 at 73.
[3] 5362/72, *Collection of Decisions* 42, 145.
[4] 3944/69, *Collection of Decisions* 33, 5.
[5] See above, p. 90.   [6] See above, p. 11.
[7] See, e.g. 2676/65, *Collection of Decisions* 23, 31 at 36.

this may be so in some civil or commercial cases and is true *a fortiori* of criminal matters.[1]

A particular example is a case where the personal character and manner of life of the party concerned are directly relevant to the formation of the court's opinion on the point which it is called upon to decide, e.g. a case in which a parent, after a divorce, makes an application to the court for a right of access to a child of the marriage.[2]

However, in criminal proceedings in cassation, where the sole task of the court was to determine whether the judgment of the lower court was in accordance with the law, the Commission held that a procedure wholly in writing met the requirements of Article 6(1), and it was unnecessary for the court to hear the oral explanations of the accused. The court did not have to decide the material facts nor the degree of his culpability or criminal liability; consequently his 'personal character and manner of life' would not have been of direct relevance.[3]

It would seem to follow that a trial held in the absence of the accused would *prima facie* be contrary to Article 6(1),[4] although in appeal proceedings it may generally be sufficient that the accused is represented by counsel.[5]

On the other hand, the right to be heard as a witness in one's own case is not as such included among the rights and freedoms guaranteed by the Convention;[6] again the question is whether there has been a fair hearing. Thus in one case the Commission found that the applicant's complaint on this score under Article 6(1) was manifestly ill-founded because he was able to present his case fully through a lawyer in all three instances.[7]

Reasoned decision

A reasoned decision, while not expressly required by Article 6, is implicit in the requirement of a fair hearing. In civil proceedings, the Commission has accepted the view that Article 6 requires reasons to be given by a court for its decisions. However, if a

[1] 1169/61, *Yearbook* 6, 520 at 570 f.
[2] 434/58, *Yearbook* 2, 354 at 370.
[3] 1169/61, *Yearbook* 6, 520 at 572.
[4] On the right to be present in person in criminal proceedings, see further under Article 6(3) (c), below, p. 117.
[5] See 3852/68, *Collection of Decisions* 32, 38 at 40, and cases there cited.
[6] 1092/61, *Yearbook* 5, 210.   [7] Ibid.

court gives reasons, then *prima facie* the requirements of Article 6 in this respect are satisfied, and this presumption is not upset simply because the judgment does not deal specifically with one point considered by an applicant to be material. On the other hand, if, for example, an applicant were to show that the court had ignored a fundamental defence, which had been clearly put before it and which, if successful, would have discharged him in whole or in part from liability, then this would be sufficient to rebut the presumption of a fair hearing.[1]

This analysis applies *a fortiori* to criminal proceedings. Thus, where a convicted person has the possibility of an appeal, the lower court must state in detail the reasons for its decision, so that on appeal from that decision his rights may be properly safeguarded.[2]

Judicial process

The notion of a fair hearing implies not only that the parties should be adequately represented but also that they should have the opportunity to comment on all evidence tendered to the court. This is part of the *procès contradictoire* which is essential to the judicial process. The point was put in a negative form by the Commission when, examining a complaint under Article 6(1), it stated that the applicant had not maintained, or adduced any evidence to show, that his conviction was arrived at by any reasoning not based on the evidence before the court.[3]

On the other hand, the courts may take judicial notice of questions of law. Where an English company complained that a German court had based its decision in a civil action on points of law without having given the parties an opportunity to make submissions on these points at the hearing, the Commission observed that:[4]

. . . it is a generally recognised principle of law that it is for the court to know the law ('Jura novit curia'); . . . . the practice in the legal systems of the High Contracting Parties varies in this respect; . . . in certain systems the concept of 'fair hearing' is interpreted in the sense that courts are required to invite the parties to make submissions on

[1] 5460/72, *Collection of Decision* 43, 99 at 107.
[2] 1035/61, *Yearbook* 6, 180 at 192.
[3] 2868/66, *Yearbook* 10, 460 at 472.
[4] 3147/67, *Collection of Decisions* 27, 119 at 126-7.

those points of law which appear to the courts to be significant; . . .
however, other legal systems do not make any such requirement; . . .
consequently, there is no generally accepted practice in this respect
within the systems of the High Contracting Parties;
    . . . the Commission finds that, when interpreting the concept of
'fair hearing' under Article 6, paragraph (1), of the Convention, allowance must be made as regards the existence of such different legal
systems; . . . the Commission finds that the established practice of the
German courts whereby the parties are not necessarily invited to make
oral submissions on all points of law which may appear significant to
the courts does not constitute an infringement of the principle of 'fair
hearing' within the meaning of this provision;
    . . . the finding does not, of course, affect the imposition under the
legal systems of any High Contracting Party of more stringent requirements in this respect . . .

Independent and impartial tribunal

The requirement of an 'independent and impartial tribunal
established by law' is obviously closely related to the requirement
of a fair hearing. There cannot be a fair trial before a biased
court. The additional specification of the necessary qualities of
the tribunal is important, however, and the alleged partiality of
the court has been in issue in a number of cases.[1]

In the Boeckmans case,[2] the applicant, who had been convicted of theft, complained that remarks made at his trial by the
President of the Chamber of the Belgian Court of Appeal were
inconsistent with, *inter alia*, the requirement of an impartial
tribunal.

The case was the first to be the subject of a friendly settlement.
The Belgian Government, while stating that the validity of the
sentence could not be questioned, agreed to pay Boeckmans
65,000 Belgian francs in compensation for remarks which were
such 'as to disturb the serenity of the atmosphere during the
proceedings in a manner contrary to the Convention and may
have caused the applicant a moral injury'.

The question may also arise, and especially under the jury
system, whether a person can be ensured a fair trial by an impartial
tribunal if his case has been the subject of adverse press and

---

[1] See also 3973/69, *Collection of Decisions* 32, 70; 3444/67, *Yearbook* 13, 302
at 324–6.
[2] 1727/62, *Yearbook* 6, 370.

television publicity before the trial. The Commission has accepted that such publicity may prejudice the rights of the accused under Article 6(1), and also the presumption of innocence under Article 6(2).[1] In a case from the United Kingdom,[2] the applicant had complained that the press had given extensive coverage to his case and that he was publicly accused in a television interview before his trial; he alleged that this publicity had a prejudicial effect. Such pre-trial publicity is common in certain countries, e.g. in France and the Federal Republic of Germany, but in these countries the verdict is never entrusted exclusively to a lay jury, which may be presumed to be more easily prejudiced. The applicant's complaints concerning the pre-trial publicity in his case were, however, rejected by the Commission as being manifestly ill-founded. The Commission noted that the Court of Appeal had extensively examined the merits of the applicant's case and had held that the conviction was well founded. Any errors committed by the jury as a result of bias would have been rectified by the decision of the Court of Appeal. The Court of Appeal had had special regard to the applicant's complaints of prejudicial publicity and found that 'there was no real risk that the jury was influenced by the publicity' and that 'the case for the Crown was so overwhelming that no jury could conceivably have returned any different verdicts". The Commission, having examined the case as it was submitted by the applicant, found no reason itself to adopt an opinion other than that expressed by the Court of Appeal.

Again, the hostile attitude of a lawyer, or a witness, which might otherwise unduly influence a jury, may be corrected by the judge. In an early Danish case declared admissible by the Commission, the Nielsen Case, one of the principal issues was whether the evidence of an expert, Dr D . . . improperly influenced the jury. The Commission stated:[3]

Although it is a matter of general experience that a bias which has once been created in the minds of the jury against an accused may not easily be eliminated, it seems to the Commission that the speech of the Public Prosecutor and the summing-up of the President must have contributed considerably to neutralise the one-sided influence which Dr D . . . 's statement may have had upon the jury.

[1] See below, p. 111.
[2] 3860/68, *Collection of Decisions* 30, 70; cf. 3444/67. *Yearbook* 13, 302 at 322–4.
[3] *Yearbook* 4, 490 at 568.

It is, of course, impossible to know what has motivated the jury to give the answers they did on the questions of Schouw Nielsen's guilt. But this does not immediately concern the Commission under the Convention. Whether the jury and the Court have appreciated the evidence correctly or not, is a question on which the Commission is not called upon to pronounce. The task under the Convention is to decide whether evidence for and against the accused has been presented in such a manner, and the proceedings in general have been conducted in such a way, that he has had a fair trial. Without in any way closing their eyes to the objectionable aspects of Dr D . . . 's statement the Commission reaches the conclusion, on an examination of the proceedings as a whole, that they do not fall short of the standard required by Article 6(1) as to the right of every accused to have a fair trial.

A person who considers a judge or juror biased may have the right under domestic law to challenge him on that ground; but such a right of challenge may be subject to reasonable limitations.[1]

In the Pfunders Case[2] the Austrian Government alleged a violation of Article 6(1) by reason of the composition of the Italian courts hearing the charges; they submitted that four out of six jurors were of 'Italian ethnic origin' and were 'particularly liable to be swayed by the Italian press campaign, the political tension, the vehement arguments of the Public Prosecutor and of the civil plaintiff'. This part of the application, however, was declared inadmissible for non-exhaustion of domestic remedies as the accused had not applied for a change of venue.[3]

Finally, reference may be made to the judgment of the Court in the Ringeisen Case. Rejecting the applicant's allegation of bias, the Court said:[4] 'it cannot be stated as a general rule resulting from the obligation to be impartial that a superior court which sets aside an administrative or judicial decision is bound to send the case back to a different jurisdictional authority or to a differently composed branch of that authority.'

Having considered the elements of a fair trial, we see that Article 6 is designed only to preclude procedural irregularities in the administration of justice and is not concerned with substantive law. Accordingly, the Commission has repeatedly rejected complaints alleging that errors of law or fact have been committed by domestic courts, on the ground that such complaints are outside

[1] 556/59, *Yearbook* 3, 288.
[3] *Yearbook* 4, 116 at 166–70.
[2] See above, p. 13.
[4] Para. 97.

its competence except where such errors might have involved a possible violation of the rights listed in the Convention.[1] Clearly, the Commission is not ordinarily concerned under Article 6(1) with, for example, the interpretation by the domestic courts of criminal law. Nor is it called upon to decide whether the domestic courts have correctly assessed the evidence before them, but only 'whether evidence for and against the accused has been presented in such a manner, and the proceedings in several have been conducted in such a way, that he has had a fair trial.'[2] But the so-called 'fourth instance' doctrine by which the Commission declines to sit as a higher instance supervising the decisions of domestic courts, cannot be taken too far. The decision of the Court in the Vagrancy cases shows that the substantive decisions of the domestic authorities are subject to a very wide degree of control under Article 5.[3] Article 7(1) may also require an interpretation of domestic law by the organs of the Convention.[4] The 'fourth instance' doctrine is to be confined to Article 6(1). Even here, of course, it is conceivable that an interpretation of domestic law may be so far-fetched as to be evidence of bias. But normally the findings of the court on fact and law will be outside the purview of Article 6(1).

Judgment within a reasonable time

The right under Article 6(1) to judgment within a reasonable time may be compared with the right under Article 5(3) to trial within a a reasonable time.[5] However, while the right guaranteed under Article 5(3) applies only to persons detained on remand on a criminal charge, the scope of Article 6(1) is wider. It extends to civil and criminal cases alike, and in criminal cases it applies whether the accused is detained or at liberty. The latter factor is important in assessing the reasonableness of the period, since, as stated above, Article 5(3) requires that there must be 'special diligence' in bringing the case to trial if the accused is detained.[6]

In criminal cases, the beginning of the period to be considered, for the purposes of Article 6(1), cannot be a single identifiable event in the proceedings against the accused which is the same in

---

[1] See, e.g. 458/59, *Yearbook* 3, 222; 1140/61, *Collection of Decisions* 8, 57; 3852/68, *Collection of Decisions* 32, 38.

[2] Report in the Nielsen Case, above, p. 105; 4428/70, *Collection of Decisions* 40, 1 at 10.

[3] See above p. 56. [4] See below, p. 122.

[5] See above, p. 67. [6] P. 70.

all cases.[1] It clearly cannot always be the date of his arrest, since he may never be arrested. On the other hand it cannot always be the date on which preliminary investigations are opened against him, as he may be unaware of the fact, and the object of the provision is to protect him from living for too long under the threat of criminal proceedings. For the same reason, it cannot be, in every case, the date on which charges are brought, as he may live for a long period in the knowledge that investigations are proceeding, although no formal charge is brought.

Thus, the Commission has said that the relevant stage is that 'at which the situation of the person concerned has been substantially affected as a result of a suspicion against him', even if no charge is brought at that date.[2]

In the Neumeister case, the accused was first examined by the investigating judge on 21 January 1960, but the indictment was not preferred until 17 March 1964. He was charged on 23 February 1961, and the Court took this date as the beginning of the period to be considered under Article 6(1).[3]

In the Wemhoff case, however, the Court considered that the period began on the date when Wemhoff was arrested. On the following day a warrant of arrest was issued, stating that he was under grave suspicion of an offence, but the indictment was not filed until the preliminary investigation was completed more than two years later.

If any general criterion is to be applied, it would seem that, in view of the aims of Articles 5 and 6, the period should be considered to begin with that act of the authorities which first substantially affects the situation of the person concerned by depriving him of that security which the law-abiding citizen is entitled to enjoy.

The period to be taken into consideration, in applying Article 6(1), lasts at least until acquittal or conviction, even if this decision is reached on appeal.[4] It is uncertain whether proceedings in cassation should be taken into account,[5] but since Article 6(1) is applicable to such proceedings in other respects,[6] it would seem that they should be included.

[1] See above, p. 83.　　　[2] 2278/64, *Collection of Decisions* 24, 8 at 18.
[3] Neumeister, para. 18 of 'The Law'.
[4] Neumeister, para. 19 of 'The Law'; Wemhoff, para. 18 of 'The Law'.
[5] Wemhoff, para. 19 of 'The Law'.
[6] Above, p. 100 (Delcourt Case).

In a case in which eight months elapsed between the delivery of the court's verdict and the date on which the accused received a copy of the court's judgment, the Commission held that the period to be considered extended to the latter date.[1] On the principles stated above, this decision is subject to a reservation. The object of Article 6(1) is to give the accused a final decision on his guilt or innocence; except where delay may prejudice his right of appeal, it does not entitle him to obtain the text of that decision within a reasonable time. Such delay therefore could not of itself infringe Article 6(1), but may result in an infringement where it prejudices or unduly delays an appeal.

In assessing whether the delay has been unreasonable, similar factors may be considered as are relevant under Article 5(3): the reasons for the delay, the complexity of the case, and whether the accused himself contributed to the delay. It must also be borne in mind, of course, that undue delays may prejudice the possibility of a fair trial.

These issues have been considered in a series of cases other than those already cited; notably in *Jentzsch* v. *Federal Republic of Germany*, *Ringeisen* v. *Austria*, *Sepp* v. *Federal Republic of Germany*, and *Huber* v. *Austria*.[2]

The right to be protected against undue delay applies also in civil cases. In such cases, it would seem that the period to be considered normally runs from the date of the institution of proceedings.

The parties have the right to a final decision within a reasonable time. But a party who has himself caused or contributed to the delay cannot complain.[3] A potential defendant should also, it would seem, have the right that proceedings be instituted within a reasonable period from the date of the alleged wrong. Thus, reasonable periods of limitation, after which the right of action will be statute-barred, may be necessary to protect a potential defendant. On the other hand, if a would-be plaintiff is debarred from instituting proceedings in the first place, it is not sufficient to satisfy Article 6(1) that he is subsequently enabled to bring proceedings before such a period of limitation has expired. The

[1] 4459/70, *Kaiser* v. *Austria*, *Yearbook* 14, 446.
[2] See the Reports of the Commission on these cases, respectively 2604/65 (see *Yearbook* 10, 218 for decision on admissibility), 2614/65 (*Yearbook* 11, 268), 3897/68 (*Yearbook* 13, 626) and 4517/70 (*Yearbook* 14, 572).
[3] 1794/63, *Yearbook* 9, 178 at 212; 4859/71, *Collection of Decisions* 44, 1.

requirement of reasonable time applies here only to the conduct of proceedings; it does not qualify the right of access to the courts.[1]

Public hearing

While there is a general right to a public hearing under Article 6(1), the second sentence contains a limitation on that right. It provides that while in all cases judgment must be pronounced in public, nevertheless the press and public may, on certain specified grounds, be excluded from all or part of the trial. Obvious examples, which could be justified on the grounds stated, are the restrictions on press reporting in juvenile courts ('the interests of juveniles') or in divorce proceedings ('the protection of the private life of the parties') and the exclusion of the public in cases involving national security 'in the interests of . . . national security in a democratic society'. The interpretation of these restrictions and of similar restrictions on other rights guaranteed in the Convention will be considered below.[2]

However, some proceedings may take place in private although they do not come within any of the permitted restrictions. In England, applications for leave to appeal against conviction or sentence are normally heard in private, and the position is similar in other countries. It would seem that this is permissible if such applications can be regarded as a step in the appellate process, and if there is a right to an appeal, heard in public, against the refusal of the application.[3] Similarly, in civil cases, interlocutory proceedings which are held in private may be permissible subject to corresponding conditions. The Commission rejected, without giving reasons, one complaint concerning such proceedings before a Master in Chambers.[4] Judgment for a very large sum of money had been given against the applicant by the Master; apparently the applicant was not present or represented. He appealed but was refused leave to defend the action by the Judge in Chambers. He appealed again to the Court of Appeal. Here he was heard in person and, presumably, in public, but his appeal was dismissed.

Clearly a person deprived of his rights in the court of first instance cannot complain if the wrong is righted on appeal. This is the very basis of the rule of exhaustion of domestic remedies.

---

[1] See Golder Report, para. 108 f.
[2] See p. 195.   [3] See above, p. 85.
[4] 3860/68, *Collection of Decisions* 30, 70.

Nevertheless it is unsatisfactory if the appeal serves not merely to correct a wrong in a particular case but to correct a defective system. A distinction should perhaps be drawn between genuine interlocutory proceedings and a determination of rights which is final rather than interlocutory, even though subject to appeal.

Article 6(2)   **Presumption of innocence**

Article 6(2) provides that 'Everyone charged with a criminal offence shall be presumed innocent until proved guilty according to law.'

The scope of this provision, and its relation to paragraph (1), have already been discussed.

The application of the principle can be considered in two separate stages. First, in pre-trial proceedings, everyone must be presumed to be innocent; this is important as limiting the use of detention on remand under Article 5(3), and also, if a person is detained, as governing the conditions of detention. He must be detained, if it is necessary at all, as an innocent person suspected of an offence, and not as a convicted prisoner.

Second, in the trial itself, the proceedings must be conducted, until conviction or acquittal, on the presumption that the accused is innocent. This requirement is closely related to that of an independent and impartial tribunal in paragraph (1).

In the Pfunders Case, the Commission interpreted the duty of the trial court under paragraph (2) as follows:[1]

This text, according to which everyone charged with a criminal offence shall be presumed innocent until proved guilty according to law, requires firstly that court judges in fulfilling their duties should not start with the conviction or assumption that the accused committed the act with which he is charged. In other words, the onus to prove guilt falls upon the Prosecution, and any doubt is to the benefit of the accused. Moreover, the judges must permit the latter to produce evidence in rebuttal. In their judgment they can find him guilty only on the basis of direct or indirect evidence sufficiently strong in the eyes of the law to establish his guilt.

Further, while Article 6(2) is primarily concerned with the attitude of mind of the judges, it may also be necessary for the

[1] *Yearbook 6*, 740 at 782–4; cf. 4124/69, *Collection of Decisions 35*, 132.

court to correct any impression of prejudice which may result from the attitude of the prosecution or of witnesses in the case. For 'the presiding judge by failing to react against such behaviour, might give the impression that the court shared the obvious animosity to the accused and regarded him from the outset as guilty.'[1]

Again, this provision precludes the courts from accepting as evidence any admissions extorted by ill-treatment; for it requires that guilt be proved 'according to law'.[2] Similarly, it would seem that improper pressure on an accused to plead guilty would be contrary to both Article 6(1) and (2).[3]

In an Austrian case, an applicant alleged that the Commissioner of Police had represented him to the Press, before he was convicted, as a fraudulent person, and that this remark was published in a Viennese daily newspaper. The Commission stated that it was conceivable that, under certain circumstances, information given to the Press by public officials before the conviction of an accused person could give rise to a question under Article 6(2). However, in the present case, the applicant had failed to produce any proof of his allegations.[4]

The question of pre-trial publicity in general must also be considered in connection with the right to a fair hearing under paragraph (1) as well as under paragraph (2), and has already been discussed above.[5] It will be recalled that in one case the Commission held that any prejudicial effect of pre-trial publicity on the jury would have been corrected in the appeal court. This is in accordance with the principle stated in the Pfunders Case that 'If the lower court has not respected the principle of presumption of innocence, but the higher court in its decision has eliminated the consequences of this vice in the previous proceedings, there has been no breach of Article 6(2).'[6]

Is it contrary to Article 6(2) for the court to be informed, in the course of the trial, of the previous convictions of the accused? The Commission examined this question under paragraphs (1) and (2) of Article 6 in the light of the practice of the Contracting States. Having found that, in a number of these countries, information as to previous convictions is regularly given during the trial before the court has reached a decision as to the guilt of the

---

[1] Ibid.   [2] Ibid.   [3] See above, p. 98.
[4] 2343/64, *Yearbook* 10, 176.
[5] See p. 104.   [6] *Yearbook* 6, 740 at 784.

accused, the Commission concluded that such a procedure does not violate any provision of Article 6,[1] even when the information is given to a jury.[2] Nevertheless, while this practice may not as such be contrary to Article 6(2), it may be that, having regard to the Commission's doctrine that the question of 'fair hearing' must be viewed in the context of the trial as a whole, it could in a particular case support a conclusion that the accused has not had a fair trial under Article 6.

The principle of the presumption of innocence is reflected in English law in the rule placing the burden of proof on the prosecution. But it cannot be equated with that rule, to which there are in any event numerous exceptions. Under the inquisitorial system of criminal procedure found in many of the Contracting Parties, it is for the court to elicit the truth in all cases. What the principle of the presumption of innocence requires here is first that the court should not be predisposed to find the accused guilty, and second that it should at all times give the accused the benefit of the doubt, on the rule *in dubio pro reo*.

Where, under English law, the burden of proof is transferred to the defence, Article 6(2) is not infringed if the presumption so created is rebuttable and is not in itself unreasonable. An applicant convicted of living on the immoral earnings of a prostitute complained of the statutory provision under which he was convicted, which states: ' . . . a man who lives with or is habitually in the company of a prostitute . . . shall be presumed to be knowingly living on the earnings of prostitution unless he proves the contrary.'[3] The effect of this provision was that when certain facts were proved by the prosecution certain other facts were to be presumed. The Commission held that the provision 'creates a rebuttable presumption of fact which the defence may, in turn, disprove. The provision in question is not, therefore, as such, a presumption of guilt. The Commission recognises, however, that this form of provision could, if widely or unreasonably worded,

---

[1] 2742/66, *Yearbook* 9, 550.
[2] 2518/65, *Yearbook* 8, 370.
[3] 5124/71, *Collection of Decisions* 42, 135; cf. the declaration by Malta, Collected Texts (1974 edn.), p. 610: 'The Government of Malta declares that it interprets paragraph 2 of Article 6 of the Convention in the sense that it does not preclude any particular law from imposing upon any person charged under such law the burden of proving particular facts.' It would seem that this declaration, not constituting a reservation under Article 64, is of no legal effect.

have the same effect as a presumption of guilt. It is not, therefore, sufficient to examine only the form in which the presumption is drafted. It is necessary to examine its substance and its effect'.

The Commission continued: 'The statutory presumption in the present case is restrictively worded. It requires the prosecution to prove that the defendant "lives or is habitually in the company of a prostitute or . . . [that he] excrcises control, direction or influence over [her] movements in a way which shows he is aiding, abetting or compelling her prostitution". Only when this has been proved is it presumed that he is knowingly living on her earnings and he is then entitled to disprove the presumption. The presumption is neither irrebuttable nor unreasonable. To oblige the prosecution to obtain direct evidence of "living on immoral earnings" would in most cases make its task impossible.'

Article 6(3)   **Rights of the accused**

Article 6(3) provides that everyone charged with a criminal offence has certain 'minimum rights'. These rights constitute essential elements of the notion of a fair trial in a criminal case. As already stated, however, the words 'minimum rights' clearly show that the rights specifically enumerated in paragraph (3) are not exhaustive, and that a trial may not conform to the general standard of a fair trial required by paragraph (1) even if the minimum rights guaranteed by paragraph (3) have been respected.[1]

The rights guaranteed by paragraph (3) apply in principle at all stages of the criminal process, from the time when the accused is charged until final conviction. However, it is obvious from their terms that the provisions of paragraph (3) (a) and (b) apply primarily to the pre-trial proceedings, while the provisions of paragraph (3) (c), (d), and (e) apply primarily to the trial itself.

(a) *the right 'to be informed promptly, in a language which he understands and in detail, of the nature and cause of the accusation against him'*

This provision has already been compared with Article 5(2), which provides that 'Everyone who is arrested shall be informed promptly, in a language which he understands, of the reasons for his arrest and of any charge against him.'[2]

---

[1] The Pfunders Case (*Austria* v. *Italy*), *Yearbook* 6, 740 at 790.
[2] See above, p. 61.

The Commission has stated that 'it is clear from a comparison of the wording of these provisions that the information to which a person is entitled concerning the charges made against him is more specific and more detailed in connection with his right to a fair trial under Article 6 than in connection with his right to liberty and security of person under Article 5.'[1]

Detailed information of the nature of the charge is necessary if the accused is to be able adequately to prepare his defence in accordance with Article 6(3) (b). The link between paragraphs (a) and (b), in the context of Article 6, was further explained in the Ofner case, where the Commission stated that 'an accused person has the right to be informed not only of the grounds for the accusation, that is, not only the acts with which he is charged and on which his indictment is based, but also of the *nature* of the accusation, namely, the legal classification of the acts in question.'[2] 'Consequently, the information on the nature of and grounds for the accusation should contain such particulars as will enable the accused to prepare his defence accordingly.'[3]

(b) *the right 'to have adequate time and facilities for the preparation of his defence'*

In the Köplinger Case,[4] the Commission declared admissible the applicant's complaint under Article 6(3) (b); the applicant alleged that he did not have the necessary time and facilities to prepare his defence, particularly with regard to the presentation of the appeals which he had lodged against the judgment of the court of first instance. He also claimed not to have been effectively assisted by his lawyers, who were appointed *ex officio* under the free legal aid system. His lawyer had frequently been changed and it was alleged that because of their late appointment they were unable to study his case in sufficient detail.

The Commission apparently assumed without argument that Article 6(3) (b) applies to appeal proceedings, and this interpretation seems to be correct.[5] It finally reached the conclusion, however, that there had been no violation of Article 6 in any of the proceedings.

The right to have adequate *time* for the preparation of the

[1] 343/57, *Yearbook* 2, 412 at 462.　　[2] 524/59, *Yearbook* 3, 322 at 344.
[3] Ibid.　　[4] 1850/63, *Yearbook* 9, 240.　　[5] See above, pp. 84 and 114.

defence has, on the whole, raised few problems under the Convention, where the opposite issue, of unduly protracted proceedings, has arisen much more often. The Commission has held that a period of fifteen days for introducing an appeal, where it was sufficient to submit a summary statement of the grounds of appeal, is consistent with Article 6(3) (b).[1]

In a United Kingdom case,[2] the applicant complained that neither he nor his solicitor had been given notice of the date on which his application for leave to appeal was to be heard by the Court of Appeal and that he was thus deprived of the possibility of putting his case before the Court. The Commission examined this complaint under Article 6(3) (b) as well as under Article 6(1). The respondent Government's observations on the admissibility of the application stated that 'It is the well-recognized duty of the legal representative of a person involved in litigation to watch the lists when cases with which they are concerned are pending. If, however, the Registrar is requested to do so by a solicitor, he also gives notice of the date to the solicitor direct.' The Commission, after examining the correspondence between the applicant's solicitors and the Registrar of the Court, finally concluded that 'it cannot be said that the Court or the Registrar and consequently the respondent Government was responsible for the fact that neither the applicant nor the solicitors had knowledge of the date of the hearing. . . '

Where in the course of proceedings the lawyer has to be replaced, the proceedings must be adjourned to allow the new lawyer adequate time to acquaint himself with the case.[3]

The right to have adequate *facilities* for the preparation of the defence may be of greater importance, especially where the accused is detained, but the difficulty may be overcome if the accused has proper legal representation. In any event, the Commission's doctrine that the rights guaranteed under the Convention may be the subject of interference in the case of lawfully detained persons[4] can have no application to Article 6, whether the accused is detained pending trial or after conviction pending appeal.

---

[1] 441/58, *Yearbook* 2, 391. Cf. 4042/69, *Yearbook* 13, 690 at 696.

[2] 3075/67, *Yearbook* 11, 466.

[3] See under Article 6(3) (c), below, p. 118, and cf. 4319/69 *Samer* v. *Federal Republic of Germany*, *Yearbook* 14, 322 at 340.

[4] See below, p. 198.

(c) *the right 'to defend himself in person or through legal assistance of his own choosing or, if he has not sufficient means to pay for legal assistance, to be given it free when the interests of justice so require'*

Under this provision, the accused has two separate rights: first, the right to defend himself in person or through legal assistance of his own choosing; secondly, to be given free legal assistance if he has not sufficient means and if the interests of justice so require.

With regard to the first limb, the Commission has stated that this does not necessarily give the accused a choice as to whether he is to appear in person or whether his case is to be presented by a lawyer. Thus, where an applicant complained that, being in detention on remand, he was not allowed to be present in person at the hearing of his appeal, the Commission held that it was for the competent authorities to decide whether he should be allowed to defend himself in person or to be represented by a lawyer.[1]

The decision of the authorities is, however, subject to the requirement that the case for the defence must be properly put forward, which in very many cases will require that the accused is legally represented, and is granted legal aid where necessary.

Indeed this requirement follows from the right to a fair hearing under Article 6(1), and to that extent applies also to civil cases. For while there is clearly no right, in civil proceedings, to legal aid as such, Article 6(3) (c) being expressly confined to persons charged with a criminal offence, the refusal of legal aid in civil cases may raise the issue of a fair hearing under Article 6(1).[2]

Where legal aid is granted, it is clear that the accused has no right to a lawyer of his own choosing; only a person who pays himself has this right.[3] In practice in many systems the lawyer is appointed by the court. It may be that in such circumstances, the court has a special duty to ensure that the accused has a fair hearing. It is well known that such systems of legal aid often impose unwanted obligations on the lawyers concerned, and these difficulties have been brought before the Commission in a different context.[4]

In an application against Austria, the applicant complained that, on his arrest, money was taken from him as security for costs

[1] 2676/65, *Collection of Decisions* 23, 31.
[2] 2804/66, *Collection of Decisions* 27, 61 at 73.
[3] 646/59, *Yearbook* 3, 272.
[4] See under Article 4 above, p. 43.

117

under a provision of Austrian law, with the consequence that he was unable to be represented by a lawyer of his choice and obliged to accept a lawyer appointed by the court.[1] The Commission held that this was consistent with Article 6(3) (c) provided that the money was not taken in order to prevent him from defending himself through a lawyer of his own choice. The decision is somewhat questionable. Under the presumption of innocence in Article 6(2), it should be presumed that the accused will not be required to pay the prosecution's costs. If the security is taken merely as a contingency, the accused should not be placed in a worse position to defend himself, with the result of making that very contingency more probable. The rights of the accused as guaranteed by the Convention must prevail over the State's claim to security for costs.

Difficulties may also arise where the lawyer appointed is frequently changed. In the Köplinger Case,[2] the Commission considered whether the frequent changes in the applicant's legal representation may have affected his right under Article 6(3) (b) to have adequate time and facilities for the preparation of his defence. It expressed the opinion that the legal aid system previously in force in Germany, under which a new lawyer was appointed at each stage of the proceedings, was scarcely satisfactory, and could give rise to doubts with regard to its compatibility with the Convention. However, under the new system, introduced while the case was before the Commission, the same lawyer was in charge of the defence throughout the proceedings.[3]

(d) *the right 'to examine or have examined witnesses against him and to obtain the attendance and examination of witnesses on his behalf under the same conditions as witnesses against him'*

This provision must be considered in the context of the accusatorial system, where it is for the parties, subject to the control of the court, to decide which witnesses they wish to call, as well as in the context of the inquisitorial system, where the court decides for itself which witnesses it wishes to hear. In the former system, again, the witnesses are examined and cross-examined by the parties or their representatives, although additional questions may be put by

---

[1] 4338/69, *Collection of Decisions* 36, 79.
[2] See above, p. 115.
[3] *Yearbook* 12, 438 at 488; and see above, under Article 6(3) (b), p. 115.

118

the judge, while in the latter system witnesses are examined by the court.

Article 6(3) (d) is intended to ensure, under both systems, that the accused is placed on a footing of complete equality, as regards the calling and examination of witnesses, with the prosecution; but it does not give him a right to call witnesses without restriction. The competent legal authorities are therefore free, provided they respect the Convention and, in particular, the above principle of equality, to ascertain whether the hearing of a witness for the defence is likely to contribute to the establishment of the truth and, if not, to refuse to call that witness.[1] A court can therefore refuse to hear a witness for the reason that his statement would be irrelevant.[2] Where the evidence is relevant, the court fulfils its obligation if it takes all appropriate steps to try to ensure the appearance of the witness.[3]

Equality alone may not be sufficient. Hence the Commission has pointed out that a court which refuses to hear a witness for the defence may violate Article 6(1) while at the same time observing the principle of equality in Article 6(3) (d).[4]

There can be no doubt that the Commission has here taken its 'fourth instance' doctrine[5] to an unacceptable length. From the premiss that it is in principle within the discretion of the national courts to establish whether a particular witness should be called, it has sometimes drawn the conclusion that the complaint was manifestly ill-founded.[6] While its decisions on such complaints have not always been so devoid of reasoning, there appears to be no case in which the Commission has reviewed the exercise by the national courts of their discretion. In this way the protection of Article 6(3) (d) has ceased to have any content.

(e) *the right 'to have the free assistance of an interpreter if he cannot understand or speak the language used in court'*

This provision, although it has been the subject of a number of

---

[1] Pfunders Case (*Austria* v. *Italy*) *Yearbook* 6, 740 at 772; cf. 4276/69, *Collection of Decisions* 33, 47.

[2] 1404/62, *Yearbook* 7, 104 at 112; 4119/69, *Collection of Decisions* 35, 127.

[3] 3566/68, *Collection of Decisions* 31, 31 at 34–5; 4078/69, *Collection of Decisions* 35, 121 at 125.

[4] See n. 2; cf. 4428/70, *Collection of Decisions* 40, 1.

[5] See above, p. 106.

[6] See, e.g. 5131/71, *Collection of Decisions* 43, 151.

applications to the Commission,[1] has not itself given rise to any particular difficulties of interpretation. Under German rules of criminal procedure, a convicted person is charged with the costs of the proceedings. The German courts have held, however, that the costs incurred in providing an interpreter could not be assessed against a foreigner. Article 6(3) (e) prevails over the normal rules, and the service of an interpreter must therefore be provided free of charge.[2]

ARTICLE 7

The principle of legality *(nulla poena sine lege)*

Article 7(1) provides that:

No one shall be held guilty of any criminal offence on account of any act or omission which did not constitute a criminal offence under national or international law at the time when it was committed. Nor shall a heavier penalty be imposed than the one that was applicable at the time the criminal offence was committed.

Article 7 embodies the principle of legality, which requires that no one should be convicted or punished except for breach of an existing rule of law. This principle, sometimes expressed in the maxim *nullum crimen, nulla poena, sine lege,* is a central part of the notion of the 'rule of law' referred to in the Preamble to the Convention. It also imposes further limitations on the lawfulness, under the Convention, of both conviction and detention.

The principle has a dual application, affecting on the one hand the legislature, on the other hand the criminal courts. In the first place, it prohibits retrospective penal legislation. Secondly, it precludes the courts from extending the scope of the criminal law by interpretation.

The issue of retrospective penal legislation was raised in the Irish Case,[3] where a separate application by the Irish Government alleged that the Northern Ireland Act 1972 infringed Article 7. The Act provided that certain limitations on the powers of the

---

[1] See, e.g. 1794/63, *Yearbook* 9, 178; 2465/65, *Collection of Decisions* 24, 50; 3914/69, *Collection of Decisions* 34, 20.

[2] See Buergenthal in Robertson (ed.) *Human Rights in National and International Law,* Manchester, 1968, 194.

[3] See above, p. 25.

Northern Ireland Parliament should not have effect, and should be deemed never to have had effect, for the purpose of certain acts of the armed forces. As a result, failure to comply with orders of the security forces might constitute a criminal offence although it was not an offence when it occurred. At the hearing before the Commission on admissibility the United Kingdom Government undertook that there would be no prosecutions under the 1972 Act for acts or omissions which occurred before its enactment, and this application was consequently withdrawn by the Irish Government.[1]

Article 7 does not merely prohibit retrospective penal legislation; it also prohibits extension of the application of the criminal law through interpretation by analogy.[2] Indeed it may well be argued that it excludes any form of extensive interpretation of penal legislation.

An applicant complained of his conviction for homosexual behaviour under a provision of the Austrian Penal Code of 1852 which makes 'unnatural indecency' an offence.[3] He maintained that a restrictive interpretation of this term, required in his view by Article 7, would prohibit only sodomy, which he had not committed, while the homosexual relations in which he had engaged, namely reciprocal masturbation, could be regarded as prohibited only by an extensive interpretation.

He stated that the Austrian Supreme Court had at one time adopted the restrictive interpretation, but changed its practice in 1902 for the extensive interpretation. The Commission appears to have accepted the argument that extensive interpretation of criminal law might infringe Article 7, but rejected the applicant's complaint since, even if the Supreme Court had changed its practice in 1902, the same principle of interpretation was applicable both when he committed the offences and when he was convicted.

A decision quoted above suggests that Article 7 'confirms . . . the principle of the statutory nature of offences and punishments'.[4] However, this should be taken in its context, not as excluding the possibility of crimes based on common law, without statutory definition, but rather as requiring that offences, whether statutory

---

[1] 5451/72, *Collection of Decisions* 41, 3.
[2] 1852/63, *Yearbook* 8, 190 at 198.
[3] 4161/69, *Yearbook* 13, 798.   [4] See n. 2.

or common law, should be defined with reasonable precision. It is very doubtful whether certain vaguely definrd offences known to English law, such as public mischief or conspiring to corrupt public morals, are consistent with Article 7.

Vagueness, however, may be as much a vice of statutory as of common law crimes.

The issue was raised by a conviction on charges of neo-Nazi activities.[1] Although not invoking Article 7 of the Convention, the applicant submitted that the Austrian law under which he was convicted, which referred to 'National Socialist activities', was vague, and that the court which convicted him, while referring generally to his participation in several youth organizations, did not indicate any particular acts which were found to be National Socialist activities. The Austrian Government argued that, while the conception of the offence was wide, it was not limitless. 'Convinced of the danger of a revival of National Socialism, the legislator deemed it essential, in addition to specifying a number of offences, to insert a general clause providing for the punishment of any "activity" of a National Socialist nature.'[2] However, this general clause was delimited in several respects, which the Government proceeded to enumerate. Its arguments appear to have satisfied the Commission, which considered the complaint under Article 7, only to reject it summarily.

In another case, however, a complaint of an extensive interpretation of criminal law was rejected by the Commission on a ground which is clearly wrong.[3] The Commission relied on the 'fourth instance' formula,[4] according to which it is not competent to examine complaints alleging that errors of fact or law have been made by domestic courts except where such errors might have involved a possible violation of the rights listed in the Convention. But, whatever merit this doctrine may have as applied to the right to a fair hearing under Article 6(1),[5] its application to Article 7 simply begs the question. For if Article 7 guarantees that criminal law will not be extended in the instant case by judicial interpretation, the Commission must always control alleged errors of law by domestic courts in these cases.[6] It must consider whether

---

[1] 1747/62, *Yearbook* 6, 424.   [2] At 430.

[3] 4080/69, *Collection of Decisions* 38, 4; cf. 5321/71, *Collection of Decisions* 42, 105, for another application of the 'fourth instance' formula to Article 7.

[4] See above, p. 106.   [5] Ibid.

[6] 1852/63, *Yearbook* 8, 190 at 198.

the domestic court, in reaching its decision, has not unreasonably interpreted and applied the relevant domestic law.[1]

The expression 'national or international law' raises the question whether, under the rules of conflict of laws, a State can enforce the law of another State even where the conduct concerned is not contrary to its own law. The Commission has held that a State may include on a person's police record an offence committed abroad, if the acts concerned constituted a criminal offence at the place where, and the time when, he was convicted.[2] The decision raises some doubts. If action relating to a police record comes within Article 7 at all, should not the conduct constituting the offence abroad also be criminal at home, before any criminal consequence should attach to it?

The fact that the acts were criminal at the place where the person was convicted may show that the foreign court had jurisdiction and consequently be relevant under private international law. But this is not sufficient under Article 7. What the principle of legality requires is that if the national law prescribes penal consequences, the conduct in question must be an offence under the substantive law of that State. The inclusion in Article 7 of the term 'international law' shows that this condition may be satisfied if the conduct in question constitutes a crime against international law; for it is of the essence of international criminal law, as it has been developed since 1945, that national courts have jurisdiction over crimes against international law. But this has no bearing on the enforcement by one State, under the rules of *private* international law, of the criminal law of another State.

Article 7 should therefore be interpreted as excluding the enforcement of a foreign criminal judgment in respect of acts which were not an offence in the enforcing State. This interpretation is confirmed by State practice. Thus, in accordance with this principle, Article 4(1) of the European Convention on the International Validity of Criminal Judgments,[3] which allows the enforcement in one Contracting State of sanctions imposed in another, provides that: 'The sanction shall not be enforced by another Contracting State unless under its law the act for which the sanction was imposed would be an offence if committed on its

---

[1] 4681/70, *Collection of Decisions* 43, 1; 5327/71, *Collection of Decisions* 43, 85.
[2] 448/59, *Yearbook* 3, 270.
[3] *European Treaty Series*, No. 70.

territory and the person on whom the sanction was imposed liable to punishment if he had committed the act there.'

Similarly, Article 2(1) of the European Convention on Extradition,[1] embodying a general rule of international law, the rule of double criminality, provides that the offence in respect of which extradition is granted must be punishable under the law of both the requesting State and the requested State.

If it is correct to interpret the provisions of the Convention, within certain limits, by reference to the domestic practice of the Contracting Parties,[2] it must be legitimate to interpret them by reference to other Conventions between Member States of the Council of Europe which may be presumed to embody a consensus on the proper limits of public authority. Conversely, these Conventions must themselves be interpreted by the Contracting Parties so as to avoid any conflict with their obligations under the Human Rights Convention.

The reference to 'international law' in Article 7(1) is elaborated in paragraph (2), which provides that: 'This Article shall not prejudice the trial and punishment of any person for any act or omission which, at the time when it was committed, was criminal according to the general principles of law recognised by civilised nations.'

The expression 'general principles of law recognised by civilised nations' is derived from Article 38 of the Statute of the International Court of Justice, as part of the law which that Court is required to apply. Although they are general principles of municipal law, they may therefore now be regarded as part of 'international law' referred to in paragraph (1). Why then was this special provision necessary?

According to the preparatory work on the Convention, the purpose of Article 7(2) is to make it clear that Article 7 'does not affect laws which, under very exceptional circumstances at the end of the second world war, were passed in order to suppress war crimes, treason and collaboration with the enemy'.[3]

Thus, Article 7(2) is designed to meet objections such as those levelled against the war crimes tribunals, that they applied retrospective legislation. It is interesting to note, however, that the

---

[1] *European Treaty Series*, No. 24.
[2] See above, p. 19.
[3] 1038/61, *Yearbook* 4, 324 at 336.

German courts, which were the courts mainly concerned with the prosecution of war crimes, have not relied on the doctrine that a person may be convicted for an offence criminal according to the general principles of law. On the contrary, the Federal Government made a reservation to Article 7 according to which: '. . . it will only apply the provisions of Article 7 paragraph 2 of the Convention within the limits of Article 103 clause 2 of the Basic Law of the German Federal Republic. This provides that "any act is only punishable if it was so by law before the offence was committed".'[1]

This reservation, instead of restricting the Government's obligations under the Convention, appears actually to extend them.[2] The Government undertook not to take advantage of the authorization to apply retrospective legislation since to do so would be unconstitutional. Rather than rely on retrospective legislation, the German courts have generally preferred to rely on the doctrine that acts which were committed under Nazi 'law' were illegal because that 'law' was invalid under a higher, unwritten law.

Article 7(2) has also been applied by the Commission in cases from countries occupied during the Second World War, such as Belgium and Denmark, which subsequently introduced retrospective legislation to punish collaborators.[3] While this practice may be in accordance with the intention of Article 7(2), it is doubtful whether its terms cover the various offences of collaboration to which it has been applied. Not all forms of collaboration with a *de facto* government, however abhorrent they may be, are criminal according to the general principles of law recognized by civilized nations.

ARTICLE 8

Privacy and family life

Article 8(1) provides that: 'Everyone has the right to respect for his private and family life, his home and his correspondence.'

Paragraph (2) allows for certain restrictions on the rights guaranteed by paragraph (1). These restrictions, which are similar

---

[1] *Collected Texts* (9th ed.) p. 604.
[2] See the Commission's comment cited by Fawcett, p. 185.
[3] See, e.g. the De Becker case, *Yearbook* 2, 214 at 226.

to those permitted under subsequent Articles of the Convention, are considered generally below.[1]

The rights protected by Article 8 are somewhat disparate. However, the fact that they are grouped together in the same Article strengthens the protection given by that Article, since each right is reinforced by its context. Thus, the right to respect for family life, the right to privacy, and the right to respect for the home may be read together as guaranteeing collectively more than the sum of their parts. This method of interpretation is justified even in the case of rights protected by separate Articles,[2] but it is all the more necessary where a single Article is concerned.

It is quite clear, for example, that wire-tapping, unless it can be justified in a particular case under paragraph (2), is prohibited by Article 8, and it matters little whether it is considered as interference with correspondence, or with privacy, or even with the home if it takes place there, since these notions should be considered together rather than in isolation. Hence, in the following pages, it will often be necessary to take together, as the Commission has frequently done, privacy and the home, or family life and the home, or privacy and correspondence.

Privacy

The scope of the protection of privacy under the Convention remains largely unexplored in the case-law.[3]

It has been suggested[4] that the Convention protects the individual, under this head, against:

1. Attacks on his physical or mental integrity or his moral or intellectual freedom.
2. Attacks on his honour and reputation and similar torts.
3. The use of his name, identity, or likeness.
4. Being spied upon, watched, or harassed.
5. The disclosure of information protected by the duty of professional secrecy.

The organs of the Convention, however, have not developed the concept of privacy, and those applications which have raised the issue have often been treated on other grounds.

In the Scheichelbauer Case,[5] the question arose whether a

---

[1] See p. 195. [2] Cf. p. 23.
[3] See *Privacy and Human Rights*, ed. Robertson, Manchester 1973.
[4] Velu, op. cit. n. 3, at 92.
[5] 2645/65, *Yearbook* 12, 156.

tape-recording of a conversation, made without the knowledge of the accused, could be used in evidence against him. The question considered by the Commission, however, was whether *use* of the recording as evidence prejudiced the applicant's right to a fair trial under Article 6(1). If it had been considered on the merits under Article 8 the question would have been whether the *making* of the recording could have been justified under paragraph (2).

In early decisions the Commission recognized that laws prohibiting homosexual behaviour constituted an interference with the right to respect for private and family life; it considered, however, that such interference was justified under paragraph (2) as being 'for the protection of health and morals'.[1] The Commission further held that Article 14 of the Convention, which prohibits discrimination between men and women in the enjoyment of the rights guaranteed, did not preclude treating men in this area differently from women.[2]

The Commission has also held that the keeping of criminal records, including photographs and finger-prints, even if it may raise an issue under Article 8, could be justified under paragraph (2) as being in the interests of public safety or for the prevention of disorder or crime.[3]

Similarly, lawful search of a person's home and the seizure of documents belonging to him may be justifiable under Article 8(2).[4] *A fortiori*, the cell of a person detained on remand may be searched in his absence.[5]

On the other hand, in the Greek Case, Article 8 was violated by the suspension of the right to respect for the home in the Greek Constitution, and by 'the consequent disregard of this right, in particular by the practice of the Greek authorities of carrying out arrests at night'.[6]

It seems likely that in future other substantial issues affecting the right to privacy will be raised under Article 8. This is one area where interferences are probably increasing rather than diminishing. The use of computers, in particular, may give rise to problems of privacy: how far, for example, does Article 8

[1] 104/55, *Yearbook* 1, 228; 167/56, *Yearbook* 1, 235; 261/57, *Yearbook* 1, 255.
[2] Ibid. [3] 1307/61, *Yearbook* 5, 230.
[4] 320/59, *Yearbook* 3, 184.
[5] 3448/69, *Collection of Decisions* 30, 56.
[6] *Yearbook* 12, The Greek Case, 152–3.

authorize the storage, and use, by the administration of personal data?

However, the main sources of infringement of privacy are not so much State agencies as bodies which may be independent of the State: the Press and other media, or private electronic data banks. It is doubtful how far the activities of such bodies can be brought within the scope of the Convention.[1]

Family life

The protection of the family, as the fundamental unit of society, figures at more than one place in the Convention. Article 12, which will be considered separately below, guarantees the right to marry and to found a family. Article 8, with which we are concerned here, prohibits in principle, and subject to the provisions of paragraph (2), interference with an existing family unit. Article 2 of the First Protocol deals with an important aspect of the rights of parents in relation to their children's education. It provides for the right of parents to ensure such education in conformity with their own religious and philosophical convictions. The relationship between this provision and Article 8 is considered below, under the right to education.[2]

The right to respect for family life, as guaranteed by Article 8 of the Convention, has as its principal element the protection of the integrity of the family. What then constitutes a 'family', and under what conditions is interference authorized under the Convention?

Applications to the Commission have raised two major aspects of the second question, and have led to the emergence of some criteria for an answer to the first. The following discussion will attempt to abstract some statements of principle from the substantial case-law on the subject.[3]

There are two types of situation which have most frequently raised issues under Article 8. First there is the case where some action by the authorities, such as expelling a person from a country, or refusing to admit someone, may result in separation of husband and wife, or of parents and children.

The second situation concerns exclusively the relationship of parents and children. It may arise after the separation or divorce

[1] See above, p. 11.   [2] P. 170.
[3] See 'Case-Law Topics', No. 2, *Family Life*, European Commission of Human Rights, Strasbourg, 1972.

128

of the parents, when the courts make an order concerning the custody of, or access to, the children of the marriage. Or it may arise, although less often, when the children of an existing marriage are taken into the care of the public authorities.

In the first type of situation, when expulsion or refusal of admission in the source of the complaint, that action in itself cannot constitute a breach of the Convention. As has already been seen, the Convention does not guarantee, at any rate outside the Fourth Protocol, any right to reside in a particular country.[1] But, as in the East African Asians Case,[2] the question may arise whether, for example, a refusal of admission does not infringe some other right which is guaranteed. Thus, while the right to reside in a particular country is not, as such, guaranteed by the Convention, the Commission has frequently examined complaints of expulsion or of refusal of admission in relation to Article 8, where such a measure might disrupt the family unit.

There have, for example, been many cases where the applicant complains of being separated from his wife as a result of his expulsion from the country where they lived together, or as a result of his not being allowed entry or permanent admission to the country in which she lives. In such cases the Commission has first examined whether there existed an effective family life between the members of the family concerned. This normally requires two elements: a close relationship; and one between persons who have been living together at the time of, or shortly before, the alleged interference.

The relationship between an uncle and a nephew or niece is not sufficiently close, at least in a case where they are not and have not been living in the same household.[3] The only cases which have been regarded as constituting a close relationship for this purpose are the relationship of husband and wife;[4] and of parent and child where there is some situation of dependence.

The last point may be illustrated by comparing the cases of Alam and Singh.[5]

---

[1] See above, p. 59.

[2] Above, p. 33.

[3] 3110/67, *Yearbook* 11, 494 at 518. The nephew and niece were children of the applicant's half-brother (p. 494).

[4] See, e.g. East African Asians, below, p. 131, and 5269/71, *Collection of Decisions* 39, 104.

[5] 2991/66 and 2992/66, *Yearbook* 10, 478.

The applicants in both cases had been resident in the United Kingdom since 1957. Alam, a citizen of Pakistan, tried in 1965 to obtain permission for his minor son, Mohamed Khan, to be admitted to the United Kingdom. Singh, a United Kingdom citizen of Indian origin, tried, also in 1965, to obtain permission for his father to enter the United Kingdom. The immigration authorities refused entry in both cases on the grounds that the applicants had failed to establish the family relationship alleged by them.

The Commission considered the applicants' complaints, *inter alia*, under Article 8 of the Convention. With regard to the applicant Singh, it found no appearance of a violation and relied on the ground that no family life was shown to exist between the applicant and his father, as both were adults who had been living apart for a considerable period.

The Alam case, however, was declared admissible, but subsequently a friendly settlement of the case was reached.[1] The United Kingdom Government agreed to grant Mohamed Khan an entry certificate, and to meet the cost of an air ticket for Mohamed Khan from Pakistan to London.

The Government also stated that it had introduced draft legislation which would confer rights of appeal against the decisions of immigration officers. The significance of this was that the case had also been considered in relation to the requirements of Article 6(1).[2] As the case was settled, the questions raised, both under Article 6(1) and under Article 8, were left open.

The rule applied in the Singh case was taken somewhat further in a later case against the United Kingdom.[3] A Cypriot citizen, married to a citizen of the United Kingdom and Colonies, was required to leave the United Kingdom, as he had been admitted only for a limited period. In examining this complaint under Article 8, the Commission, in accordance with its general practice,[4] treated as a relevant factor the possibility for the wife to follow her husband. In this case, however, the Commission stated:

another aspect of her family life should be considered as her departure from the United Kingdom would mean that she would no longer be able to live permanently with her parents as she and her husband

---

[1] *Yearbook* 11, 788.   [2] See below, p. 256.
[3] 5269/71, *Collection of Decisions* 39, 104.
[4] See below, p. 131.

are doing at present. The question therefore arises whether her relationship with her parents is also to be regarded as 'family life' within the meaning of the said Article. However, even if it were assumed that the relationship between an adult daughter and her parents with whom she still lives may in particular circumstances constitute family life, the circumstances of the present case, as they have been presented by the applicants, do not show that there is such a close link between the second applicant and her parents as could be described as amounting to 'family life' within the meaning of Article 8. In this respect the Commission has taken into particular consideration that she is 26 years of age, married and living together with her husband and is working full time. The Commission also notes that there is no suggestion that her parents are financially dependent on her nor she on them.

The Commission accordingly rejected the complaint as manifestly ill-founded.

These, then, are the criteria which the Commission has applied in deciding whether family life exists for the purposes of Article 8. However, even if a sufficiently close relationship exists, it does not follow that expulsion, or refusal of admission, will constitute an interference with the right to respect for family life.

The Commission will next enquire whether the family unit could not be preserved by establishing the family's residence in the country to which the member of the family is to be expelled, or from which he seeks admission.[1] If it could, then the State has not interfered with the right to respect for family life. Such a limitation on the notion of interference is necessary; for otherwise there would be an effective prohibition on expulsion, and on refusal of admission, whenever family life was established.

If, however, it is doubtful whether the family could establish itself elsewhere, then the complaint must be examined on the merits. This was the situation in two applications in the first group of East African Asians Cases.[2] In each of the two, the applicant had been refused permission to enter the United Kingdom from Uganda to join his wife, who had lawfully entered the United Kingdom, in one case with six children, some time previously. The complaints were declared admissible, but shortly afterwards all the applicants in this group of cases were admitted for permanent residence.

[1] See, e.g. 2535/65, *Collection of Decisions* 17, 28.
[2] *Yearbook* 13, 928 at 1004.

The conclusion seems to be that the Convention does not guarantee the right to family life in a particular country, but only an effective family life as such, no matter where. This principle, however, appears to be modified in the case of the relationships between parents and their children, if the latter are not admitted to the country where the former have their residence. In the Alam Case, the Commission did not reject the application on the ground that the father could leave the country and establish the family unit by joining his child.[1]

It would seem to follow that, while the admission of a person to permanent residence may not imply any obligation to admit his spouse (present or future), it may imply an obligation to admit his dependent children.

A final point that has arisen in some of these cases is whether the immigration laws involve an element of discrimination based on sex which might raise an issue under Article 14 taken together with Article 8. In the United Kingdom, as in other European countries, the rule is frequently applied that a woman may normally be admitted to join her husband, but that only exceptionally may a man be admitted to join his wife. In the East African Asians Cases, the Government submitted that the place of residence of a family is normally the place of residence of the husband, and that Article 8 does not safeguard any right for husband and wife to live together permanently in any other place than the place of residence of the husband, or at a place where he is entitled to be.[2] The question is whether such differential treatment of men and women in this field is justifiable under Article 14, or whether it constitutes discrimination under that Article. The question arose again in the Cypriot case mentioned above. The applicant alleged that not merely the decision which was challenged, but the immigration rules, were in breach of Article 14.[3] The point is passed over in the Commission's decision.

Most of the other cases on family life which have been brought before the Commission concern the rights of parents in relation to their children. The situations giving rise to these cases have been extremely varied, but certain principles can be found in the Commission's decisions.[4]

[1] 'Case-Law Topics', No. 2, *Family Life*, pp. 40–1.
[2] *Yearbook* 13, 928 at 978; cf. 1004.
[3] 5269/71, *Collection of Decisions* 39, 104 at 107.
[4] 'Case-Law Topics', No. 2, p. 13 *et seq.*

First, the family life of parents with their children does not cease owing to the separation or divorce of the parents. Where, in such cases, the courts award custody of the children to one parent, there is inevitably an interference with the family life of the other parent. However, in these cases, 'it may be legitimate, or even necessary, for the national law to provide rules governing the relationship between parents and children which differ from the rules which are applicable when the family unit is still maintained.'[1] Thus, where an applicant complained of court decisions awarding the custody of his son to his divorced wife, the Commission stated that the terms of paragraph (2) leave a considerable measure of discretion to the domestic courts when deciding on questions concerning the custody of the children of divorced parents. It found that the courts had taken full account of the situation of each parent in relation to the general well-being of the child, and that there was no indication that the courts, in reaching their various findings, had interfered with the applicant's family life in a manner not permitted under paragraph (2).[2]

If a parent is not awarded custody of his child, he may not be prevented from access to it unless special circumstances, as defined in paragraph (2), so require.[3] The domestic courts and other authorities must therefore examine whether the grounds mentioned in paragraph (2) justify the denial of access. They may consider factors such as the health or morals of the child,[4] including its psychological well-being,[5] and the prevention of crime.[6]

Such considerations apply with still greater force to questions of custody.[7]

The Commission has also considered a number of complaints by applicants, in some cases still married and living together, whose children have been made wards of public or judicial authorities, and have subsequently been placed in Childrens' Homes where care and education can be properly assured.[8]

---

[1] 2699/65, Yearbook 11, 366 at 376.

[2] Ibid.; cf. 4284/69, Collection of Decisions 37, 74.

[3] 172/56, Yearbook 1, 211 at 217.

[4] 911/60, Yearbook 4, 198; 2792/66, Collection of Decisions 21, 64.

[5] 2808/66, not published.

[6] 1449/62, Yearbook 6, 262.

[7] Ibid.

[8] 'Case-Law Topics', No. 2, p. 23 et seq.

In a United Kingdom case[1] which is not untypical of many others, the applicants (husband and wife) complained of a violation of Article 8. Their two children had been taken into custody by the Kent County Council when local authorities found that the family had insufficient accommodation and that the well-being of the children was affected. The Commission noted that the removal of the applicants' children was pursuant to an order made under the relevant law by a competent court and was consequently itself lawful. It further observed that the court had found that the applicants' children were not receiving the care, protection, and guidance that a good parent may reasonably be expected to give and that the lack of such care, protection or guidance was likely to cause them unnecessary suffering or seriously to affect their health or proper development. The Commission held that the finding of the court would clearly justify, under Article 8(2), the removal of the applicants' children.

The fundamental question in all these cases is how far the Commission and the Court can control the decisions of the national authorities. In reading the Commission's case-law, one may sometimes have the impression that it is too ready to rely on those decisions as themselves justifying the measures complained of, and to allow the national authorities a 'margin of discretion'[2] in considering the relevant factors under Article 8(2), which precludes effective control. This is a problem which arises under a number of Articles of the Convention; Articles 9 to 11, for example, have a paragraph (2) which serves a similar function to paragraph (2) of Article 8. It raises issues of general importance in the interpretation and application of the Convention and is examined in some detail below.[3]

The protection of Article 8 extends also to illegitimate children. The mother of an illegitimate child may in some cases be entitled to its custody, and the rights of the mother, as well as the child, must be respected.[4]

The father of the illegitimate child is also entitled to certain parental rights. The German legislation on this subject, which

---

[1] 4004/69, *Collection of Decisions* 33, 18; cf. 4185/69, *Collection of Decisions* 35, 140.

[2] See, e.g. 2648/65, *Collection of Decisions* 26, 26; 4396/70, *Collection of Decisions* 36, 88, and cf. p. 201, below.

[3] See pp. 201 and 205.   [4] 514/59, *Yearbook* 3, 197.

was at that time probably in breach of the Convention, came before the Commission in the following circumstances.[1]

The applicant was engaged to a woman who declared she would only marry him if they could have a child together. However, after she had had a child she refused to marry him and left him, taking the child with her. In court the applicant acknowledged that he was the father and was ordered to pay maintenance for the child. He was, however, refused an order giving him access to his child, since the law recognized no such right. The paternity of an unmarried father was unrecognized by German law, unless a declaration of legitimacy was issued; but this required the consent of the mother, which she refused to give.

The German Government stated, in its observations on admissibility, that it had submitted to the Federal Parliament a Bill on the legal status of illegitimate children, which would shortly enter into force. The new legislation would first of all do away with the provision of the German Civil Code according to which the illegitimate child and the father were deemed not to be relatives. Secondly, it would provide for the possibility for the father to acquire parental power by adopting the child or by having it declared legitimate, while the necessary consent of the mother could be replaced by that of the guardianship court in cases where it would be in the interest of the child.

Thirdly, the person having custody of the child would be entitled to decide whether, and to what extent, the father should have access to the child. If personal contact with its father would benefit the child, the guardianship court could take the decision.

The Commission, having received this communication and the applicant's reply, decided to strike the application off its list of cases as 'the new legislation concerning the status of illegitimate children . . . gives a natural father some possibility, not hitherto available, to claim access to, or exert influence over, the situation of his child.' It added that the new legislation gave the applicant reasonable satisfaction in regard to his complaint.

The family life of prisoners

Applicants detained in prison have frequently complained of

---

[1] 3100/67, *Collection of Decisions* 31, 16; cf. 5288/71, *Collection of Decisions* 44, 25.

interference with the right to respect for family life.[1] Some have complained that they have been refused permission to have visits from their children. The Commission has rejected such complaints under paragraph (2), for example on the ground that such interference with family life was necessary for the prevention of crime.[2]

In an Austrian case,[3] the Commission was of the opinion that the refusal of the Austrian authorities to allow a child to visit her father in prison or to correspond with him, because he was serving a sentence of more than one year's imprisonment, was, in the light of Article 8, a rather serious measure. The Commission first established that this refusal was a consequence of Austrian law, which provides that a person who is convicted to a prison sentence of more than one year loses his paternal rights and that a guardian is to be appointed for his children. In the circumstances of the above case, the refusal by the authorities concerned was properly designed to protect the interests of minors. The Commission decided that such measures did not exceed the margin of discretion[4] which, according to its case-law, is left to the authorities under Article 8(2). It is unsatisfactory that the decision of the authorities appears to have been based on a general legal rule rather than on a full examination of the merits of the particular case.

Again, the Commission's control of the decisions of national authorities under paragraph (2) is not always sufficiently rigorous. An example is a case[5] where a prisoner complained that he was refused permission to attend his daughter's funeral. The Commission here adopted the formula used by the Court in the Vagrancy Cases[6] and found that in view of all the circumstances, including the fact that the child was born after the applicant was imprisoned and that he had never seen her:

while there was interference by a public authority with the exercise of the right enshrined in Article 8(1), such interference was in accordance with the law, and the authorities did not transgress the limits of the power of appreciation which Article 8(2) leaves to them. There is no

---

[1] See 'Case-Law Topics', No. 1, *Human Rights in Prison*, 1971, p. 20 *et seq.*
[2] 1983/63, *Collection of Decisions* 18, 19; cf. 2515/65, *Collection of Decisions* 20, 28.
[3] 2306/64, *Collection of Decisions* 21, 23.   [4] See below, p. 201.
[5] 4623/70, *Collection of Decisions* 39, 63.   [6] See below, p. 201.

other element in the present case which might indicate that the prison authorities did not have sufficient reason to believe that it was necessary to impose this restriction for the purpose of the prevention of disorder or crime, the protection of health or morals, and the protection of the rights and freedoms of others.

No attempt is made to assess the reasons given by the authorities; indeed so far as can be seen from the Commission's decision, no reasons were given, and, since this part of the application was not communicated to the respondent Government, there is no indication of what reasons might have been used to justify the decision of the authorities.

It is evident that the Commission can scarcely supervise the 'power of appreciation' or exercise of discretion by the national authorities if it does not even know on what grounds they based their decision. When this information cannot be provided by the applicant, it must be obtained from the respondent Government. Otherwise there can be no effective control.

It is also important to ensure that the grounds advanced under paragraph (2) to justify an interference with family life are the real grounds of the decision. Restrictions on the rights guaranteed by the Convention can never be imposed as a punishment. To do so would be contrary, not only to the express terms of the limiting clauses themselves, but also to Article 18, which provides that: 'The restrictions permitted under this Convention to the said rights and freedoms shall not be applied for any purpose other than those for which they have been prescribed.'

Quite apart from purely legal considerations, it would be contrary to modern penological standards to restrict unnecessarily the family life of prisoners. If they are to be able to take their place again in society, they should have the greatest contact with the outside world that is consistent with the fact of their detention. Progressing standards of penal policy may even be legally relevant, since it is sometimes legitimate to interpret the Convention in the light of the practice of the Contracting Parties. Thus, restrictions which would at one time have been justified may cease to be permitted as standards are raised.[1]

In this way, a degree of marital life for prisoners may come to be recognized as part of the right to respect for family life guaranteed by Article 8.

[1] See above, p. 18.

The Commission considered, from the viewpoint outlined above, the complaint of a prisoner that he was refused permission to receive visits from his wife over week-ends in order to maintain their conjugal life in prison.[1] The Commission examined the question in the light of a comparative survey of the relevant law and practice of the States Parties to the Convention.

As a result of these inquiries the Commission noted that in eleven of the member States of the Council of Europe no system existed which gave prisoners the opportunity of continuing their marital life. On the other hand, these issues were under discussion in four States, and in three of them there was a very limited system for such access. In one State only, legislation allowed regular home leave for prisoners; and in one other State, home leave and conjugal visits in prison were allowed.

Having 'noted with sympathy the reformative movement in several European countries as regards an improvement of the conditions of imprisonment and the possibilities of detained persons to continue their conjugal life to a limited extent', the Commission finally rejected the application on the ground that such interference with the right to family life was 'necessary in the interests of public safety'.

The decision is significant as demonstrating the potential value of a 'dynamic' approach to the interpretation of the Convention.[2]

Respect for correspondence

'Correspondence' refers primarily to communication in writing.[3] Article 8 prohibits, subject to the exceptions in paragraph (2), any form of interference with correspondence, whether by censorship or otherwise.

Applications to the Commission have mainly been concerned with prisoners' correspondence. Interference here may take different forms. Prisoners' letters may be stopped or intercepted. There may be censorship of incoming and of outgoing letters. Or there may be a restriction on the number of letters that may be written.

The subject may be treated in three parts: restrictions on prisoners', and other detained persons', correspondence in general; restrictions on correspondence with defence counsel;

[1] 3603/68, *Collection of Decisions* 31, 48.
[2] See above, p. 18.   [3] See Fawcett, 194–5.

and finally, restrictions on correspondence with the Commission itself.

Often, of course, interference with prisoners' letters can be justified on one of the grounds stated in paragraph (2), as being necessary, for example, for the prevention of crime,[1] or for the protection of the rights of others.[2]

For some years, however, in dealing with complaints concerning correspondence in general, the Commission applied the doctrine that certain forms of restriction were an 'inherent feature' of imprisonment. The 'normal control' of prisoners' correspondence did not constitute, on this view, an interference with the right to respect for correspondence, requiring justification under Article 8(2), since it was an inherent feature of detention lawfully imposed under Article 5. Thus, in the De Courcy case,[3] which appears to be the first fully considered decision to rely on the doctrine, the Commission stated that 'the limitation of the right of a detained person to conduct correspondence is a necessary part of his deprivation of liberty which is inherent in the punishment of imprisonment.'

The notion of certain restrictions on the rights guaranteed by the Convention being regarded as an 'inherent feature' of detention is objectionable on a number of grounds, which are set out below.[4] Nevertheless, in the Vagrancy cases[5] the Commission developed this notion in examining the censorship of the applicants' correspondence while they were detained. It stated[6] that 'the fact of being detained necessarily involves restrictions on the rights and freedoms guaranteed by the Convention. These restrictions are a consequence of the fact of being detained and are not permissible except insofar as they are justified by the cause of such detention, provided always that the detention itself is in accordance with Article 5'.

In the present cases the Commission considered that, bearing in mind the cause of detention, such a control could not be justified as an inherent feature of the concept of detention. The Commission concluded, partly on this ground, but partly also on the

[1] See below, p. 140. [2] 3717/68, *Collection of Decisions* 31, 96.
[3] 2749/66, *Yearbook* 10, 388 at 412; cf. 4144/69, *Collection of Decisions* 33, 27 and (on Article 10) 1860/63, *Yearbook* 8, 204 at 216, and 4101/69, *Yearbook* 13, 720 at 728.
[4] See p. 198. [5] Above, p. 55.
[6] 'Publications of the Court', Series B, p. 97.

ground that the applicants' detention did not comply with the requirements of Article 5, that the censorship of the applicants' correspondence during their detention constituted a violation of Article 8.

The Court, however, found that there had been no violation of Article 8. Nevertheless, the Court did not find it necessary to rely on the 'inherent feature' argument. Instead the Court relied exclusively on Article 8(2). It found that the supervision of the applicants' correspondence constituted 'unquestionably' an interference with their rights under Article 8(1). But the interference was authorized under paragraph (2). In reaching this conclusion, the Court first found that the supervision in question was 'in accordance with the law' within the meaning of Article 8(2), referring in this connection to the relevant provisions of Belgian law. It then referred expressly to the grounds provided in Article 8(2) on which interference is authorized. It observed that 'the competent Belgian authorities did not transgress in the present cases the limits of the power of appreciation which Article 8(2) of the Convention leaves to the Contracting States: even in cases of persons detained for vagrancy, those authorities had sufficient reason to believe that it was "necessary" to impose restrictions for the purpose of the prevention of disorder or crime, the protection of health or morals, and the protection of the rights and freedoms of others'.[1]

It seems that since the judgment in the Vagrancy Cases the Commission has ceased to rely on the 'inherent feature' doctrine, at least in complaints concerning intereference with correspondence.

However, it would be unfortunate if the Commission fell back on the general formula adopted by the Court of relying on a margin of discretion in the authorities to assess the factors under Article 8(2). It is necessary, first, to distinguish the different elements involved in 'control' of correspondence, and secondly to differentiate more clearly the grounds of exception permitted under Article 8(2).

Some aspects of the control of prisoners' correspondence would present no difficulties on this analysis.

The *stopping* of a particular letter could obviously be justified

[1] Para. 93.

in a particular case on one of the grounds mentioned in paragraph (2) (e.g. 'for the prevention of crime'), if the object of the letter were for example to effect an escape from prison. This in turn would justify, on the same ground, the reading by prison authorities of *all* letters, both incoming and outgoing. Finally, the fact that all letters may have to be read by prison authorities, who are responsible for good order in prisons, might in turn be said to justify the imposition of a limit to the number of letters which a prisoner may send or receive. In each case, however, the interference would have to be properly justified on one of the grounds stated in paragraph (2), and the reasons given by the authorities ascertained and assessed on this basis.

The correspondence of detained persons with their defence counsel is specially privileged. This follows from Article 6(3) (b) of the Convention which guarantees to everyone charged with a criminal offence the right to have adequate time and facilities for the preparation of his defence. This provision applies equally, as has been seen, to proceedings on appeal.[1] One of the questions considered on the merits in the Köplinger case[2] was the applicant's complaint that the written communications he had addressed to his defence counsel had been transmitted belatedly by the prison authorities. In the event, the Commission considered that there had been no violation.

The correspondence of detained persons with the Commission requires separate consideration. Even if a certain control of correspondence in general is permitted, correspondence with the Commission has a special protection.

In the first place, States which have accepted the Commission's competence to receive individual applications undertake, by the terms of Article 25(1), not to hinder in any way the effective exercise of this right. Complaints by detained persons of interference with their correspondence with the Commission are therefore examined under Article 25, even if they do not raise any issue under Article 8. Here the Commission does not apply the rules of admissibility applicable to complaints under Section I of the Convention, although it may ask the Government for its observations on the question.[3] It has frequently drawn the attention of Governments to the need to give prison authorities adequate

---

[1] See above, pp. 84 and 114.   [2] See above, p. 115.
[3] 3591/68, *Collection of Decisions* 31, 37.

instructions in order that prisoners can fully exercise their right under Article 25.[1]

The Commission has, however, interpreted Article 25 rather restrictively, as meaning that, even if a particular complaint of interference has not been refuted, the requirements of the system are satisfied if the applicant has been able to present his case in a completely adequate manner.[2] But where a particular letter has been stopped, for example, it is difficult to see how the Commission can judge from the material that is not suppressed that the case has been adequately presented. It would be preferable to interpret Article 25 as requiring an unqualified freedom of correspondence with the Commission.

The need to protect the effective exercise of the right of petition is recognized in the legislation of the Contracting States; in Austria, for example, the Act concerning the Execution of Sentences expressly guarantees the right of prisoners freely to communicate with the Commission without restriction.[3]

In addition, the position of persons participating in proceedings under the Convention, including applicants to the Commission, is protected by a separate Agreement, the European Agreement relating to persons participating in proceedings of the European Commission and Court of Human Rights. By Article 3(1) of this Agreement, the Contracting Parties undertake to respect the right to correspond freely with the Commission and the Court. Paragraph (2) provides that, subject to the usual limitations set out in paragraph (3):

As regards persons under detention, the exercise of this right shall in particular imply that:
(a) if their correspondence is examined by the competent authorities, its despatch and delivery shall nevertheless take place without undue delay and without alteration;
(b) such persons shall not be subject to disciplinary measures in any form on account of any communication sent through the proper channels to the Commission or the Court;
(c) such persons shall have the right to correspond, and consult out of

---

[1] 'Case-Law Topics', No. 1, European Commission of Human Rights, Strasbourg, 1971, p. 41.
[2] 3827/68, *Collection of Decisions* 32, 27; 3868/68, *Yearbook* 13, 600 at 620; 4225/69, *Yearbook* 13, 864 at 886.
[3] Op cit. n. 1, p. 45.

hearing of other persons, with a lawyer qualified to appear before the courts of the country where they are detained in regard to an application to the Commission, or any proceedings resulting therefrom.

These provisions of the Agreement may be regarded as simply elucidating the notion of the effective exercise of the right of petition under Article 25. It is substantially in accordance with the Commission's interpretation of that Article.[1] Thus, while the Commission cannot deal with alleged infringements of the Agreement as such, it can take account of its provisions in construing Article 25.[2] Further, the Agreement cannot in any way limit the protection given by Article 25, since Article 6 of the Agreement provides that: 'Nothing in this Agreement shall be construed as limiting or derogating from any of the obligations assumed by the Contracting Parties under the Convention.'

The importance of allowing unrestricted access to the Commission does not need elaboration. It provides in itself a safeguard of the rights of persons in detention, since the authorities will be aware of the constant availability of this remedy. On the other hand, the provision of Article 3(2) (a), recognizing that correspondence may be examined by the competent authorities,[3] is clearly eminently sensible, as it may enable a legitimate complaint to be remedied without the need for further proceedings. It is the practice in some countries for prisoners' complaints to be photocopied and copies sent to the appropriate government department; this has sometimes led to the applicant obtaining satisfaction and withdrawing his complaint. In these ways, the Convention may have done much to improve the situation of persons in detention.

ARTICLE 9

Freedom of thought, conscience and religion

Article 9(1) provides that:

Everyone has the right to freedom of thought, conscience and religion; this right includes freedom to change his religion or belief and freedom,

---

[1] Op. cit., p. 42 f.   [2] See e.g. 3672/68, *Collection of Decisions* 31, 92.

[3] Ibid.; cf. 4144/69, *Collection of Decisions* 33, 27 and 3914/69, *Collection of Decisions* 34, 20 (letters from the Secretary of the Commission to the applicant opened by the prison authorities).

either alone or in community with others and in public or private, to manifest his religion or belief, in worship, teaching, practice and observance.

Freedom of thought, conscience and religion thus includes freedom to manifest one's religion or belief.[1] Only the *manifestation* of religion or belief is subject to the limitations set out in paragraph (2); otherwise the protection of these freedoms is absolute and not subject to any restriction whatever. It is doubtful whether even the derogations permitted under Article 15 could have any application here.

The freedoms guaranteed are closely related to the freedom of opinion guaranteed by Article 10. Religious education which is a subject of special difficulty is also dealt with by Article 2 of the First Protocol.

Norway, when ratifying the Convention, found it necessary to make a reservation to Article 9, as the Norwegian Constitution of 1814 provided for a ban on Jesuits. In 1956 this provision was abrogated, and the reservation withdrawn.[2] Similarly in Switzerland, a reservation was considered necessary pending revision of the denominational articles of the Federal Constitution;[3] the revision was subsequently effected.

Article 9 may appear, *prima facie*, to give a right to conscientious objection to military service. Such a right is in fact recognized in many countries; consequently, a refusal to recognize it could not easily be justified under paragraph (2) as being 'necessary in a democratic society'.

However, in accordance with the principle that the Convention must be read as a whole, Article 9 must be interpreted in the light of Article 4, which makes express reference to conscientious objectors. Article 4(3) (b) provides that, for the purposes of that Article, the term 'forced or compulsory labour' shall not include, 'in case of conscientious objectors in countries where they are recognised', service exacted instead of compulsory military service.

[1] Thus, liberty of conscience has been defined as 'the right to hold and profess what principles we choose, and to live in accordance with them', Plamenatz, *Man and Society*, Volume I, p. 49.

[2] *Collected Texts*, 9th edn., p. 605.

[3] See Federal Council's Report to the Federal Assembly on the Convention, *Yearbook* 12, 502 at 508.

Two conclusions seem to follow from the wording of this provision. First, since it speaks of conscientious objectors 'in countries where they are recognised', it seems that States are not obliged, under Article 9, to recognize them. Secondly, since it makes express provision for substitute service, it follows that where conscientious objectors are recognized, and are permitted to perform substitute service in lieu of military service, they cannot claim, under Article 9, exemption from substitute service. Hence no one is entitled under Article 9 to exemption on grounds of conscience either from military service or from substitute service.

The issue was examined by the Commission in the Grandrath Case.[1] The applicant was a member of the sect of Jehovah's Witnesses and exercised within this sect the function of Bible study leader. Like other members of the sect, he objected, for reasons of conscience and religion, not only to performing military service but also to any kind of substitute service. The German authorities recognized him as a conscientious objector but required him to perform substitute civilian service. When he refused to do so, criminal proceedings were instituted against him and he was convicted and sentenced to eight months' imprisonment, a sentence which was reduced on appeal to six months. In addition to the applicant's complaint under Article 9, the Commission considered *ex officio* the question whether, under Article 14 in conjunction with Article 9 or Article 4, he had been subject to discrimination as compared with Roman Catholic or Protestant ministers.

In the Commission's opinion, there were two aspects to be considered under Article 9.[2] First there was the question whether the civilian service which the applicant was required to perform would have restricted his right to manifest his religion. The Commission considered that it would not in fact have interfered either with the private and personal practice of his religion, or with his duties to his religious community, which were in any case a spare-time activity. Secondly there was the question whether Article 9 had been violated by the mere fact that he had been required to perform a service which was contrary to his conscience or religion. Here the Commission was of the opinion that, having regard to the provisions of Article 4, it must be concluded that objections of

---

[1] *Yearbook* 10, 626; cf. 5591/72, *Collection of Decisions* 43, 161.
[2] At p. 672.

conscience do not, under the Convention, entitle a person to exemption from substitute service.

In relation to Article 14, the Commission first expressed the view, subsequently confirmed by the Court in the Belgian Linguistic Case,[1] that the application of Article 14 does not depend upon a previous finding that another Article of the Convention has been violated. Article 14 provides that the enjoyment of the rights and freedoms set forth in the Convention shall be secured without discrimination on grounds of, *inter alia*, religion. The Commission stated that, in certain cases, Article 14 may be violated in a field dealt with by another Article of the Convention, although there is otherwise no violation of that other Article.

In the present case, it is necessary to refer to the limitative provisions contained in various Articles of the Convention. For example, in each of Articles 8 to 11, a certain right is guaranteed by paragraph (1), but the Contracting Parties are, under paragraph (2), allowed, subject to specific conditions, to restrict that right. When using this power to restrict a right guaranteed by the Convention, the Contracting Parties are bound by the provisions of Article 14. Consequently, if a restriction which is in itself permissible under paragraph (2) of one of the above Articles, is imposed in a discriminatory manner, there would be a violation of Article 14 in conjunction with the other Article concerned. The situation under Article 4 is similar. Although the types of work and service, enumerated in paragraph (3), are not expressly described as exceptions to the general prohibition against 'forced labour', they nevertheless operate as such in the present context.[2]

Thus, while certain forms of service are permitted under Article 4(3), a State may not impose such forms of service in any way which would constitute religious discrimination. There was no doubt that the German legislation on compulsory military service differentiated between ministers of different religions. Under that legislation, Evangelical and Roman Catholic ministers were exempt from military service, and therefore also from substitute service, if they were ordained. Ministers of other religions, however, were exempt only if the ministry was the principal occupation of the person concerned, and if his functions were equivalent to those of an ordained Evangelical or Roman Catholic Minister.

However, the Commission considered that the question whether

[1] See below, p. 189.   [2] At p. 678.

or not this difference in treatment amounted to a discrimination in violation of Article 14 depended upon an evaluation of the grounds on which the difference was based. In accordance with general theory on the subject of discrimination, certain differentiations may be legitimate and therefore not precluded by Article 14.[1] It was therefore necessary to examine the reason for which the German legislature had agreed to grant exemption from service to ministers who were neither of Roman Catholic nor of Evangelical faith only if their ministry was their principal occupation. The Commission found that that reason was the desire to prevent a large-scale evasion of the general duty to perform military service. If this limitation were abandoned, the result might well be to exempt an entire religious community. To prevent this result, the law laid down such criteria that only those ministers whose functions required their constant and continued attendance at their ministerial office would be exempted from compulsory service. The real basis of the distinction made by the law was in the function performed by different categories of ministers and was not according to the religious community to which they belonged. Hence the law was not discriminatory.

While the Commission's analysis of Article 14 is persuasive, its application of the Article to the facts of this case is more questionable. It would have been acceptable if exemption from compulsory service had been based solely on the criterion of the minister's function; but it was not. There was the additional requirement in the case of a minister who was neither Roman Catholic nor Evangelical that his ministry must be his principal occupation. The Commission's finding with regard to the reason for the distinction made by German law also raises some doubts. Even if this were in fact the reason, and even if differential treatment can be justified in some cases by the objects of the legislation, as the Court held in the Belgian Linguistic case,[2] it seems doubtful whether this would be adequate justification for this distinction. For it would have been open to the legislature simply to provide that any minister of religion should be exempt whose ministry was his principal occupation.

An apparently serious interference with religious freedom was brought before the Commission in an application against the

[1] At p. 682. Cf. below, p. 190.
[2] See below, p. 191.

United Kingdom.[1] A church practising a certain cult and also having educational functions, the Church of Scientology of California, was considered by the United Kingdom authorities to be harmful. They accordingly decided to take certain measures against it, including the denial or withdrawal of student status for members of the church, the refusal or termination of work permits and employment vouchers, and the refusal of extensions of stay within the United Kingdom to continue studies at its establishments. The application, which alleged violations *inter alia* of Article 9, was summarily rejected. In so far as the application was brought by the church, the Commission considered that a legal as opposed to a natural person is incapable of having or exercising the rights mentioned in Article 9(1). In so far as it was brought by or on behalf of the individual members of the church, the Commission simply found that there had been no restriction on the rights guaranteed under Article 9(1).[2] The only reason given was that the measures complained of did not prevent the members, whether resident or coming from abroad, from attending the college of the church or its other branches in the United Kingdom, or otherwise manifesting their religious beliefs. Yet this is precisely what the measures *prima facie* appear designed to prevent.

The decision is inadequate in many respects. It examines the complaints *ex officio* under Article 2 of the First Protocol, in relation to the right to education,[3] but not in relation to the freedom to receive and impart information and ideas, under Article 10. It deals with the complaints under Article 14 by stating baldly that the members of the church enjoy their rights under Article 9 to the same extent as members of other religious groups. And its rejection of the principal complaints under Article 9 is wholly unsatisfactory.

To criticize the Commission's decision is not, of course, to suggest that the United Kingdom authorities did not have good reason to take the measures they did. But these reasons should have been examined by the Commission under paragraph (2) of Articles 9 and 10, and under Article 14. The treatment of the application, which does not appear even to have been communicated to the respondent Government for its observations on admissibility, contrasts strikingly with the thorough examination on the

---

[1] 3798/68, *Yearbook* 12, 306.   [2] At p. 318, cf. 322.   [3] See below, p. 176.

merits of the Grandrath Case and the careful reasoning of the Commission's opinion.

Apart from these two cases, few restrictions of religious liberty have been brought before the Commission. The Commission has held that a Dutch system of old age pension insurance, alleged to interfere with the religious duty of caring for old people, does not violate Article 9.[1] Nor was Article 9 infringed by Dutch legislation on compulsory motor insurance. The applicant was convicted for driving without insurance. He objected for religious reasons to any form of insurance on the ground that, according to his beliefs, prosperity and adversity are meted out to human beings by God, and it is not permissible to attempt to prevent or reduce the effects of possible disasters. The Commission considered that compulsory motor insurance could be justified under Article 9(2) as being necessary 'for the protection of the rights and freedoms of others'.[2]

In two applications against Austria, the Commission found that freedom of conscience is not infringed by a system of compulsory voting.[3] No doubt this finding is subject to the existence of a choice of candidates, for otherwise the elections would not be free as required by Article 3 of the First Protocol,[4] or subject at least to an option, as there was in the cases under consideration, to leave the voting paper blank.

Article 9 is not infringed by the requirement that dairy farmers become members of the Health Service.[5] The Dutch legislation in question was enacted in order to prevent tuberculosis among cattle; and the term 'protection of health' used in Article 9(2) could reasonably be extended to cover schemes for the prevention of cattle disease.

Presumably the same term might be used to justify, in certain circumstances, medical treatment, such as blood transfusions, to which a patient objected on religious grounds.

Another issue which could arise under Article 9 is whether individuals may be compelled to disclose their religion to the authorities for such purposes as the registration of births or marriages, or the taking of a census. In an application against Austria,[6]

---

[1] 1497/62, *Yearbook* 5, 286; 2065/63, *Yearbook* 8, 266.
[2] 2988/66, *Yearbook* 10, 472.
[3] 1718/62, *Yearbook* 8, 168; 4982/71, *Collection of Decisions* 40, 50.
[4] See below, p. 178.   [5] 1068/61, *Yearbook* 5, 278.
[6] 2854/66, *Collection of Decisions* 26, 46.

a father refused to disclose the religion of the parents when registering the birth of his child. The registrar then declined to issue a certificate since the law required that the certificate should state the religion of the parents. The problem under Article 9 was not resolved as the applicant had not complied with the condition of exhaustion of domestic remedies. The question might also be considered in relation to the protection of privacy under Article 8.[1]

There have been few complaints by prisoners of interference with religious liberty. It remains doubtful how far a prisoner can claim under Article 9 facilities to practise a religion which is not generally practised in that State. Where a British prisoner complained of the absence of the services of a Church of England priest in a German jail, the Commission appears to have considered that a German Protestant pastor might have been sufficient to comply with Article 9 in such a case.[2] The Commission has stated that a refusal by the prison authorities to provide special food required by a religion which was not a religion usually practised in that State was permitted under Article 9(2).[3] Nor, in the Commission's opinion, does Article 9 impose any obligation to put at the disposal of prisoners books which they consider necessary for the exercise of their religion or for the development of their philosophy of life.[4] The Commission might, however, have considered this complaint under Article 10 of the Convention,[5] or even under Article 2 of the First Protocol.[6] In the same case, the applicant's complaint that the prison authorities had refused him permission to grow a beard, as prescribed by his religion, was rejected under Article 9(2). The respondent Government had submitted, somewhat curiously, that the refusal was justified as being necessary in order to be able to identify the prisoner.

The decision is not satisfactory and the reported cases taken together give the impression that the Commission is somewhat unsympathetic to complaints of interference with religious freedom.

[1] See above, p. 126.
[2] 2413/65, *Collection of Decisions* 23, 1 at 8.
[3] Not published; see 'Case-Law Topics', No. 1, *Human Rights in Prison*, p. 31.
[4] 1753/63, *Yearbook* 8, 174 at 184.
[5] See below, p. 154.
[6] See below, p. 172.

ARTICLE 10

Freedom of expression

Article 10 guarantees a single, though fundamental, right, the right to freedom of expression. This right is defined, in Article 10(1), as including 'freedom to hold opinions and to receive and impart information and ideas without interference by public authority and regardless of frontiers'.

As already stated, freedom of opinion is closely related to freedom of thought guaranteed by Article 9, and the two Articles have frequently been considered together.

Certain restrictions are expressly allowed. Article 10(1) itself provides that 'This Article shall not prevent States from requiring the licensing of broadcasting, television or cinema enterprises.' Paragraph (2) provides that the exercise of freedom of expression, since it carries with it duties and responsibilities, may be subject to such formalities, conditions, restrictions or penalties as are necessary for the purposes there specified.[1] Further, restrictions on the reporting of judicial proceedings are expressly allowed by Article 6(1),[2] while Article 16 allows restrictions on the political activity of aliens.

Subject to these provisions, freedom of expression under Article 10 should be considered as prohibiting censorship, whether in the form of prior authorization or subsequent prosecution, of books, the Press, television and radio, the cinema and theatre, or any other vehicle for the expression of ideas.

In the Greek case,[3] the Commission considered that the system of Press censorship operated in Greece was inconsistent with Article 10, and in particular that: (1) the prohibition of the publication of any text, local or foreign, 'criticising directly or indirectly' the Government in the discharge of its duties was a restriction of the freedom of expression which could not be justified under Article 10(2); (2) the general prohibition of notices of 'left-wing organisations', without further specification of their purpose, involved a discrimination on grounds of 'political opinion' under Article 14 read together with Articles 9 and 10.[4]

The only other case in which the Commission considered that there had been a violation of Article 10 was the De Becker Case.

[1] See below, p. 195.   [2] See above, p. 110.   [3] See above, p. 26.
[4] Report, para. 369; *Yearbook* 12, the Greek Case, 164.

De Becker, a Belgian journalist, had been condemned to death in 1946 on the ground that during the Second World War he had collaborated with the German authorities in Belgium, in particular in the exercise of his functions as editor of the Belgian daily newspaper *Le Soir*. The judgment carried with it the forfeiture of certain rights prescribed by the Belgian Penal Code. Subsequently the death sentence was commuted to life imprisonment, but the forfeiture of these rights was confirmed.

At the time of his application to the Commission in 1956, De Becker was deprived for life of the right, among others, to take part in the management, editing, publication or distribution of a newspaper or any other publication.

In its Report, the Commission expressed the opinion that the relevant provisions of the Belgian Penal Code,

insofar as they affect freedom of expression, were not fully justifiable under the Convention, 'whether they be regarded as providing for penal sanctions or for preventive measures in the interests of public security. They are not justifiable in so far as the deprivation of freedom of expression in regard to non-political matters, which they contain, is imposed inflexibly for life without any provision for its relaxation when with the passage of time public morale and public order have been re-established and the continued imposition of that particular incapacity has ceased to be a measure 'necessary in a democratic society' within the meaning of Article 10, paragraph (2), of the Convention.[1]

However, after the Commission had referred the case to the Court, the Belgian law was amended. The applicant stated that the new legislation satisfied his claim and gave everyone the possibility of regaining his full rights and free expression. He concluded that he now had no interest in proceeding with the case and withdrew his application. The Court struck the case off its list, the applicant, the Commission and the Belgian Government having expressed their agreement with this course.

There might seem to be the possibility of a conflict between the guarantee of freedom of expression under Article 10 and the protection of privacy under Article 8. But laws for the protection of privacy fall within Article 10(2), as being necessary 'for the protection of the reputation or rights of others', the more clearly as such laws are required by Article 8 itself.

[1] *Yearbook* 5, 320 at 326.

The protection of official secrets is provided for not only by the usual reservation for national security, but also by one 'for preventing the disclosure of information received in confidence', which includes official secrets[1] but goes much further.

In the Televizier case,[2] the question arose of a conflict between the freedom of expression and the protection of copyright. The Dutch Supreme Court had held that the publication in a weekly magazine of material concerning forthcoming radio and television programmes could amount to an infringement of copyright. The Televizier company which published the magazine complained that, as a consequence of the court's decision, the Dutch broadcasting corporations, which also publish weekly magazines, or have a financial interest in them, had an unjustifiable monopoly of the material. It alleged a violation of Articles 10 and 14. The application was declared admissible, but the case was subsequently struck off the list after the parties reached a settlement. The copyright law, on which the proceedings against the company had been based, had been replaced by a new Broadcasting Act, and the proceedings against the applicant for infringement of copyright were to be discontinued. The Televizier Company had entered into an agreement with one of the five broadcasting corporations, and was publishing the complete programmes of all the corporations. The settlement was subject to the conditions that the company should withdraw its application and that the Commission would not deal further with the case.

The Commission, with the agreement of the applicant and of the respondent Government, accordingly struck the case off its list.[3] It did not, however, pay any attention to the requirement that the general interest should be satisfied. Normally, before accepting the withdrawal of an application or approving a friendly settlement of a case, the Commission has regard not only to the question whether the applicant has received satisfaction in respect of his complaint, but also to the question whether any modification of the law or practice in issue is required by the Convention. This is part of the Commission's duty, under Article 19 of the Convention, to ensure the observance of the undertakings of the Contracting Parties; but it also has a practical justification, since otherwise the same question is likely to be reopened in future

---

[1] 4274/69, *Yearbook* 13, 888.   [2] 2690/65, *Yearbook* 9, 512.
[3] *Yearbook* 11, 782.

cases. It was therefore to be expected that the issues raised by the Televizier case would come before the Commission again; and a few years later an application raising similar issues was declared admissible.[1]

In dealing with complaints by prisoners under Article 10, the Commission has occasionally invoked the dubious doctrine that certain limitations are an inherent feature of imprisonment.[2] Thus, where an applicant complained that he had been refused permission to buy a copy of the prison regulations, the Commission stated that 'the limitations imposed on the right referred to in Article 10 are the consequence of a prisoner's special situation', and that 'the very purpose served by carrying out a penalty involving deprivation of liberty entails the restriction of certain rights and freedoms.'[3] However, the Commission went on to find that the restriction was justified 'for the prevention of disorder' under paragraph (2), as it appeared from the observations of the parties that the applicant's object in requesting the regulations was not to understand better his rights and duties in prison, but to discuss the prison system with the press. More doubtful is the Commission's rejection on the same ground of the applicant's complaint that the authorities would not permit him to take out a joint subscription with other prisoners to a daily newspaper.

In another case, an applicant complained that he was refused permission to buy a certain commentary on the German Code of Criminal Procedure which he needed to prepare his application for a re-trial. The Commission again referred to its notion of inherent feature, but also found that there had been no interference with the applicant's rights under Article 10(1), since he had on the facts had access to all the information he wanted.[4] Access in prison to books of an educational character may also raise an issue under Article 2 of the First Protocol.[5]

The position is somewhat different with obscene or pornographic materials. An applicant complained of the withdrawal of certain privileges which he had previously enjoyed, namely permission to study, to write scientific and technical works, to paint and to draw. The respondent Government stated that the privileges

[1] 5178/71, *Collection of Decisions* 44, 13.
[2] See below, p. 198, and see the cases cited under Article 8, above, p. 139.
[3] 1860/63, *Yearbook* 8, 204 at 216.
[4] 2795/66, *Collection of Decisions* 30, 23.
[5] See below, p. 172.

had been withdrawn because he had been found in possession of pornographic drawings and poems; but the applicant claimed that they had been executed by fellow-prisoners at the request of warders who sold them outside the prison. The Commission, referring to the special situation of prisoners and invoking paragraph (2) at large, rejected the complaint.[1]

Another applicant, a wholesale newsagent in Germany, had been convicted of circulating publications liable to corrupt the young. He alleged a violation of freedom of the press guaranteed by Article 10, in that the obligation was imposed on him, a newsagent, to censor publications. His application was supported by a trade organization of which he was a member. The Commission, asserting that a State has a certain 'margin of appreciation'[2] in determining the limits that may be placed on the freedom of expression, found that the measures complained of were justified under paragraph (2) as being necessary 'for the protection of morals' of young persons.[3]

A different decision was reached on an application concerning the publication in the United Kingdom of 'The Little Red School Book'. The publisher had been convicted on an obscenity charge and his conviction upheld on the ground that the book was likely to deprave and corrupt a significant proportion of the children likely to read it. His complaint under Article 10 was declared admissible.[4]

There may be a special justification under Article 10 for allowing States a certain measure of discretion in deciding, for example, to what extent seditious, blasphemous or obscene publications should be allowed. It is obvious that standards in these areas vary widely among the Contracting States, and may change quite rapidly within a society. It is hardly possible, or perhaps even desirable, to lay down general criteria of universal application in this field. Nevertheless, the restraints imposed must be controlled by the Commission and the Court, to ensure that they do not go beyond the limits necessary for the purposes set out in Article 10(2). In particular, although the limitations on the freedom of expression are expressed in very general terms, they must in every case be found to be 'necessary in a democratic society'.

[1] 1760/63, *Yearbook* 9, 166.   [2] See below, p. 201.
[3] 1167/61, *Yearbook* 6, 204 at 218.
[4] *Handyside* v. *United Kingdom*, Council of Europe Press communiqué C (74) 9.

The provision permitting licensing of broadcasting or television does not of itself preclude a State monopoly in these fields.[1]

In a case where an applicant complained that he had been refused a licence to set up a commercial radio station in the United Kingdom, the Commission held expressly that Article 10 permits the banning of private broadcasting.[2] It did not consider it necessary to examine the complaint under Article 14.

If, however, private broadcasting were permitted, licences would have to be granted in a manner which avoided discrimination contrary to that Article.

In an application against Italy, the owner of a private cable television business at Biella (Telebiella), complained of a decision of the Ministry of Posts and Telecommunications by which he was obliged to close his business, and following which some of his offices were forcibly closed.[3] The measures were based on a decree by the President of the Republic which in 1973 granted to the State-controlled Italian Radio and Television Corporation (RAI–TV) a monopoly of television broadcasting including cable transmissions. The ban on private cable television, which precipitated the fall of the Italian Government, was subsequently declared unconstitutional by the Italian Constitutional Court.

A French declaration, on ratifying the Convention, also suggests a doubt about the legality of a State radio or television monopoly. The Government declared that it interpreted the provisions of Article 10 as being compatible with the system established in France under the Act determining the legal status of French radio and television (O.R.T.F.).[4]

Whether or not private broadcasting is permitted, the law must ensure that there is freedom for political views to be expressed without discrimination, especially during election campaigns. Thus, the Commission has stated[5] that an issue might arise under Article 10 alone or in conjunction with Article 14 of the Convention if, for example, one political party were excluded from broadcasting facilities at election time while other parties were given broadcasting time.

[1] 3071/67, *Collection of Decisions* 26, 71 at 75.
[2] 4798/71, *Collection of Decisions* 40, 31.
[3] Council of Europe Press communiqué C (74) 13.
[4] See Debbasch, 'La Convention européenne des Droits de l'Homme et le régime de l'O.R.T.F.', *Revue des droits de l'homme* 1970, 638.
[5] 4515/70, *Yearbook* 14, 538 at 545–6.

This view seems a logical inference from the impact of television on public opinion. Political freedom, which once depended largely on freedom of assembly and freedom of association, now rests as much on freedom of expression and independence in the Press, radio, and television.

Freedom of assembly and freedom of association

Article 11 guarantees the right to freedom of peaceful assembly and to freedom of association with others.

'Freedom of assembly is a major part of the political and social life of any country. It is an essential part of the activities of political parties . . . and the conduct of elections under Article 3 of the First Protocol, which are to ensure the free expression of the opinion of the people.'[1] In the Greek Case,[2] the Commission found that the Greek Government had infringed both the freedom of assembly and the freedom of association.[3]

Freedom of association under Article 11(1) expressly includes the right to form and to join trade unions. However, the Commission has drawn a distinction between the right to set up an association or a trade union, or to be affiliated to it, and the right to be associated with its administration or management.

In circumstances somewhat similar to the De Becker case,[4] an applicant had forfeited certain rights for life, under a sentence imposed by a Belgian war tribunal. The rights forfeited included the right to be associated in any way with the administration, management, or direction of a professional association or a non-profit-making association. The Commission stated that this right 'is not covered by the traditional notion of freedom of association as laid down in Article 11'.[5]

Nor does freedom of association include the freedom *not* to join an association. Thus, Article 11 does not prohibit the 'closed shop' system, whereby a man cannot be employed in a particular trade unless he is a member of a particular union. The preparatory

---

[1] The Greek Case, Report of the Commission, para. 392, *Yearbook* 12, The Greek Case, pp. 170–1.
[2] See above, p. 26.
[3] Paras. 393–6, pp. 171–2.
[4] See above, p. 151.
[5] 1028/61, *Yearbook* 4, 324 at 338.

work on the Convention shows that, on account of the difficulties raised by the 'closed shop' system, it was considered undesirable to include the principle set out in Article 20(2) of the Universal Declaration of Human Rights, that no one may be compelled to belong to an association.[1]

On the other hand, the right to freedom of association may be infringed by acts of intimidation against a trade union official. A shop steward working with the Irish Electricity Supply Board claimed, in effect, that he had been victimized. The respondent Government denied that there had been any interference with the exercise of the applicant's duties as shop steward and that in any event the rights invoked were outside the scope of Article 11. The Commission stated that it 'cannot share the opinion of the respondent Government that threats of dismissal or other actions intended to bring about the relinquishment by an employee of the office of shop steward held by him, as alleged in the present case, could not in principle raise an issue under Article 11 of the Convention; . . . on the contrary, such interference could, in certain circumstances, seriously restrict or impede the lawful exercise of the freedom of association in relation to trade unions which that Article aims at securing.'[2] The Commission found, however, that the Government had discharged its obligations under Article 11 by ensuring that domestic law provided an effective remedy for any violation of its provisions.[3]

The system of collective bargaining in Sweden has raised several issues under Article 11.

In the Schmidt and Dahlstrom case, two applicants, a professor at Stockholm University and a captain in the Swedish Army, complained that the Government had violated their rights under Article 11 after their respective unions had proclaimed a strike in certain sectors following the collapse of negotiations for a new collective agreement.[4] When a final settlement was reached, the new salaries agreed were not backdated in the case of the applicants, as they were members of unions which had organized the selective strikes. The increases were, however, back-dated in the case of members of other unions, and non-union members who

[1] Fawcett, p. 223. But see 4072/69, *Yearbook* 13, 708 at 718, where it seems to have been assumed *per incuriam* that freedom of association implies freedom not to join an association.

[2] 4125/69, *Yearbook* 14, 198 at 222.   [3] See below, p. 227.

[4] 5589/72, *Collection of Decisions* 42, 123.

had not joined the strike. The applicants complained that this differential treatment of members of unions which organized strikes and employees who did not join unions was a deterrent to joining a union, and contrary to Articles 11 and 14. An interesting feature of this case was that the Swedish Government, while maintaining that there had been no violation of the Convention, did not raise objections to the application being declared admissible. It stated that the application gave rise to a number of important questions relating to the interpretation of Article 11, and that it was prepared to accept that the case should be examined on its merits. This approach represents a welcome development in the attitude of the States parties to the Convention, as well as considerably simplifying the proceedings.[1]

In the case brought by the Swedish Pilots Association (Svenska Lotsförbundet), the association, which represented the majority of Swedish pilots, complained of the refusal of the National Collective Bargaining Office to conduct negotiations with a view to concluding an agreement with it. The Office had applied a policy of entering into collective agreements only with the four major labour organizations and, after the pilots' association ceased to be affiliated to one such organization, the Office refused to conclude a separate agreement with the association. The Commission declared the application admissible,[2] joining to the merits the question whether it complied with the rule that an application must be introduced within six months of the final decision under domestic law.[3] However, the application was subsequently declared inadmissible under Article 29,[4] after the Commission had established that it did not in fact comply with the six months rule.[5] This shows that the initial decision to join that question to the merits was incorrect.

A similar complaint was brought before the Commission by the Swedish Engine Drivers' Union (Svenska Lokmannaförbundet) whose 1,200 members represented about twenty per cent of all engine drivers employed by the Swedish State Railways. Again the National Collective Bargaining Office had refused to conclude a separate collective agreement with the applicant. The applica-

---

[1] See below, p. 272.   [2] 4475/70, *Yearbook* 14, 496.
[3] See below, p. 241.   [4] See below, p. 251.
[5] *Collection of Decisions* 42, 1. This decision contains a summary of the submissions of the parties on the merits.

tion, alleging violations of Articles 11 and 14, was declared admissible without any reservations.[1] In the proceedings on the merits the Swedish Government submitted that Article 11 was not applicable in the case, since the Swedish system of collective bargaining with civil servants' trade unions was not covered by the right to freedom of association and, further, that the union in any event was not discriminated against within the meaning of Article 14, since the differential treatment was justified by the fact that the four big federations of unions, with whom collective agreements were concluded, were the most representative unions in their field.[2]

It is uncertain how far the trade union rights of civil servants are protected by Article 11. Paragraph (2) includes a special provision that 'This Article shall not prevent the imposition of lawful restrictions on the exercise of these rights by members of the armed forces, of the police or of the administration of the State.' In the practice of the Contracting States, the position seems to vary with respect to the different categories. In the armed forces trade unions are generally not recognized at all. The police often have the right to form or join trade unions, although they may be subject to special restrictions in the exercise of these rights. Civil servants normally have the right to freedom of association, and in some countries full trade union rights.

The position of the police forces under Article 11 came before the Commission in an application brought by a police organization in Belgium (Syndicat National de la Police Belge).[3] It complained in particular of the refusal of the Belgian authorities to accept it as one of the representative organizations for consultations on legislation in social and economic fields. While paragraph (2) makes special provision for the trade union rights of the police, the case, which is still pending, raises issues about the scope of freedom of association under paragraph (1). Is freedom of association respected if a union has been formed without any interference and there has been no attempt to prohibit its meetings or to prevent any one from joining it, as the Belgian Government submitted in the proceedings on admissibility; or does it extend to recognizing the rights of trade unions to participate in the process of democratic government?

[1] 5614/72, *Collection of Decisions* 42, 130.   [2] B(73) 47, p. 43.
[3] 4464/70, *Collection of Decisions* 39, 26 and 34.

In a high proportion of cases declared admissible in recent years, the Commission has been concerned with trade union rights under Article 11, although for many years this Article had almost never been invoked by applicants or considered by the Commission. The two Swedish cases and the Belgian case just mentioned have now been referred to the Court of Human Rights. A difficulty of principle is raised by these cases, since there is other international machinery for dealing with complaints concerning trade union rights, in particular under the conventions of the International Labour Organisation and under the European Social Charter. The danger of overlap may be partly avoided by Article 27(1) (b) which provides that the Commission cannot deal with an application which has already been submitted to another procedure of international investigation or settlement. But there remains the unresolved question of how far such complaints should be dealt with by the Human Rights Commission and Court and how far they should be dealt with by bodies with a more specialized expertise. The provisions of the other international instruments are naturally more detailed, and within the International Labour Organisation, in particular, a substantial body of law has been developed, to which the Commission has referred in interpreting the provisions of Article 11.[1] To ensure uniformity in the development of international law in this area, further measures of co-ordination between the bodies concerned may be desirable.

ARTICLE 12

The right to marry and to found a family

Article 12 guarantees the right to marry and to found a family. These rights are not subject to limitations of the kind set out in paragraph (2) of Articles 8 to 11. Instead, limitations are to be found in the provision that men and women of marriageable age have the right to marry and to found a family, 'according to the national laws governing the exercise of this right'.

The scope of this qualification is not clear. It is evident that the exercise of the rights guaranteed cannot be wholly governed by national law. In that case, the protection of Article 12 would

[1] See, e.g. 4125/69, *Yearbook* 14, 198 at 216.

extend only to cases where there was a breach of national law. But the purpose of the Convention, here as elsewhere, is to guarantee certain minimum rights irrespective of the provisions of national law.[1]

The correct view, therefore, would seem to be that Article 12 imposes an obligation to recognize, both in principle and in practice, the right to marry and to found a family. This obligation implies that the restrictions placed on these rights by national law must be imposed for a legitimate purpose, for example, to prevent polygamy or incest, and must not go beyond a reasonable limit to attain that purpose. On the other hand, the precise scope of the restrictions may vary among the Contracting States, as does, for example, the marriageable age.

Article 14 is also of special importance in relation to Article 12, since it prohibits discrimination not only, for example, on racial or religious grounds, but also on grounds of sex. Thus, in relation to marriage and the founding of a family, there must be no discrimination between men and women. Not all forms of differential treatment, of course, constitute discrimination, so that there is no requirement that marriageable age, for example, should be the same for both men and women, but all differential treatment must be examined by reference to its purpose and justification to ensure that it is not unlawful.

While the right to marry and the right to found a family are two separate rights, it seems from the wording of the Article that only married couples can claim the right to found a family. If the Article had been worded 'Everyone has the right to marry and to found a family', it might have been easier to infer that unmarried people also had the right to found a family.

It may be significant, also, that the Article ends with a reference to 'this right', rather than 'these rights', thus apparently envisaging a close connection between the two.

But while the unmarried may have no right under Article 12 to found a family, the term 'family' in Article 8 has a wider meaning, and the relations of a parent with an illegitimate child are protected under that Article.[2] It cannot be argued that the meaning of 'family' in Article 8 is as restricted as in Article 12, for it is necessary to give it a wider interpretation in other respects also.

[1] See Opsahl in *Privacy and Human Rights*, ed. Robertson, Manchester, 1973, at 190.   [2] See above, p. 134.

'Family' in Article 8 must include the family into which a person is born, as well as the family which he founds. Otherwise the absurd conclusion would follow that only parents, and not children, could claim the right to respect for family life. It is therefore reasonable to interpret Article 8, as the Commission has done, as extending in principle to any close relationship, whether by blood or marriage, and whether legitimate or not.

National laws may restrict the right of prisoners to marry. In an application against the Federal Republic of Germany, the Commission held that not merely a convicted prisoner, but a person detained on remand, may be refused permission to marry. The applicant, who had been arrested on charges of theft, was refused permission to marry by the German authorities and objected in particular to the reasons given for their decision. The courts had taken into account the applicant's criminal record and the probability that, if he were convicted, he would be given a long prison sentence and perhaps an indefinite period of detention. This the applicant complained infringed his right to be presumed innocent until convicted. The authorities had also considered the applicant's personality, and the fact that the marriage of prisoners inevitably affected the maintenance of order within prison establishments. The Commission appears to have approved all these grounds.[1]

In another case,[2] a man sentenced to prison in England and later deported to Pakistan complained that the authorities had refused to allow him to marry, while in prison, a woman living in England who was the mother of his child. After obtaining observations from the Government and the applicant, then in Pakistan, the Commission found that, according to the information available at the time at which the prison authorities refused the applicant's petition to marry, he already had a wife and children in Pakistan. The applicant subsequently stated that he had been divorced from his wife before his deportation, but this statement was only made during the proceedings before the Commission and after he had already been deported. The Commission also observed that the applicant's submissions had not been substantiated by any evidence and that the applicant had not shown that he made it clear to the United Kingdom authorities,

[1] 892/60, *Yearbook* 4, 240 at 256.
[2] 3898/68, *Yearbook* 10, 666.

before his deportation, that he no longer had a wife in Pakistan. The Commission accordingly rejected the application as manifestly ill-founded.

The right of men and women, once married, to found a family may be subject to increasing strain in a society preoccupied with the dangers of over-population. Article 12 plainly does not preclude the provision of family planning services; at the other extreme, sterilization, according to the Commission, may even, in certain circumstances, involve a violation of Articles 2 and 3 of the Convention.[1] Fiscal and other non-coercive disincentives are probably not contrary to Article 12.

ARTICLE 1 OF THE FIRST PROTOCOL

Property rights

The First Protocol guarantees additional rights in three fields, property, education, and political rights, where it proved impossible to agree on the text at the time of the signature of the Convention in November 1950.[2] Further discussions were necessary and the First Protocol was finally concluded and signed in March 1952. It entered into force on 18 May 1954. All parties to the Convention except Switzerland have ratified the First Protocol and the additional rights guaranteed by its Articles 1 to 3 may be regarded as on the same basis as the rights guaranteed by the Convention. All the provisions of the Convention, including Articles 13 to 18, apply equally to the rights guaranteed by the First Protocol.[3] These rights are also subject in the same way to the control of the organs set up by the Convention. No separate provision is made in the First Protocol for acceptance of the Commission's competence to receive applications from individuals, or for accepting the compulsory jurisdiction of the Court. Consequently, in contrast to the Fourth Protocol, declarations by States accepting these optional provisions apply automatically to the First Protocol as well.

The first paragraph of Article 1 provides that: 'Every natural or legal person is entitled to the peaceful enjoyment of his possessions. No one shall be deprived of his possessions except in the

---

[1] 1287/61, not published.
[2] See Robertson, *Human Rights in Europe*, p. 12 f.
[3] Article 5 of the First Protocol.

public interest and subject to the conditions provided for by law and by the general principles of international law.'

The structure of the paragraph can best be understood by comparing it with that of Article 2(1) of the Convention. Having formulated the right as a general principle in the first sentence, it continues by specifying the conditions in which the most extreme form of interference with that right is authorized. The second sentence, however, does not exhaust the protection of the first.[1]

Under the terms of the second sentence, three conditions must be satisfied before a person may be deprived of his possessions. Of these conditions the last, which requires that the taking be subject to the conditions provided for by the general principles of international law, has posed the most serious problem of interpretation.

The Commission has held that Article 1 of the First Protocol does not require a State which deprives its nationals of their possessions in the public interest and subject to the conditions provided for by law to pay compensation;[2] the general principles of international law referred to in Article 1 are the principles which have been established in general international law concerning the confiscation of the property of foreigners.[3] Measures taken by a State with respect to the property of its own nationals are therefore not subject to these general principles of international law in the absence of a particular treaty clause specifically so providing.

Further, the preparatory work confirmed that the Contracting Parties had no intention of extending the application of these principles to the case of the taking of the property of nationals.

The curious consequence of this interpretation is that in a system introduced to protect human rights independently of the individual's status, the national is in a different position from that of the alien; and this in a Convention which by Article 1 expressly extends to everyone within the jurisdiction of the Contracting Parties, and which expressly prohibits, in Article 14, discrimination on grounds of national origin. Moreover, it seems contrary to the whole object of a provision designed to protect property rights that it should permit expropriation without compensation.

Of course, the general prohibition of discrimination between

---

[1] Cf. above, p. 24.   [2] 1870/63, *Yearbook* 8, 218 at 226.
[3] 511/59, *Yearbook* 3, 394 at 422–4.

nationals and aliens in Article 14 does not preclude differential treatment where this is expressly provided for. Article 16, for example, expressly authorizes discrimination against aliens in their political activities. But this simply reinforces the argument that differential treatment must not be read into the Convention by implication.

It would be possible to construe Article 1 of the First Protocol in quite a different way, so as to extend to nationals the protection given to aliens by international law.[1] For if the first paragraph affords only the protection already afforded by international law, it achieves nothing; and it can hardly be argued that the sole object of this provision was to give aliens an additional remedy, of proceedings on the European level, in addition to the classic remedy under international law of diplomatic protection.

In a case concerning steel nationalization in Great Britain, the applicants complained of the compulsory acquisition of their debenture stock in a steel company.[2] The applicants, who also complained of the price proposed in the nationalization Act, submitted that the compulsory acquisition of the debenture stock was unnecessary to achieve the object of the Act, since the company could be brought into public ownership merely by the acquisition of the shares in the company.

The Commission found that the United Kingdom Government had not exceeded the 'margin of appreciation'[3] as to what measures were in the public interest. The considerations referred to in the decision as showing that the measure was in the public interest, in particular the fact that the House of Commons had reversed certain amendments by the House of Lords, seem of doubtful relevance and certainly inadequate to justify the Commission's findings without further examination. The application, which raised both legal and political issues of major importance, was rejected as inadmissible without communication to the respondent Government.

The second paragraph of Article 1 provides that: 'The preceding provisions shall not, however, in any way impair the right of a

---

[1] See further Egon Schwelb, 'The Protection of the Right of Property of Nationals under the First Protocol to the European Convention on Human Rights', *American Journal of Comparative Law*, 1964, 518–41; cf. Böckstiegel, 'Gilt der Eigentumsschutz der Europäischen Menschenrechtskonvention auch für Inländer', *Neue Juristische Wochenschrift*, 20, 1967, 905.

[2] 3039/67, *Yearbook* 10, 506.   [3] Below, p. 201.

State to enforce such laws as it deems necessary to control the use of property in accordance with the general interest or to secure the payment of taxes or other contributions or penalties.'

In the British Steel case, however, the Commission held that the compulsory acquisition of the applicants' debenture stock was a deprivation of possessions and not a control of their use. Hence the second paragraph had no application, and the applicants' argument that the acquisition was not 'necessary' could not avail. The conclusion again is strange: the mere control of the use of property must be deemed to be necessary in the general interest, while the actual deprivation of property need only be in the public interest without any requirement of necessity.

However, the difficulties of interpretation are partly a consequence of the defective drafting of the Article, which clearly represents a compromise designed to protect property rights without prejudicing the power of the State to nationalize property in the public interest.

It is nevertheless surprising that the Article does not clearly enunciate a right to compensation for the taking of property.[1] Nor does it prohibit, as such, a wealth tax,[2] nor a form of capital gains tax such as that introduced as part of the financial and monetary reforms in Germany after the Second World War.[3]

The last part of the second paragraph allows not only for taxes and fines[4] but also for compulsory pension and social security contributions.[5]

Rights acquired under a contributory pension scheme may, however, be protected by Article 1. In an application against the United Kingdom, the applicant complained that she did not receive a widow's pension to which she claimed she was entitled by virtue of her own and her late husband's contributions.[6] The Commission recognized that a question might arise under Article 1 if contributions made many years before to a compulsory contributory pensions scheme, which had subsequently been replaced by a comprehensive National Insurance system, could be regarded

---

[1] See Fawcett, p. 347 f.
[2] *Gudmundsson* v. *Iceland*, 511/59, *Yearbook* 3, 394.
[3] 551/59, *Yearbook* 3, 244; 673/59, *Yearbook* 4, 286.
[4] 323/57, *Yearbook* 1, 241 at 246.
[5] 2065/63, *Yearbook* 8, 266; 2248/64, *Yearbook* 10, 170.
[6] 4288/69, *Yearbook* 13, 892.

as creating a vested interest in a pension which might be described as 'possessions' within the meaning of Article 1.

The Commission found, however, after examining the legislation in force at the time, that the applicant had not acquired any such vested interest. A widow's pension was payable under that legislation only in respect of her late husband's contributions; and at the relevant period the applicant had not been married.

The Commission also left open the question whether even contributions to a general national insurance system might give rise to acquired rights capable of coming within Article 1. The better view probably is that while Article 1 may protect rights arising out of compulsory contributory pension schemes, where the amount of the pension is directly related to the amount of contributions, it has no application to general social security systems where there is no direct correlation of contribution and benefit.

This view was adopted by the Commission in a subsequent case concerning pension schemes in the Netherlands.[1] After examining the system of financing the schemes, the Commission concluded:

It is therefore clear, both from the manner in which the funds are administered and from the system of distribution adopted, that this branch of the Dutch social insurance legislation is based on the principle of solidarity which reflects the responsibility of the community as a whole to provide a minimum financial basis for its aged members and for survivors. The contributions which the younger members of the community are obliged to make are collected in a revolving fund from which the older or surviving members of the community receive their pension. The distribution of the pension funds takes into account the economic realities of the period concerned to the extent that persons benefiting from this system receive their pension in accordance with the wage index established for the period in which the pension is paid and not according to that established for the periods in which they made contributions. There is, therefore, no relationship between the contributions made and the pension received in the sense that the amounts paid by the insured person are accumulated with a view to covering the pension benefits accruing to him when reaching pensionable age. Consequently, a person does not have, at any given moment, an identifiable share in the fund claimable by him but he has an expectancy of

[1] 4130/69, *Collection of Decisions* 38, 9.

receiving old-age or survivors pension benefits subject to the conditions envisaged by the Acts concerned.

Hence, the benefits accruing under the schemes did not constitute a property right which could be described as 'possessions' under Article 1.

Another issue which has arisen under this Article is whether money may be taken from a person on his arrest and kept as security for the costs of criminal proceedings against him. Austrian law provides that the Austrian Government acquires, as security for costs in criminal proceedings, a lien with regard to money and other movable objects found in the possession of an accused person at the time of his arrest. In accordance with this provision, an applicant's possessions, including a substantial sum of money, were taken away by the prison authorities on his arrest.[1] They then refused to release a sum to meet the fee of his own lawyer, and he was advised to accept a lawyer appointed by the court under a legal aid scheme. The applicant invoked the presumption of innocence under Article 6(2) and his rights under Article 6(3) (c). The Commission also examined this complaint *ex officio* under Article 1 of the First Protocol, but found that the taking of the applicant's money was authorized by the second paragraph as the payment of prosecution costs which might have been awarded against the applicant was a 'contribution' within the meaning of this paragraph. The decision seems to be more questionable under Article 6(3) (c).[2]

ARTICLE 2 OF THE FIRST PROTOCOL

The right to education

Article 2 of the First Protocol provides, in its first sentence, that 'No person shall be denied the right to education'.

The negative formulation of this right has given rise to doubts about its scope. What significance is to be attached to the fact that Article 2 does not provide, on the model of other Articles, that everyone has the right to education, but only that no one shall be denied it? Does Article 2 oblige States to provide adequate educa-

---

[1] 4338/69, *Collection of Decisions* 36, 79.
[2] See above, p. 117.

tional institutions at different levels of education? Does it only guarantee access to existing institutions? Or does it merely prohibit States from taking action that might prevent persons under their jurisdiction from educating themselves?

The issue was raised in the Belgian Linguistic Case. Six groups of applicants claimed that various aspects of the Belgian legislation governing the use of languages in schools were inconsistent with the Convention. The applicants, who were French-speaking residents in the Dutch-speaking part of Belgium and in the Brussels periphery, wanted their children to be educated in French.

The first issue in the case was the scope of Article 2, and in particular whether the first sentence of the Article imposes any positive obligations, and if so, what. Different views were expressed on this issue by the applicants, by the Belgian Government and by the Commission.[1] The interpretation adopted by the Court was as follows.[2]

Article 2 does not recognize such a right to education as would require States to establish at their own expense, or to subsidize, education of any particular type or at any particular level. It does, however, guarantee a right of access to educational institutions existing at a given time. Such access, moreover, constitutes only a part of the right to education. For the right to education to be effective, it is necessary that the individual should have the right to obtain official recognition of the studies which he has completed. A specific complaint of the applicants was that the authorities refused to recognize studies at secondary schools which did not comply with the language laws. The Court finally held, however, that this refusal was not contrary to Article 2 itself, nor to Article 2 read in conjunction with Article 14, since those who had completed such studies could obtain recognition of them by passing an examination before a central board, a condition which did not, in all the circumstances, impose unreasonable requirements.

The Court further held, following the opinion of the Commission in this respect, that measures taken in the field of education may also affect the right to respect for private and family life or

---

[1] Case 'relating to certain aspects of the laws on the use of languages in education in Belgium' (merits), judgment of 23 July 1968, pp. 19–22; *Yearbook* 11, 832 at 834–40.
[2] 'Judgment of the Court', p. 31; *Yearbook* 11, 832 at 858.

derogate from it. This would be the case, for instance, if their aim or result were to disturb private or family life in an unjustifiable manner, *inter alia* by separating children from their parents in an arbitrary way.[1] Consequently, the case had to be examined under Article 8 of the Convention.

The Court considered in this connection the applicants' complaint that the State refused to establish or subsidize, in the Dutch-speaking region concerned, primary school education using French as the language of instruction. The Court held that there was no violation of Article 8. If the parents sent their children to a Dutch-language school, there was a 'certain impact' upon family life; but Article 8 does not guarantee the right to be educated in the language of one's parents by the public authorities or with their aid. If, on the other hand, parents sent their children to school in Brussels, or the French-speaking region, or abroad, so that they should be taught in French, the consequent separation was not imposed by the Belgian legislation but resulted from the parents' own choice.[2]

Ultimately, the Court found that the Belgian legislation failed to comply with the provisions of the Convention and Protocol in only one respect. It infringed Article 14 of the Convention, read in conjunction with the first sentence of Article 2 of the First Protocol, in so far as it prevented certain children, solely on the basis of the residence of their parents, from having access to the French-language schools in certain communes on the periphery of Brussels. The law provided that the language of instruction in these communes was Dutch, but that French-speaking classes should be provided at the nursery and primary levels, on condition that it was asked for by sixteen heads of family. However, this education was not available to children whose parents lived outside these communes, even though there were no French-speaking schools in the communes where they lived. The Dutch classes, on the other hand, accepted all children, whatever the place of residence of the parents. Applying the criteria of discrimination which it elaborated in this case,[3] the Court held that this differential treatment could not be justified under Article 14.[4]

---

[1] 'Judgment of the Court', p. 33; *Yearbook* 11, 832 at 862.
[2] 'Judgment of the Court', p. 43; *Yearbook* 11, 832 at 882–4.
[3] See below, p. 191.
[4] 'Judgment of the Court', pp. 69–71; *Yearbook* 11, 832 at 938–42.

Certain legislative reforms have been considered by the Committee of Ministers, which has the duty of supervising the execution of the judgment of the Court.[1] Other cases concerning Belgian language legislation are still under consideration by the Commission and the Committee of Ministers,[2] and the problems have clearly not been resolved.

The concept of education has perhaps a wider significance today than at the time when the Protocol was drafted. It is frequently now regarded as a continuing process in the life of human beings, rather than a stage through which they pass as children. The Council of Europe itself has done much to promote the idea of 'permanent education'.[3]

The implications of this development for the States parties to the Protocol are not unduly alarming, if it is accepted that, as stated by the Court in the Belgian Linguistic case, they are not required by Article 2 to establish at their own expense, or to subsidize, education of any particular type or at any particular level. They are, however, in accordance with that judgment, obliged to provide access to those educational institutions which exist, and to recognize the studies completed there. This requirement may ordinarily create no difficulty in relation to adult education.

Special difficulties may arise, however, in relation to convicted prisoners, especially since Article 2 contains no escape clause allowing interference in the interests of public order, security, etc. The question has not yet been fully examined. Two unpublished decisions of the Commission in which the question arose do not seem to contain any considered view on the problem.[4] In the Golder case, which has been considered above,[5] the applicant referred to certain examination facilities which he was trying to obtain, but did not make any specific complaint in this respect. An application against Austria which put the question clearly was rejected for non-exhaustion of domestic remedies.[6] The applicant alleged that his right to further education was being denied by the prison authorities. Although the Austrian law on the Execution of Sentences provided that prisoners should be given the opportunity for further education, such provisions were ineffec-

---

[1] See below, p. 268.   [2] B (73) 47, pp. 14–15.
[3] See the Studies published by the Council of Europe under this title.
[4] 1854/63 and 2617/65, not published; see *Human Rights in Prison*, p. 38.
[5] See above, p. 91.   [6] 4511/70, *Collection of Decisions* 38, 84.

tive because they were required to pay for their books and other educational material, which they could not afford out of their prison earnings.

Again, it may be possible to apply by analogy the reasoning of the Court in the Belgian Linguistic case and to argue that States have no positive obligation to subsidize prisoners' education, but may not take steps to interfere with it. In this sense, the obligation under Article 2 is a negative one.

The second sentence of Article 2 provides that: 'In the exercise of any functions which it assumes in relation to education and to teaching, the State shall respect the right of parents to ensure such education and teaching in conformity with their own religious and philosophical convictions.' This provision reflects a very long tradition of conflict in many European countries over the place of religion in schools. In the Belgian Linguistic case, the applicants argued that 'philosophical convictions' should be interpreted to include the cultural and linguistic preferences of the parents. There is, of course, a close connection between the language of education, which has a fundamental role in cultural development, and philosophical beliefs. Nevertheless, it would probably go too far to say that the parents' right in question includes the right to ensure the teaching of their children in a language of their choice.

The Commission, which was followed by the Court in this respect, was unanimous in considering that the second sentence of Article 2 was not intended to guarantee respect for preferences or opinions in cultural or linguistic matters, whether such opinions were considered in themselves or as part of the 'personalist philosophy' of the applicants. The Commission pointed out that at one stage in the preparatory work on the Protocol the text referred solely to the protection of religious opinions, but that the team 'philosophical' was added in order to cover agnostic opinions.[1] Nevertheless, the term is certainly too wide to be given so restricted an interpretation; the preparatory work cannot be invoked to support a meaning contrary to the text.[2] To draw too narrow a distinction, in deciding what beliefs are protected by this provision, would in any event infringe Article 14.

[1] Opinion of the Commission, para. 379; 'Publications of the Court', Series B, p. 282.
[2] See above, p. 21.

It seems clear that the second sentence of Article 2 obliges States to respect the wishes of parents in matters of religious education in state schools. It is a different question how far it applies to private schools.[1] The provision is plainly the result of a compromise and has provoked more reservations than any other. Reservations of varying scope have been made by Greece, Malta, Sweden, Turkey, and the United Kingdom.[2] Some at least of these reservations, as will be seen, are consistent with the interpretation stated above, that Article 2 imposes an obligation to respect the wishes of parents in matters of religious education, at least in state schools.

However, in a case concerning compulsory sex education in schools,[3] the Danish Government argued that the State had fulfilled its obligations under Article 2 by allowing parents to have their children educated in private schools. This interpretation would seem to devoid the Article of its content. It would seem to mean that Article 2, or at least its second sentence, is satisfied if private schools are tolerated.

On the assumption that there is an obligation, where education is provided in state schools, to allow for the religious and philosophical convictions of the parents, what is the extent of the obligation? It will be noticed that Article 2 does not merely require such allowance to be made in relation to religious instruction as such; it extends to education and teaching generally. But religious instruction is the clearest example; where compulsory religious instruction is provided in state schools, it may be inferred from Article 2 that parents must be allowed, if they wish, to make alternative arrangements.

The issue arose in the Karnell and Hardt case.[4] The applicants, who were members of the Evangelical-Lutheran Church of Sweden, complained that they were prevented from giving their children appropriate religious instruction. Their children, who were attending state schools, had compulsory religious instruction at school, and their Church had been refused permission to provide alternative religious instruction. The applicants maintained that the reservation made by Sweden when ratifying the First Protocol did not apply to their case. This reservation was to the effect that parents could not obtain, by reason of their philoso-

---

[1] See below, p. 175.   [2] See *Collected Texts*, 9th edn., section 6.
[3] See below, p. 177.   [4] 4733/71, *Yearbook* 14, 676 at 690.

phical convictions, dispensation for their children from taking part in certain parts of the education in state schools; nor could they obtain dispensation from taking part in the teaching of Christianity unless their children were of another faith than the Swedish Church and satisfactory religious instruction had been arranged for them.

The application was originally introduced by the Evangelical–Lutheran Church itself, but the four individual applicants later joined themselves to it. The Commission, following its decision in the case mentioned below,[1] decided that the application was inadmissible in so far as it had been introduced by the Church, since a corporation, being a legal and not a natural person, is incapable of having or exercising the rights mentioned in Article 2. It was irrelevant, in this connection, that permission to provide religious instruction in lieu of the school could be given, under Swedish law, only to a religious community and not to individual parents. This part of the reasoning seems correct, since although it was the church which had been refused permission to provide alternative religious instruction, the second sentence of Article 2 refers only to the rights of parents.

In so far as the application was introduced by the four individual applicants, it was declared admissible after the Swedish Government had stated that, although it did not consider the applicants' rights to have been violated, it was prepared to accept that the application should be examined on its merits.

Subsequently the Commission approved a friendly settlement of the case. The applicants asked to withdraw their application in view of a decision of the Swedish authorities by which they were given full satisfaction with regard to their complaints. By the terms of this decision, pupils belonging to the Evangelical–Lutheran Church would, if their parents so requested, be exempted from compulsory religious instruction; such instruction would remain separate from instruction in other subjects in classes where exempted pupils participate; and any such exempted pupil would not be at any disadvantage by reason of not having received religious instruction at school.

An important question which has not yet been resolved is to what extent the second sentence of Article 2 applies to private

[1] p. 176.

schools. In the Belgian Linguistic case the applicants maintained, in effect, that by the words 'In the exercise of any functions which it assumes in relation to education and to teaching', this provision applies not only to state schools but also to 'independent teaching subsidized, regulated and controlled' by the public authorities.[1] It may indeed be argued that the State's obligations in this field extend to any school subsidized, or even recognized, by the public authorities. On the other hand, it may go too far to hold that it applies to all schools whose courses are recognized by the State, since the Court held in the Belgian Linguistic case that everyone has the right to obtain official recognition of the studies which he has completed.

The question of recognition of independent educational establishments arose, among others, in a case which has already been considered above under Article 9.[2] A church which had a substantial educational programme, the Church of Scientology of California, complained of measures taken by the United Kingdom authorities, including the denial or withdrawal of student status for members of the Church, and the refusal of extensions of stay within the United Kingdom to continue studies at its establishments. The Commission held that, in so far as the application was brought by the Church, a corporation, being a legal and not a natural person, was incapable of having or exercising the rights mentioned in Article 2 of the First Protocol. In so far as the application was brought by individual members of the Church, the Commission followed the ruling by the Court in the Belgian Linguistic case that the first sentence of Article 2 serves merely to guarantee the right, in principle, to avail oneself of the forms of education existing at a given time, and that the Convention lays down no specific obligations concerning the organization of the system of education. The Commission inferred from this that a State is not obliged to recognize, or to continue to recognize, any particular institution as an educational establishment. The Commission did not, however, mention the Court's ruling that this provision guarantees the right of access to existing educational institutions. Nor did it refer to the second sentence of Article 2, or consider whether parents' rights under that provision had been

---

[1] 'Judgment of the Court', p. 22, *Yearbook* 11, 832 at 840; cf. 3789/68, *Collection of Decisions* 33, 1 at 3.

[2] See above, p. 147.

infringed. It is not possible to ascertain from the Commission's decision whether or not this issue arose.

Even if there is no obligation to recognize an institution as an educational establishment, the decision whether or not to recognize it as such does not remain entirely within the discretion of the State. The State must not differentiate between institutions in any way which would amount to discrimination under Article 14. This issue, also, was inadequately treated in the Commission's decision.[1]

The refusal of admission to aliens to attend an educational establishment is consistent with Article 2, but not for the reason given by the Commission. The Commission relied on the ground that the Convention does not guarantee any right of a foreign national to enter or reside in a country other than his own. But, as the Commission has frequently recognized, such a right may exist in particular cases where a right guaranteed by the Convention is in issue, for example under Article 3[2] or Article 8[3]. The reason why an alien cannot claim the right of admission to a country to attend an educational establishment there is that, as the Court stated in the Belgian Linguistic case, the right of access to an educational establishment is guaranteed only to persons within the jurisdiction of the State concerned.

An application against Denmark has raised the question whether compulsory sex education in schools is consistent with Article 2.[4] Sex education was an optional subject in Danish state schools for many years. In 1970 a law was enacted to make it obligatory in these schools. According to the law, sex education would not be presented as a separate subject, but would be integrated with the teaching of other subjects. The applicants, the parents of a girl aged ten, objected that this law infringed their right to ensure education and teaching in conformity with their own religious and philosophical convictions. This complaint was declared admissible by the Commission.

---

[1] See above, p. 146.
[2] See above, p. 31.
[3] See above, p. 129.
[4] *Kjeldsen* v. *Denmark*, 5095/71, *Collection of Decisions* 43, 44; cf. *Pedersen* v. *Denmark*, 5926/72, *Collection of Decisions* 44, 93 and 96.

ARTICLE 3 OF THE FIRST PROTOCOL

Free elections

Article 3 of the First Protocol provides that: 'The High Contracting Parties undertake to hold free elections at reasonable intervals by secret ballot, under conditions which will ensure the free expression of the opinion of the people in the choice of the legislature.'

This provision 'presupposes the existence of a representative legislature, elected at reasonable intervals, as the basis of a democratic society'.[1] It goes further than requiring free elections; it requires that the exercise of political power be subject to a freely elected legislature. Examination of the rights and freedoms guaranteed by the Convention has shown the importance of all those rights and freedoms being guaranteed by law, and of all restrictions on them being subject to the law. Article 3 of the First Protocol underpins the whole structure of the Convention in requiring that laws should be made by a legislature responsible to the people. Free elections are thus a condition of the 'effective political democracy' referred to in the Preamble, and of the concept of a democratic society which runs through the Convention.

Free elections imply a genuine choice. Hence, as the Commission stated in the Greek Case, the suspension of political parties is also contrary to Article 3.[2] On the other hand, it is consistent with the Convention, in accordance with Article 17, to prohibit political parties with totalitarian aims.[3]

Although Article 3, in contrast to Article 21(3) of the Universal Declaration of Human Rights, does not refer expressly to universal suffrage, the Commission has expressed the view that it implies recognition of universal suffrage.[4] On the other hand, its form is different from that in which the other rights in the Convention and Protocol are expressed. It does not provide that everyone has the right to vote. If a person complains that he is disqualified from voting, the Commission's task is to consider whether such disqualification affects the 'free expression of the opinion of the people' under Article 3.[5]

[1] The Greek Case, Report of the Commission, *Yearbook* 12, The Greek Case, 179.
[2] Op. cit., 180. [3] See below, p. 210.
[4] 2728/66, *Yearbook* 10, 336 at 338; cf. 5302/71, *Collection of Decisions* 44, 29 at 48. [5] Ibid.

In a case where an applicant had forfeited the right to vote in Belgium, among other civic rights, for offences of collaboration during the Second World War, the Commission adopted a somewhat different formulation. It stated that Article 3 does not guarantee the right to vote but solely the right that the Contracting States should hold free elections.[1]

The formulation is important if only because of the question of the effect of Article 14. If Article 3 implied the right to vote, any disqualification would have to be examined under Article 14. If the only right under Article 3 is as stated by the Commission, however, then it is doubtful whether a person can allege discrimination in the enjoyment of the right guaranteed. Either the obligation to hold free elections is respected, or it is not. If it is not, Article 14 is otiose. If it is, a person cannot claim that he has been the victim of discrimination, in being disqualified from voting, because the only question will be whether the disqualification complained of affects the free expression of the opinion of the people.

The Commission does not so far seem to have considered the question under Article 14, but has accepted that certain categories of citizen may be excluded from voting, without the free expression of the opinion of the people being prejudiced. Thus, Belgians resident in the Congo complained unsuccessfully that they were denied the right to vote in the metropolis.[2] Convicted prisoners may also be refused permission to vote.[3]

On the other hand, wider disqualifications, such as, for example, the disqualification of women, might be considered as affecting the free expression of the opinion of the people, even without regard to Article 14. An argument to this effect might be based on the general spirit of the Convention as well as the modern understanding of a democratic society.

In any event, it is clear that Switzerland regarded as an obstacle to ratification of the Convention and First Protocol the fact that women did not, until recently, have the right to vote in federal legislative elections or, even now, in certain of the cantons.[4]

[1] 1028/61, *Yearbook* 4, 324 at 338.
[2] 1065/61, *Yearbook* 4, 260.
[3] 2728/66, *Yearbook* 10, 336.
[4] Federal Council's Report to the Federal Assembly on the Convention, *Yearbook* 12, 502 at 509–10.

The former disability was removed by revision of the federal constitution.

Of the member States of the Council of Europe, Switzerland is the clearest proof that Article 3 cannot be confined to the central power. It must extend to the Swiss cantons, which have a very high degree of autonomy, and to all provincial legislatures where there is a measure of decentralization of power. The only federal States apart from Switzerland in the Council of Europe are the Federal Republic of Germany and Austria, the German *Länder* having more power than the Austrian *Bundesländer*.

In a case referred to above, where a convicted prisoner was refused permission to vote, his complaints related both to *Land* elections and to federal elections in Germany, and the Commission did not distinguish between them.[1] It would certainly be incorrect to exclude *Land* elections from the scope of Article 3.

In the United Kingdom, a unitary State, questions arise in relation, in particular, to Northern Ireland. Article 3 should be interpreted as presupposing, in so far as there is a degree of autonomy in Northern Ireland, the existence of a representative legislature there, and as requiring the holding of free elections, in the conditions laid down by the Article, for the Northern Ireland legislature as well as for the United Kingdom Parliament at Westminster. However, in the event of direct rule in Northern Ireland by the Westminster Government, the requirements of Article 3 are transferred to Westminster, with the result that the citizens in Northern Ireland have rights in relation to the United Kingdom parliament alone. There is, of course, no right to the devolution of power under Article 3. There is only a right that political power, wherever exercised, should be subject to democratic control.

However, it is doubtful how far Article 3 applies to municipal government. Does it require, here too, a representative legislature, and free elections?

This issue arose in the first Northern Irish cases.[2] The applicants submitted that the most important elections there were the local government elections. Under special laws, approximately thirty per cent of the adult population was disfranchised in local elections. In particular, only a householder or spouse of a

[1] 2728/66, *Yearbook* 10, 336.
[2] 3625/68, etc., *Yearbook* 13, 340.

householder had the right to vote; and it was the policy of the Northern Ireland authorities, according to the applicants, to make public housing available only to its supporters. In addition, the applicants alleged that the authorities used gerrymandering of electoral districts as a device to control elections and to prevent representative government.[1]

The United Kingdom Government submitted, in its observations on admissibility, that it was clear both from the text of Article 3 and from the preparatory work that the term 'choice of legislature' did not include elections to a local authority which is subordinate to a national or provincial authority and has only limited powers to pass bye-laws of purely local application.[2] As the cases were struck off the list, the issue was not resolved, but, with a growing tendency in Europe to the devolution of power, it is likely that the question of the scope of Article 3 will arise again. It seems clear that, as the situation was in Northern Ireland, the Government's submissions were correct on this point. A distinction can be drawn in all modern States between the legislative bodies which have supreme legislative powers, and subordinate authorities which are empowered only to enact subordinate legislation, however general it may be in its application. The term 'legislature', used without qualification in Article 3, should be interpreted as extending to a provincial legislature which has a degree of autonomy, but not to such subordinate authorities.

The requirement that elections be held 'under conditions which will ensure the free expression of the opinion of the people' excludes devices such as gerrymandering which would distort that expression. It is uncertain, however, how far it excludes, for example, multiple or plural voting. In Northern Ireland, businessmen, according to the applicants in the above case, were given six votes in respect of each business which they operated. Article 3, in contrast to Article 21(3) of the Universal Declaration of Human Rights, does not speak of 'equal suffrage'. But too great a departure from the principle of 'one man, one vote' would be inconsistent with Article 3.

Article 3 does not require any particular system of voting, such as proportional representation, again subject to the requirement that the system will ensure that the will of the people is expressed in the election result. Nor is the Article infringed by a law impos-

[1] At 344.   [2] At 412.

ing a duty to vote in a case where the voter has the opportunity of recording a blank vote.[1]

Article 3, like Articles 1 and 2 of the First Protocol but to a lesser extent, reflects the difficulties which prevented these rights from being incorporated in the text of the Convention.[2] Those difficulties are preserved in an unsatisfactory draft, the result of a compromise, and continue to give rise to problems of interpretation.

FOURTH PROTOCOL

Personal liberty and freedom of movement

The Fourth, like the First, Protocol guarantees certain additional rights. The other Protocols, the Second, Third, and Fifth, do not deal with substantive rights and are considered elsewhere. The Fourth Protocol was concluded in September 1963 and entered into force on 2 May 1968. It has not, however, been ratified by all the parties to the Convention. It has not yet been ratified by Cyprus, Greece, Italy, Malta, the Netherlands, Switzerland, Turkey, and the United Kingdom.

The rights guaranteed by the Fourth Protocol, in Articles 1 to 4, all relate to liberty of the person and freedom of movement.

As between the States parties to the Protocol, its provisions are to be regarded as additional Articles of the Convention, and all the provisions of the Convention are to apply accordingly.[3]

However, in contrast to the First Protocol, States must make a separate declaration in respect of the Fourth Protocol to recognize the Commission's competence to receive applications from individuals, or to accept the compulsory jurisdiction of the Court.[4] Further, such a declaration may be limited to one or more of Articles 1 to 4 of the Protocol.[5] It is difficult to see why, if a State is prepared to accept the obligations of the Fourth Protocol, it should not be willing to accept the optional provisions in respect of all of them. In fact, no State which has made these declarations has so far limited its acceptance in this way.

Article 1 of the Fourth Protocol provides that: 'No one shall be

[1] 1718/62, *Yearbook* 8, 168; 4982/71, *Collection of Decisions* 40, 50.
[2] See above, p. 164. [3] Article 6(1).
[4] Article 6(2). [5] Ibid.

deprived of his liberty merely on the ground of inability to fulfil a contractual obligation.'

Its wording shows that it is conceived as an extension of the protection of liberty of the person guaranteed by Article 5 of the Convention. It limits further the conditions specified by Article 5(1) under which alone a person may be arrested or detained. In particular, it limits the scope of Article 5(1) (b), which authorizes arrest or detention for non-compliance with the lawful order of a court or in order to secure the fulfilment of any obligation prescribed by law. Under the Fourth Protocol, a person may not be arrested or detained merely on the ground of inability to pay a debt or otherwise meet a contractual obligation.

In the view of the experts who drafted the Protocol, the Article aims 'at prohibiting, as contrary to the concept of human liberty and dignity, any deprivation of liberty for the sole reason that the individual had not the material means to fulfil his contractual obligations'.[1]

However, the obligation must arise out of contract. The Article does not apply to obligations arising from legislation in public or private law.[2]

Further, the Article does not apply if a debtor acts with malicious or fraudulent intent; or if a person deliberately refuses to fulfil an obligation, irrespective of his reasons therefor; or if inability to meet a commitment is due to negligence. In these circumstances, the failure to fulfil a contractual obligation may legitimately constitute a criminal offence.[3] The object of the Article is primarily, it seems, to prohibit arrest or imprisonment for civil debt.

The scope of Article 1 was examined *ex officio* by the Commission in a case where the applicant was detained in civil proceedings brought by a creditor. The German Code of Civil Procedure enables a court, at the request of a creditor, to order the detention of a debtor who fails to make an affidavit of his possessions. The Commission found that the applicant was lawfully detained under Article 5(1) (b), since there was a specific obligation under German law to make an affidavit.[4] Nor was the complaint admissible under the Fourth Protocol. The applicant had been detained in

---

[1] Explanatory Reports on the Second to Fifth Protocols to the Convention, Strasbourg 1971, p. 39.
[2] Ibid. [3] Ibid. [4] See above, p. 50.

order to secure the fulfilment of his obligation to swear an affidavit. Consequently, his detention was not based merely on the ground of inability to fulfil a contractual obligation.[1]

Article 2(1) provides that: 'Everyone lawfully within the territory of a State shall, within that territory, have the right to liberty of movement and freedom to choose his residence.' Paragraph 2 provides that: 'Everyone shall be free to leave any country, including his own.'

These provisions are based on Article 13(1) and (2) of the Universal Declaration of Human Rights, whose wording they follow closely. A person's right to return to his country, which is also included in Article 13(2) of the Universal Declaration, is dealt with separately by Article 3 of the Fourth Protocol. While Article 2 deals with freedom of movement within a country, and the right to leave it, Article 3 precludes a State from expelling, or refusing to admit, its own nationals. Thus, Article 2 applies to everyone, in relation to any country, but Article 3 applies only to nationals in relation to their own State.

The reference, in Article 2(1), to 'Everyone lawfully within the territory of a State ' includes all that State's nationals present within its territory, since it follows from the provisions of Article 3 that, subject to the possible exception of extradition,[2] the presence of a person in the State of which he is a national cannot be unlawful. As for persons who are not nationals, they are lawfully within the territory so long as they comply with any conditions of entry that may have been imposed. Such conditions may, of course, include restrictions as to the length of stay, after the expiry of which their presence will be unlawful. But, subject to the limitations permitted under paragraphs 3 and 4, these conditions cannot, under Article 2(1), include any restrictions on their liberty of movement, or on their freedom to choose their residence.

The freedom to leave a country, under Article 2(2), is subject to the restrictions set out in paragraph 3. These restrictions are, of course, sufficient to preclude a convicted prisoner from leaving the country in which he is detained. The reference to 'the maintenance of *ordre public*' in paragraph 3 was included, as is shown by the preparatory work, expressly to allow for the case of persons lawfully detained under Article 5.[3] Similarly, a person who has

---

[1] 5025/71, *Yearbook* 14, 692 at 696.   [2] See below, p. 185.
[3] 4256/69, *Collections of Decisions* 37, 67.

been detained with a view to deportation or extradition, under Article 5(1) (f), cannot claim the right to leave the country freely.[1]

As already stated, Article 3 precludes a State from expelling, or refusing to admit, its own nationals.

There is no provision for any restrictions to the rights guaranteed by Article 3, which is curious since the provision of Article 3(1) that 'No one shall be expelled, by means either of an individual or of a collective measure, from the territory of the State of which he is a national' makes no exception for the practice of extradition. It is extraordinary that the explanatory report on the Fourth Protocol merely says that 'It was understood that extradition was outside the scope of this paragraph.'[2] Such understandings are not an adequate basis for drafting a legal text. In any event, on the accepted principles of treaty interpretation, this explanatory report cannot be invoked to interpret the text, since the text is clear and unambiguous.[3]

The European Convention on Extradition does not preclude the extradition of nationals, but provides that a Contracting Party shall have the right to refuse extradition of its nationals.[4] The extradition of nationals is prohibited by the law of many Member States of the Council of Europe.[5] But the Convention on Extradition permits a State to refuse the extradition of its nationals even if this would not be contrary to its own law. It would seem that States Parties to the Fourth Protocol are precluded from extraditing their nationals in the absence of a reservation to the contrary.

It appears that the Committee of Experts which drafted the Fourth Protocol also considered the hypothesis of a State expelling one of its nationals after first depriving him of his nationality, but 'thought it was inadvisable in Article 3 to touch on the delicate question of the legitimacy of measures depriving individuals of nationality'.[6]

---

[1] 4436/70, *Collection of Decisions* 35, 169.
[2] Explanatory Reports on the Second to Fifth Protocols to the Convention, Strasbourg 1971, p. 47.
[3] See Article 32 of the Vienna Convention on the Law of Treaties and above, p. 18.
[4] European Convention on Extradition, ETS No. 24, Article 6(1).
[5] e.g. Cyprus, the Federal Republic of Germany, Netherlands, Switzerland.
[6] Op. cit., pp. 47–8.

However, the effect of Article 3(1) must be to preclude a State from depriving a person of his nationality in order to expel him. Otherwise it would offer no adequate protection. The Commission, indeed, has gone further, and has considered whether it may be contrary to Article 3(1) to refuse to grant a person nationality, if the object of the refusal is to be able to expel him.

An applicant complained both of his imminent expulsion, and of the refusal of the German authorities to recognize him as a German citizen. The Commission stated that, although the Convention confers no right to a nationality as such, the question arose whether there existed, between the decision to refuse him nationality and the order for his expulsion, a causal relation creating the presumption that the refusal had as its sole object his expulsion from German territory. There was no evidence of that, however, in the present case.[1]

Similar considerations apply to paragraph 2, which provides that: 'No one shall be deprived of the right to enter the territory of the State of which he is a national.'

A State could not refuse a person nationality if he fulfils the conditions laid down by its law, or deprive him of his nationality, in order to be able to refuse him admission.

Article 5 of the Fourth Protocol, like Article 4 of the First Protocol, makes provision for a declaration concerning the application of the Protocol to dependent territories on the model of Article 63 of the Convention.[2]

In addition, however, Article 5(4) provides that, for the purposes of Articles 2 and 3 of the Protocol, the territory of a State to which the Protocol applies by virtue of ratification, and each territory to which it applies by a declaration under Article 5, shall be treated as separate territories. The effect of this provision is that a State which ratifies the Protocol, and extends its application under Article 5 to its dependent territories, guarantees freedom of movement within each of those territories without also guaranteeing freedom of movement from one territory to another. The Committee of Experts explains paragraph 4 as follows:[3]

The Committee decided to add a paragraph 4 to Article 5 in order to take account of a problem which may arise in connection with States which are responsible for the international relations of overseas terri-

---

[1] 3745/68, *Collection of Decisions* 31, 107.
[2] See above, p. 14.   [3] Op. cit., p. 55.

tories. Thus, for example, insofar as nationality is concerned, there is no distinction between the United Kingdom and most of the territories for whose international relations it is responsible; in relation to these territories and the United Kingdom there is a common citizenship, designated as 'citizenship of the United Kingdom and Colonies'.

Persons who derive the common nationality from a connection with one such territory do not, however, have the right to admission to, or have immunity from expulsion from, another such territory. Each territory has its own laws relating to admission to and expulsion from its territory. Under these laws admission can be refused to persons who, though they possess the common nationality, do not derive it from connection with the territory in question, and in certain circumstances such persons can be expelled from that territory. Equally, persons who derive the common nationality from a connection with a dependent territory can in certain circumstances be refused admission to the United Kingdom or, if admitted, be expelled from the United Kingdom. What is said above is relevant to Article 3 of this Protocol, but a similar situation would arise as regards the interpretation of 'territory'for the purposes of Article 2.

Accordingly, it is desirable that the references in Articles 2 and 3 to the territory of a State should relate to the metropolitan territory and each non-metropolitan territory separately, and not to a single geographical entity comprising the metropolitan and other territories.

This interpretation would apply only to Article 2, paragraph 1, and to Article 3 of this Protocol.

Article 4 prohibits the collective expulsion of aliens. The Article does not regulate in any way the individual expulsion of aliens. Its scope is thus extremely limited. The reasons given for this omission by the Committee of Experts are set out in the explanatory report.[1] One reason given was that the matter had already been dealt with in the European Convention on Establishment. However, that Convention does not deal with the expulsion of aliens in general; it deals only with the expulsion of nationals of other States parties to that Convention.[2] Possibly a difficulty for the governments was that if any rights were recognized in the Protocol in relation to the expulsion of aliens generally, then the rights granted on a reciprocal basis, under the Establishment Convention or under other treaties, to the nationals of other State

[1] Op. cit., pp. 50–1.
[2] European Treaty Series No. 19, European Convention on Establishment, Article 3.

parties to those instruments might have had to be extended, through the effect of Article 14, to all aliens.

ARTICLE 14

Freedom from discrimination

Article 14 of the Convention contains a general prohibition of discrimination in relation to the rights guaranteed by the Convention and Protocols. It provides that:

The enjoyment of the rights and freedoms set forth in this Convention shall be secured without discrimination on any ground such as sex, race, colour, language, religion, political or other opinion, national or social origin, association with a national minority, property, birth or other status.

The term 'Convention' in this Article must be understood as including the First and Fourth Protocols, which themselves provide that all the provisions of the Convention apply to them.[1] Since Article 14 applies equally to the rights guaranteed by the First and Fourth Protocols, it seems appropriate to consider it after those rights have been discussed.

The enunciation of the principle of equality, and the prohibition of discrimination, were considered so fundamental as to be placed at the beginning of the Universal Declaration of Human Rights (Articles 1 and 2) and of the United Nations Covenants on Economic, Social and Cultural Rights and on Civil and Political Rights (Articles 2 and 3). These principles also have a prominent place in many national constitutions, for example in the Basic Law of the Federal Republic of Germany (Article 3), in the 'equal protection' clauses of the United States Constitution, and in the constitutions of many Commonwealth countries. Several international instruments prohibiting particular forms of discrimination, or discrimination in particular fields, have been drawn up, in the United Nations, in the International Labour Organisation, in UNESCO, and elsewhere. There is thus a substantial body of law on the subject. Nevertheless, Article 14 of the European Convention has given rise to a number of major problems of interpretation.

[1] Article 5 of the First Protocol, and Article 6(1) of the Fourth Protocol.

188

Before the judgment of the Court in the Belgian Linguistic Case, there was some doubt as to the relation between Article 14 and the Articles which define the other rights and freedoms guaranteed. It is clear that Article 14 does not prohibit discrimination as such, in any context, but only in 'the enjoyment of the rights and freedoms set forth in this Convention'. On the other hand, does Article 14 only come into play if there has been a violation of one of those rights? The view that Article 14 has such a subsidiary role, advanced by the Belgian Government before the Court in the Belgian Linguistic Case, derived some support from certain earlier decisions of the Commission.[1]

However, this interpretation would, as the Commission itself argued in the Belgian Linguistic Case, have deprived Article 14 of its effectiveness, and it was rejected by the Court. The breach of Article 14 does not presuppose the violation of the rights guaranteed by other Articles of the Convention.

While it is true that this guarantee has no independent existence in the sense that under the terms of Article 14 it relates solely to 'rights and freedoms set forth in the Convention', a measure which in itself is in conformity with the requirements of the Article enshrining the right or freedom in question may however infringe this Article when read in conjunction with Article 14 for the reason that it is of a discriminatory nature.

Thus, persons subject to the jurisdiction of a Contracting State cannot draw from Article 2 of the Protocol the right to obtain from the public authorities the creation of a particular kind of educational establishment; nevertheless, a State which had set up such an establishment could not, in laying down entrance requirements, take discriminatory measures within the meaning of Article 14.

To recall a further example, cited in the course of the proceedings, Article 6 of the Convention does not compel States to institute a system of appeal courts. A State which does set up such courts consequently goes beyond its obligations under Article 6. However it would violate that Article, read in conjunction with Article 14, were it to debar certain persons from these remedies without a legitimate reason while making them available to others in respect of the same type of actions.

In such cases there would be a violation of a guaranteed right or

---

[1] M.-A. Eissen, 'L'autonomie de l'article 14 de la Convention européenne des droits de l'homme dans la jurisprudence de la Commission', *Mélanges Modinos*, Paris 1968, 122; Belgian Linguistic Case (Merits), 'Judgment of the Court', pp. 25–50, *Yearbook* 11, 832 at 846–56.

freedom as it is proclaimed by the relevant Article read in conjunction with Article 14. It is as though the latter formed an integral part of each of the Articles laying down rights and freedoms. No distinctions should be made in this respect according to the nature of these rights and freedoms and of their correlative obligations, and for instance as to whether the respect due to the right concerned implies positive action or mere abstention. This is, moreover, clearly shown by the very general nature of the terms employed in Article 14 'the enjoyment of the rights and freedoms set forth in this Convention shall be secured'.[1]

Thus, to put the matter differently, while there can never be a violation of Article 14 considered in isolation, there may be a violation of Article 14, considered together with another Article of the Convention, in cases where there would be no violation of that other Article taken alone.

The example selected by the Court emphasizes the potential scope of Article 14. It might have selected, as an example of an 'independent' violation of Article 14, the type of situation considered by the Commission in the Grandrath case.[2] Here a limitation on a right is expressly authorized, for example by paragraph (2) of one of Articles 8 to 11; but a State may not limit the right in a discriminatory way, although that would not violate the Article in question, since it would infringe that Article in conjunction with Article 14.

The right of appeal, however, in the example given by the Court, is as such outside the scope of the Convention altogether, whether in civil or in criminal cases. Nevertheless, Article 14 together with Article 6 prohibit discrimination in access to the courts throughout the whole of the judicial system.

The conclusion is, therefore, that discrimination is prohibited, not only in the restrictions permitted, but also in laws implementing the rights guaranteed, even if those laws go beyond the obligations expressly provided by the Convention.

A second, and more difficult, major problem of interpretation raised by Article 14 was also dealt with by the Court in the Belgian Linguistic Case. What forms of differential treatment constitute 'discrimination'?

To argue that Article 14 prohibits all inequalities of treatment based on the grounds stated would lead to manifestly unreasonable

---

[1] Judgment, pp. 33–4; *Yearbook* 11, 832 at 862–4.
[2] See above, p. 145.

results, since the inequality might actually be designed to benefit the less privileged class. For example, the provision of additional educational facilities for the children of poorer families would not necessarily constitute discrimination. On the other hand, if only certain forms of inequality are prohibited, by what objective criteria can they be identified?

In spite of the very general wording of the French version ('sans distinction aucune'), Article 14 does not forbid every difference in treatment in the exercise of the rights and freedoms recognised. This version must be read in the light of the more restrictive text of the English version ('without discrimination'). In addition, and in particular, one would reach absurd results were one to give Article 14 an interpretation as wide as that which the French version seems to imply. One would, in effect, be led to judge as contrary to the Convention every one of the many legal or administrative provisions which do not secure to everyone complete equality of treatment in the enjoyment of the rights and freedoms recognised. The competent national authorities are frequently confronted with situations and problems which, on account of differences inherent therein, call for different legal solutions; moreover, certain legal inequalities tend only to correct factual inequalities. The extensive interpretation mentioned above cannot consequently be accepted.

It is important, then, to look for the criteria which enable a determination to be made as to whether or not a given difference in treatment, concerning of course the exercise of one of the rights and freedoms set forth, contravenes Article 14. On this question the Court, following the principles which may be extracted from the legal practice of a large number of democratic States, holds that the principle of equality of treatment is violated if the distinction has no objective and reasonable justification. The existence of such a justification must be assessed in relation to the aim and effects of the measure under consideration, regard being had to the principles which normally prevail in democratic societies. A difference of treatment in the exercise of a right laid down in the Convention must not only pursue a legitimate aim: Article 14 is likewise violated when it is clearly established that there is no reasonable relationship of proportionality between the means employed and the aim sought to be realised.[1]

The Court thus adopted, and applied in its examination of the legislation in question, the weaker of two alternative theses on the

---

[1] Judgment, p. 34; *Yearbook* 11, 832 at 864–6.

meaning of discrimination. On this weaker thesis, differential treatment is justified if it has an objective aim, derived from the public interest, and if the measures of differentiation do not exceed a reasonable relation to that aim.

A stronger thesis would be that differential treatment is justified only if, without regard to the purpose of the measures in question, the facts themselves require or permit differential treatment.

This view of Article 14 was clearly formulated by a member of the Commission, Mr. Balta, in an individual opinion in the Grandrath case.[1] He stated:

In my view, the intention of Article 14 is to establish the principle of complete equality in the enjoyment of the rights and freedoms set forth in the Convention. This being so, enjoyment of those rights and freedoms may not be made subject to any kinds of discrimination other than those which are either inherent in the nature of the right in question or are designed to remedy existing inequalities.[2]

The two theses both start from the idea that a difference of status, of sex, race, language, etc., cannot of itself justify differential treatment; but whereas on the first thesis differential treatment might be justified by the purpose of the measures in question, on the second thesis it could only be justified if the difference of status implied certain objective factual differences which required or permitted different legal treatment.

The distinction is of considerable practical importance, since on the thesis adopted by the Court it found a violation on only one aspect of the Belgian legislation; on the stronger thesis, other provisions might also have been inconsistent with the Convention.[3]

The point may be illustrated by a hypothetical case. Suppose that, in a particular country's educational system, higher standards of qualifications are required of women than of men for admission to universities. The difference might be justified on policy grounds, for example by the argument that the university education of men yielded higher returns than that of women. On the Court's interpretation of Article 14, that argument might be accepted. On the other view, what is in issue is simply that men and women have

---

[1] See above, p. 145.   [2] *Yearbook* 10, 626 at 686.
[3] See Khol, 30 *Zeitschrift für ausländisches öffentliches Recht und Völkerrecht* (1970), 263.

equal rights to education, and that this equality cannot be affected by the purpose of the measures in question.

A difficult question is the scope of the domestic remedies rule in relation to complaints of discrimination. The difficulty here is that there may be no remedy against the exercise of a power which is lawful in itself, and unlawful through the effect of Article 14. An example would be measures to prohibit political meetings on the ground that they would lead to breaches of the peace. Such a measure might be justified under Article 11(2), but it would be contrary to Article 14 if only the meetings of the opposition parties were banned, while the government's supporters continued to hold public meetings. Yet it would be difficult to challenge the banning of a particular meeting without consideration of the general policy; and where national law contained no prohibition of discrimination, corresponding to Article 14, which could be invoked in the courts, it would probably be impossible to succeed. More generally, it may be said that whenever the executive has a discretionary power, it may be difficult to secure, by an action in an isolated case, that this power is not exercised in a discriminatory manner.

Discrimination on certain of the grounds referred to in Article 14 has already been discussed: in relation to sex, under Article 8;[1] to race, under Article 3;[2] to language, under Article 2 of the First Protocol;[3] to religion, under Article 9.[4]

Finally, it should be noted that the grounds listed in Article 14 are not exhaustive. Discrimination based on any 'other status' is prohibited. The French text, 'toute autre situation', seems to go even further in this respect.

[1] See above, p. 132. [2] See above, p. 33.
[3] See above, p. 170. [4] See above, p. 145.

PART III RESTRICTIONS

1. EXPRESS RESTRICTIONS

Certain restrictions or limitations upon the rights guaranteed by the Convention and Protocols are expressly authorized. They may be authorized in the very Article setting out the right in question; for example, the limitations authorized under paragraph (2) of Articles 8 to 11. Or they may be authorized under the general provisions of the Convention in Articles 15 to 17.

Some rights are so fundamental that no derogation is allowed under Article 15; even in time of war, no one may be subjected to servitude, to inhuman treatment, or to retroactive penal law.[1] Some rights, on the other hand, admit of special exceptions; thus freedom of expression, freedom of assembly and freedom of association are subject to additional restrictions, in that, by Article 16, those freedoms do not qualify the right of a State to impose restrictions on the political activities of aliens.

Again some rights are so formulated that the Article setting out the right does not make provision for any restrictions. This is the case with Article 3 of the Convention and Articles 3 and 4 of the Fourth Protocol.

Where there is an express limitation contained in a particular Article, this limitation may take various forms. Sometimes, as in Article 4, a particular term is defined in such a way as to indicate the limits of the right guaranteed; thus 'forced or compulsory labour' is defined so as to allow for certain forms of work which might otherwise have been regarded as prohibited.[2] Sometimes, as in Article 12, the limitation is contained in the very articulation of the right.[3] Sometimes, as in Article 2, certain specified exceptions are allowed.[4] Sometimes, again, as in Articles 8 to 11, general provisions allow for interference by the authorities under certain prescribed conditions.

The important consideration, however, is that logically it makes no difference how the right is limited. The drafting technique is of

[1] See below, p. 204.
[2] See above, p. 37.
[3] See above, p. 161.
[4] See above, p. 22.

no significance; and in particular, it makes no difference whether the scope of the right is limited by its very definition, in the articulation of the right, or by separate express provisions.

This is essential for the understanding of the two basic principles concerning the restrictions on the rights guaranteed. The first principle is that only the restrictions expressly authorized by the Convention are allowed.

That principle is nowhere stated in the Convention, but, as will be seen in a moment, it is presupposed by the whole system of the Convention. Further, it is presupposed, in particular, by the second basic principle, which is expressly stated by Article 18. This principle is that 'the restrictions permitted under this Convention to the said rights and freedoms shall not be applied for any purpose other than those for which they have been prescribed'.

Logically, therefore, it is unsound to deal separately with the restrictions to the rights guaranteed. The question of such restrictions is inseparable from the question of the scope of the rights as discussed in Part II above.[1] Nevertheless, this procedure has a practical justification, in that there are certain considerations common to the various restrictions, or to put it differently to the scope of the various rights, which can conveniently be treated together.

The importance of requiring that restrictions must, in every case, be justified by an express provision of the Convention is very great. It enables the Commission and the Court to control the alleged interference by reference to those express provisions, rather than to fall back on the vague and undefined notion of inherent limitations, considered in the next section.

First it must be shown that the restriction was in each case 'in accordance with the law' (Article 8(2) of the Convention and Article 2(3) and (4) of the Fourth Protocol), or 'prescribed by law' (Articles 9(2), 10(2), 11(2)), or 'subject to the conditions provided for by law' (Article 1 of the First Protocol).

These references are of course to municipal law, and the Commission and Court must accept the interpretation of national law adopted by the national courts. This is not because the Commission and the Court are not a 'fourth instance',[2] or higher court of

---

[1] See Report of the Commission in the Golder case, para. 88.

[2] See above, p. 107.

appeal above the national courts. It is rather because questions of municipal law are, for the Commission and the Court, simply questions of fact.

Thus German laws passed during the Nazi period must be accepted as law if they are regarded as valid by the German legal system. Again, in considering whether a law which had been declared invalid by the Austrian Constitutional Court could subsequently be applied to facts arising prior to its annulment, the Commission referred to that Court's own case-law on the subject.[1]

Next, in addition to being lawful, the restriction must be 'necessary in a democratic society' (Articles 8(2) to 11(2) and Article 2(3) of the Fourth Protocol) for one of the purposes there prescribed; or it must be justified by the public interest (Article 1 of the First Protocol and Article 2(4) of the Fourth Protocol).

The requirement that a restriction must be *necessary* in a democratic society for the prescribed purposes has perhaps not been given sufficient weight by the Commission, especially in view of its acceptance of an area of discretion, considered below.

If, however, we look, not at the exercise of discretion by the authorities in applying a rule to a particular case, but at the content of the rule itself, there is an element in the Commission's practice which might be justified by reference to this requirement.

The Commission has frequently interpreted the provisions of the Convention with the aid of a comparative survey of the relevant laws and practices in the Contracting States. An example is a summary of vagrancy laws in force in various European countries, set out in Appendix IV of the Commission's Report on the Vagrancy cases.[2] This technique, already mentioned,[3] is not always easy to justify. But, when examining a particular rule restricting the exercise of a right, such as a rule restricting the right of persons detained as vagrants to respect for their correspondence, there may be good reason to compare other systems of law within the Council of Europe. For if other systems manage without such a restriction, it can hardly be said to be 'necessary in a democratic society'.

Finally, the Commission and the Court must ensure, in accor-

---

[1] 3500/68, *Collection of Decisions* 37, 1.
[2] 'Publications of the Court', Series B, p. 143.
[3] See above, p. 19.

dance with Article 18, that the restrictions permitted have not been applied for any purpose other than that for which they have been prescribed. Thus restrictions on the rights guaranteed by the Convention may not be applied to a convicted prisoner, in a particular case, as a punishment. This question is considered further below.

2. 'INHERENT LIMITATIONS'

The first principle stated above, that only the restrictions expressly provided by the Convention are allowed, has not always been accepted. The idea that, over and above the limitations expressly permitted by the Convention, there are certain 'inherent' limitations, has been used by the Commission in dealing with applications by convicted prisoners and other detained persons.[1] It has also been supported by some writers on the Convention.[2] The issue raises a number of questions of general importance, which justify somewhat full treatment.

In the first place certain general remarks must be made about the position of convicted prisoners and other detained persons.

A high proportion of applications to the Commission—at one time it was more than half—come from applicants detained or interned.[3] Such persons are plainly more likely to suffer grievances, both real and imaginary. It is therefore of great importance to decide how far the guarantees of the Convention are applicable to them.

In an application brought by Ilse Koch, wife of the commandant of Buchenwald concentration camp, the Commission stated that, although 'the applicant is imprisoned in execution of a sentence imposed on her for crimes against the most elementary rights of men', this circumstances did not deny her the guarantee of the rights and freedoms defined in the Convention.[4]

The Commission has nevertheless felt compelled to apply a double standard in dealing with complaints by convicted prisoners. For some years it adopted the doctrine that many restrictions complained of were an 'inherent feature' of imprisonment, and did not require to be justified under one of the exceptions expressly provided by the Convention.

[1] See above, p. 139.   [2] See, e.g. Fawcett, 69.
[3] The annual statistics are given in the Yearbook.
[4] 1270/61, *Yearbook* 5, 126 at 134.

The doctrine was applied most frequently to complaints under Article 8 of interference with correspondence; the Commission, as has been seen above,[1] often did not deal with such complaints by considering whether they fell within one of the exceptions in Article 8(2), but stated that the 'normal control' of prisoners' correspondence was an inherent feature of imprisonment. Thus, in the De Courcy case,[2] the Commission stated that 'the limitation of the right of a detained person to conduct correspondence is a necessary part of his deprivation of liberty which is inherent in the punishment of imprisonment.'

A study of the Commission's decisions on this issue reveals a scarcely perceptible slide from the view that certain restrictions are a necessary feature of imprisonment, and therefore the interference complained of can be justified under paragraph (2), to the position that, since these restrictions are necessary, there is an inherent limitation in the right stated in paragraph (1), so that there has not been any interference with that right such as would require justification under paragraph (2).

The doctrine of 'inherent feature' has also, though less frequently, been applied to other complaints, for example, under Articles 8,[3] 9,[4] and 10.[5] It is so imprecise that, once adopted, it is hard to see its limits. Does it apply, for example, to the right of access to the courts under Article 6(1)? In the Golder case,[6] the Commission thought not.

It seems plain that this doctrine is both incorrect and unnecessary. It is incorrect because to apply special limitations to one class of persons is contrary to the whole scheme of the Convention, which is intended to apply equally to all human beings, and which is extended by Article 1, and indeed by the opening word of almost every Article in Section I, to 'everyone' within the jurisdiction of the Contracting States.

It is unnecessary because the permitted limitations are sufficient to allow for those restrictions on the rights of prisoners which are really necessary.[7] In fact the doctrine of inherent limitations seems to be based on a German theory (of *immanente Schranken*) developed in the context of a system which appeared to guarantee funda-

---

[1] p. 139.   [2] 2749/66, *Yearbook* 10, 388 at 412.
[3] 3819/68, *Collection of Decisions* 32, 23.
[4] 4517/70, *Collection of Decisions* 38, 90 at 97.
[5] 2795/66, *Collection of Decisions* 30, 23; see above, p. 154.
[6] See above, p. 91.   [7] See above, p. 140.

mental rights without any restriction; the system of the Convention is quite different and leaves no place for inherent limitations.

It is evident that the drafters of the Convention had continually before their minds the situation of the convicted prisoner. In the case of one Article, Article 3, they specifically protect the prisoner by setting limits to the possibilities of punishment; Article 4(3), on the other hand, recognizes the legitimacy of compulsory labour in prison. In Article 5 provision is made for the lawful detention of persons duly convicted. Articles 2, 6 and 7 make no special provision for convicted prisoners, from which it may be deduced that they have the same rights under these Articles as persons at liberty. Articles 8 to 11 contain, in paragraph (2) of each Article, limited exceptions which allow for a proper balance to be struck between the protection of human rights and the restrictions on the exercise of those rights which may be necessary in a free society in the special condition of a detained person. It is evident that these restrictions must be found in every case in paragraph (2) of the Article concerned, or elsewhere in the express terms of the Convention, and that they cannot be implied.

Indeed, if there were any inherent limitation it might be expected in the case of a person detained in prison who complains, under Article 2(2) of the Fourth Protocol, that he is not free to leave the country! Yet here the Commission itself pointed out that the refusal to release the applicant was justified under Article 2(3), and that it was clear from the preparatory work of the Protocol that the notion of *ordre public* was explicitly included in that paragraph in order to cover such cases.[1]

If the issue were still in doubt, the wording of Article 18 would be conclusive; in providing that the restrictions permitted 'shall not be applied for any purpose other than those for which they have been prescribed', it makes it clear that the only restrictions permitted are express restrictions, prescribed for a particular purpose; and that there can be no implied restrictions for which *ex hypothesi* no purpose is prescribed.

The Commission's doctrine that certain restrictions are an 'inherent feature' of detention seems to have been disapproved by the Court in the Vagrancy Cases. The Court held, as we have seen,[2] that there was unquestionably an interference with the

---

[1] 3962/69, *Collection of Decisions* 32, 68; see above, p. 184.
[2] See above, p. 140.

right to respect for correspondence; it thus rejected the notion that there was no need to find justification under paragraph (2). Since this judgment the Commission's decisions suggest that it has rightly abandoned the doctrine.

However, the Court relied, under paragraph (2), on a notion which is at first sight equally vague and unwarranted, the notion of a 'power of appreciation' which Article 8(2) leaves to the Contracting States. The Court held, 'in the light of the information given to it, that the competent Belgian authorities did not transgress in the present cases the limits of the power of appreciation which Article 8(2) of the Convention leaves to the Contracting States: even in cases of persons detained for vagrancy, those authorities had sufficient reason to believe that it was "necessary" to impose restrictions for the purpose of the prevention of disorder or crime, the protection of health or morals, and the protection of the rights and freedoms of others.'[1] While this approach seems somewhat lacking in logical rigour, it is possible to give it some precision.

3. CONTROL OF DISCRETION

The idea underlying the notion of a 'power of appreciation' is that the Convention leaves the authorities a certain area of discretion. Interference with the rights guaranteed by the Convention does not have to be shown to be actually necessary in order to be justified under paragraph (2); it has to be shown only that the authorities had sufficient reason to believe that it was necessary.

The term sometimes used by the Commission, 'margin of appreciation', is evidently a 'translation' from the French and the concept of a 'power of appreciation' is derived from those continental systems of administrative law which are based on the doctrines of the French *Conseil d'Etat*. For the purposes of judicial review of administrative action within these systems, the question is not whether the reasons given by the authorities actually did justify the measures taken. The question is whether, in the circumstances, they could in principle justify it.

It is necessary, therefore, to distinguish the functions of the national authorities, on the one hand, and of the Commission and the Court on the other. The national authorities, in drawing up

[1] Para. 93.

legislation and administrative rules authorizing, under certain conditions, interference with the rights guaranteed by Articles 8 to 11, must make it a condition of such interference that it is necessary for one of the purposes specified in the second paragraph of the Article concerned. In applying these laws and rules, again, they must be satisfied that the interference in the particular case is in fact necessary for one of those purposes. However, it is for the national authorities, not for the Commission and Court, to decide whether the interference was in fact necessary in the particular case. For the Commission and Court, reviewing their decisions, the question becomes: did the national authorities *have sufficient reason* to believe that it was necessary?

It need hardly be added that the test is objective—the question is not: did the authorities think they had sufficient reason, but did they have sufficient reason in fact. The alternative explanation can be supported only by the logic of Humpty Dumpty.[1] Thus, in each case, the Commission and the Court must first ascertain on what grounds the national authorities acted, and then decide whether those grounds gave them sufficient reason to believe that their action was necessary. This is the extent of the national authorities' power of appreciation.

It must be admitted that, although the Commission has in its more recent decisions dropped an express reference to the 'margin of appreciation',[2] it has put undue weight on this concept. It has often used it at the wrong place: instead of ascertaining the facts and the grounds on which a decision was taken by the national authorities, and then considering whether they did not exceed the limits of their discretion, it has simply assumed that the discretion was properly exercised.[3]

4. ABUSE OF POWER (ARTICLE 18)

It remains to consider, under this head, the scope of Article 18, which provides that 'The restrictions permitted under this Convention to the said rights and freedoms shall not be applied for any purpose other than those for which they have been prescribed.'

---

[1] See the dissenting opinion of Lord Atkin in *Liversidge* v. *Anderson*, [1942] A.C. 206 at 225, 245.

[2] 'Case-Law Topics', No. 4, p. 2.

[3] See, e.g. above, p. 136.

This Article, as already stated, shows that there can be no inherent or implied limitations on the rights guaranteed. Each limitation must be express and have an explicit purpose. Further, Article 18 limits the area of discretion of the national authorities. In effect, it excludes *détournement de pouvoir*,[1] or abuse of power, notions familiar in many systems of domestic law. The principle is that where the real purpose of the authorities in imposing a restriction is outside the purposes specified, one of the specified purposes cannot be used as a pretext for imposing that restriction. The restriction may be one which is legitimate in itself, and lawfully imposed in accordance with the proper procedure. But it will still be prohibited if imposed for an improper purpose. To take an example already cited, where the right of a convicted prisoner to respect for family life is subject to a restriction on the grounds set out in Article 8(2), such a restriction may be imposed only for the purposes there specified, and not, for example, as a punishment.

In *Kamma* v. *The Netherlands*,[2] the applicant complained that while he was detained on remand the police took advantage of his detention to conduct investigations against him in connection with a murder, although he was not detained on account of that crime nor had any such judicial investigations been authorized. He submitted that Article 18, read in conjunction with Article 5, had been violated in this respect. The Dutch Government argued that it was normal procedure, and in no way inconsistent with the Convention, to conduct police inquiries into criminal charges before their investigation was authorized by a judicial decision. The application was declared admissible by the Commission.

It is not clear why Article 18 was included in the Convention. There is no equivalent provision in the Universal Declaration of Human Rights nor in the United Nations Covenant on Civil and Political Rights.[3] Nor is there much guidance in the preparatory work.[4] Article 18 may seem to add little to the Convention except

---

[1] Cf. 753/60, *Yearbook* 3, 310; Lawless Case, Judgment, *Yearbook* 4, 438 at 480.

[2] *Collection of Decisions* 42, 22.

[3] But see Article 30 of the American Convention on Human Rights: 'The restrictions that, pursuant to this Convention, may be placed on the enjoyment or exercise of the rights or freedoms recognized herein may not be applied except in accordance with the laws enacted for reasons of general interest and in accordance with the purpose for which such restrictions have been established.'

[4] See Guradze, *Europäische Menschenrechtskonvention*, Berlin 1968, 204.

to make explicit what is either implicit in other provisions or else may be thought to be well established under the general principles recognized by international law.[1] But it is useful as putting beyond doubt the scope of the restrictions permitted, and as making clear the requirement of good faith in the application of these restrictions.

5. EMERGENCY POWERS (ARTICLE 15)

Article 15(1) provides that: 'In time of war or other public emergency threatening the life of the nation any High Contracting Party may take measures derogating from its obligations under this Convention to the extent strictly required by the exigencies of the situation, provided that such measures are not inconsistent with its other obligations under international law.'

By paragraph (2), however, no derogation is permitted from Article 2, except in respect of deaths resulting from lawful acts of war, or from Articles 3, 4 (paragraph 1) and 7. Paragraph (3) requires a State availing itself of this right of derogation to keep the Secretary General of the Council of Europe fully informed of the measures which it has taken and the reasons therefor.

Article 15 incorporates, in effect, the principle of necessity common to all legal systems. Most States have provisions for emergency legislation, empowering them to take measures in a state of emergency which would not otherwise be lawful.

However, under Article 15, such measures are subject to the control of the organs of the Convention. If a State avails itself, in a case, of its right of derogation, it is for the Commission and the Court to consider, first, whether a public emergency threatening the life of the nation could be said to exist at the material time; and secondly, whether the measures taken were in fact strictly required by the exigencies of the situation. Finally, such measures must be consistent with other obligations under international law.

The issue arose for the first time in the Cyprus cases, two applications brought by Greece against the United Kingdom when Cyprus was still under British rule.[2]

The Commission considered that it was 'competent to pronounce on the existence of a public danger which, under Article 15, would grant to the Contracting Party concerned the right to

[1] Cf. Kiss, *L'abus de droit en droit international*, Paris 1953.
[2] 176/57, *Yearbook* 2, 174 and 182; 299/57, *Yearbook* 2, 178 and 186.

derogate from the obligations laid down in the Convention'. The Commission also considered that it was 'competent to decide whether measures taken by a Party under Article 15 of the Convention had been taken to the extent strictly required by the exigencies of the situation'. It added that 'the Government should be able to exercise a certain measure of discretion in assessing the extent strictly required by the exigencies of the situation.'[1]

Subsequently a political solution to the Cyprus problem was reached, and the Committee of Ministers decided that no further action was called for.

The notion of a government's 'measure of discretion' (French: *marge d'appréciation*) was to have an influential career. The expression, which was sometimes rendered 'margin of appreciation' as a 'translation' of the French term, reappears in a variety of contexts.[2] Its scope in relation to derogations is considered below. For the moment it is sufficient to observe that it qualifies, but does not exclude, the control by the Commission and the Court of the application of Article 15.

The existence of this control was confirmed by the Court in the Lawless case.[3]

The Irish Government had contended that, provided measures taken under Article 15 were not contrary to Article 18, they were outside the control of the Convention bodies. The Court said, however: 'It is for the Court to determine whether the conditions laid down in Article 15 for the exercise of the exceptional right of derogation have been fulfilled'.[4] It accordingly considered, first, whether there could be said to be a public emergency threatening the life of the nation; second, whether the measures taken in derogation from obligations under the Convention were 'strictly required by the exigencies of the situation'; and third, whether the measures were inconsistent with other obligations under international law.

Some indication of the scope of the 'margin of appreciation', an expression which recurs in the Commission's Report in the Greek Case,[5] can be found in the Court's judgment in the Lawless case. The Court held that 'the existence at the time of a "public emergency threatening the life of the nation" *was reasonably deduced*

---

[1] *Yearbook* 2, 174 at 176.   [2] See above, p. 201.
[3] See above, p. 50.   [4] *Yearbook* 4, 438 at 472.
[5] *Yearbook* 12, The Greek Case, at 72.

by the Irish Government from a combination of several factors, which the Court proceeded to enumerate.[1] Thus, as in the case of other authorized limitations,[2] the Commission and Court must consider whether the national authorities had *sufficient reason to believe* that a public emergency existed, within the meaning of Article 15.

What then constitutes such a public emergency? In the Lawless case, the Court defined it as 'an exceptional situation of crisis or emergency which affects the whole population and constitutes a threat to the organized life of the community of which the State is composed'.[3] The Court found, as we have seen, that the existence of a public emergency was 'reasonably deduced' by the Irish Government. The Court had regard, in particular to three factors: the existence of a secret army (the Irish Republican Army—IRA); the fact that this army was also operating outside the territory of the State; and the steady and alarming increase in terrorist activities in the period before the emergency was declared.[4]

In the Greek Case, the Commission had to consider the validity of a derogation by a revolutionary government. The respondent Government, which had seized power in Greece by a *coup d'état* on 21 April 1967 and had suspended parts of the Constitution, invoked Article 15 of the Convention. The Commission considered that the Convention applied in the same way to a revolutionary as to a constitutional government.[5]

As regards the definition of a 'public emergency threatening the life of the nation', the Commission followed the definition given by the Court in the Lawless Case.[6] Methodologically, too, the Commission followed the Court, but only in part. It sought to answer the question whether there was such a public emergency in Greece by examining the elements indicated by the respondent Government as constituting in its view such an emergency.[7] These elements were examined by the Commission under three heads: the danger of a Communist take-over; the crisis of constitutional government; and the breakdown of public order in Greece.[8]

The Commission considered that in the present case the burden lay upon the respondent Government to show that the conditions

---

[1] *Yearbook* 4, 438 at 474.   [2] See above, p. 201.
[3] *Yearbook* 4, 438 at 472–4.   [4] Ibid.
[5] *Yearbook* 12, The Greek Case, at 32.
[6] At 71–2.   [7] At 44.   [8] At 45.

justifying measures of derogation under Article 15 had been and continued to be met.[1] It concluded that the Government had not satisfied it that there was on 21 April 1967 a public emergency threatening the life of the Greek nation.[2]

However, in one respect the Commission did not follow the Court's view of Article 15. The Commission, while referring to the government's 'margin of appreciation', did not merely consider whether the Greek Government had sufficient reason to believe that a public emergency existed; it considered whether such an emergency existed in fact. This difference of approach is of great importance since it makes more stringent the requirements of Article 15.

If it is established that this first condition of Article 15 is satisfied, it must next be asked whether the measures which are the subject of the application were 'strictly required by the exigencies of the situation'.

In the Greek Case, as the Commission was not satisfied that there was a public emergency, the measures could not in any event be justified under Article 15. It was not therefore necessary to consider whether the measures taken were strictly required by the exigencies of the situation. Nevertheless, the Commission decided to examine that question also, on the hypothesis that there was a public emergency in Greece threatening the life of the nation.[3] The Commission found that, even on that hypothesis, the measures taken could not be justified under Article 15, because they went beyond what the situation required.[4]

In the Lawless case, the Court held, following the opinion of the Commission, that detention without trial was justified under Article 15. In considering whether such a measure was strictly required by the exigencies of the situation, the Court had particular regard, not only to the dangers of the situation, but also to the existence of a number of safeguards designed to prevent abuses in the operation of the system of administrative detention.[5]

Finally, measures which may be taken by a State under Article 15(1) must not be 'inconsistent with its other obligations under international law'. Thus, they must not conflict with its other treaty obligations, or obligations under customary international law. Any such measures are not permitted under Article 15. Hence,

[1] At 72.   [2] At 76.   [3] At 104.
[4] At 135–6 and 148–9.   [5] At 478.

a State could not avail itself of Article 15 to release itself from its obligations, for example, under other human rights instruments. This would in any event be precluded by Article 60 of the Convention, which provides that: 'Nothing in this Convention shall be construed as limiting or derogating from any of the human rights and fundamental freedoms which may be ensured under the laws of any High Contracting Party or under any other agreement to which it is a Party.'

Issues relating to Article 15 have normally been examined on the merits and cannot usually be disposed of at the stage of admissibility. In inter-State cases, this is indeed inevitable, since such a case cannot be rejected as being manifestly ill-founded.[1] In the case brought by Ireland against the United Kingdom, the respondent Government invoked, at the stage of admissibility, the notification of derogation which it had made in respect of Northern Ireland. The Irish Government accepted that a public emergency within the meaning of Article 15 existed in Northern Ireland, but denied that the measures taken by the United Kingdom Government were strictly required by the exigencies of the situation. The Commission held that this question could not be determined at the stage of admissibility.[2]

Indeed, even on an individual application, it would be difficult to justify a decision holding that all the conditions of Article 15 were plainly fulfilled at the stage of admissibility; normally such an application should be examined on the merits if Article 15 is invoked.[3]

Three remarks should be added on the scope of derogations *ratione temporis*. First, in considering whether the measures were permissible under Article 15, regard must be had to the situation before the emergency is declared. This was of course done by the Court in the Lawless case and by the Commission in the Greek Case. Secondly, notification under Article 15(3) may have a limited retroactive effect. No time limit is laid down for notifications, but the Court appeared to consider in the Lawless case that communication without delay is an element in the sufficiency of information required by that provision.[4] In the

---

[1] See below, p. 222.
[2] *Ireland* v. *United Kingdom, Collection of Decisions* 41, 3 at 88.
[3] But see 493/59, *Yearbook* 4, 302 at 310–16.
[4] *Yearbook* 4, 438 at 482–6.

Greek Case the Commission considered that the initial notice of derogation was given within a reasonable time, but that there was undue delay in communicating the reasons for the measures of derogation.[1] Thirdly, it is evident that if the measures in question remain in force after the circumstances which justify them have disappeared, they represent a breach of the Convention.[2] In the Greek Case, accordingly, the Commission examined the evolution of the situation from the date of the *coup* to the time of compiling its Report.[3]

Article 15 necessarily requires the Commission and the Court to make judgments of an essentially political character. It was for this reason, among others, that successive French Governments hesitated for many years before ratifying the Convention, and other governments hesitated to accept the optional clauses.[4] Article 16 of the French Constitution confers on the President of the Republic wide-ranging powers in the event of a state of emergency, which is itself widely defined. The Article provides that if the institutions of the Republic, the independence of the Nation, the integrity of its territory or the fulfilment of its international undertakings are seriously and immediately threatened, and the regular operation of the public authorities is interrupted, the President of the Republic shall, after certain consultations, take 'the measures required by these circumstances'.

When ratifying the Convention in 1974, the French Government made a far-reaching reservation to Article 15. This reservation is to the effect that 'the circumstances specified in Article 16 of the Constitution regarding the implementation of that Article . . . and in which it is permissible to apply the provisions of those texts, must be understood as complying with the purpose of Article 15 of the Convention.' The reservation also relates to certain legislation in the same field. Finally, the reservation provides that, for the interpretation and application of Article 16 of the Constitution, the terms 'to the extent strictly required by the exigencies of the situation' shall not restrict the power of the President of the Republic to take 'the measures required by the circumstances'.

[1] Op. cit., at 42–3.
[2] De Becker case, Report of the Commission, 'Publications of the Court', Series B, p. 133.
[3] Op. cit., at 92–103.
[4] See, e.g. for the attitude of the United Kingdom Government in 1959, *Yearbook* 2, 548 at 558.

6. ABUSE OF RIGHTS (ARTICLE 17)

Article 17 provides that: 'Nothing in this Convention may be interpreted as implying for any State, group or person any right to engage in any activity or perform any act aimed at the destruction of any of the rights and freedoms set forth herein or at their limitation to a greater extent than is provided for in the Convention.'

This fundamental provision, the Commission has stated, is designed to safeguard the rights listed in the Convention, by protecting the free operation of democratic institutions.[1] In an early case introduced by the German Communist Party, the Commission quoted, from the preparatory work, the statement that the object was to prevent adherents to totalitarian doctrines from exploiting the rights guaranteed by the Convention for the purpose of destroying human rights.[2]

The object of Article 17, therefore, is to limit the rights guaranteed only to the extent that such limitation is necessary to prevent their total subversion, and it must be quite narrowly construed in relation to this object.

In the above case, the German Communist Party had, in 1956, been declared 'anticonstitutional' by the Federal Constitutional Court. The Court had consequently dissolved it and ordered the confiscation of its property. The Party challenged this decision as contrary to Articles 9, 10, and 11 of the Convention. The Commission, applying Article 17, rejected the application as incompatible with the provisions of the Convention. The avowed aim of the Communist Party, according to its own declarations, was to establish a communist society by means of a proletarian revolution and the dictatorship of the proletariat. Consequently, even if it sought power by solely constitutional methods, recourse to a dictatorship was incompatible with the Convention because it would involve the suppression of a number of rights and freedoms which the Convention guaranteed.

In a sequel to this case, a company incorporated under Swiss law, Retimag S.A., complained of the confiscation without compensation of two of its properties in Germany.[3] The German court which ordered the confiscations had held that the company was unquestionably a legal front which had the dual purpose of

[1] 250/57, *Yearbook* 1, 222 at 224.   [2] Ibid.
[3] 712/60, *Retimag S.A.* v. *Federal Republic of Germany, Yearbook* 4, 384.

safeguarding real property belonging to the dissolved Communist Party and of continuing communist subversive activities. Article 17 was invoked by the German Government but the application was rejected for non-exhaustion of domestic remedies. Whether, however, Article 17 can be invoked in relation to a claim based on Article 1 of the First Protocol must be doubtful in view of the judgment of the Court in the Lawless case.

In that case[1] the Irish Government maintained that the activities of the IRA, in which Lawless was engaged, fell within the terms of Article 17, and that he was therefore not entitled to rely on Articles 5, 6, 7, or any other Article of the Convention. The Commission expressed the view that Article 17 was not applicable. It stated that the general purpose of Article 17 was to prevent totalitarian groups from exploiting the principles enunciated by the Convention. But to achieve that purpose, it was not necessary to deprive the persons concerned of all the rights and freedoms guaranteed in the Convention. Article 17 covered essentially those rights which, if invoked, would enable them to engage in the activities referred to in Article 17. The Court, in somewhat different language, followed in substance the view of the Commission.[2] Thus Article 17 applies only to rights, such as those in Articles 9, 10, and 11, which entitle a person to engage in activities; it prevents him from relying on those Articles to engage in subversive activities. A person engaging in subversive activities does not, therefore, forfeit the right to a fair trial under Article 6; but he cannot claim the freedom to organize political meetings, for instance, if his purpose in using that freedom is to undermine all civil liberties. It is always a question of the purpose for which the rights are used; the principle is that 'no person may be able to take advantage of the provisions of the Convention to perform acts aimed at destroying the aforesaid rights and freedom'.[3] Hence, Article 17 cannot be used to deprive an individual of his political freedom simply on the ground that he has supported a totalitarian government in the past.[4]

It follows also that even persons engaging in terrorist activities for subversive ends cannot be deprived of their protection under the Convention. In the result, those who pursue anarchy, for

---

[1] See above, p. 50.   [2] *Yearbook* 4, 438 at 450–2.   [3] Ibid.
[4] Cf. De Becker case, Report of the Commission, 'Publications of the Court', Series B, 137, 138.

example, by organizing political meetings on a peaceful basis may in a sense be at a disadvantage compared with those who resort to violence. The former may lose, through the application of Article 17, the political freedoms guaranteed by Articles 9, 10, and 11 ; the latter, since they do not seek to exercise political activities, lose nothing. If, however, the scale of violence is such as to create a national emergency, the rights guaranteed under Articles 5 and 6 may also be suspended in application of Article 15.

7. RESERVATIONS (ARTICLE 64)

International law recognizes that a State, in accepting a treaty, may in certain circumstances attach a reservation, that is, make its acceptance subject to some new term which limits or varies the application of the treaty to that State.[1]

Article 64(1) of the Convention provides that:

Any State may, when signing this Convention or when depositing its instrument of ratification, make a reservation in respect of any particular provision of the Convention to the extent that any law then in force in its territory is not in conformity with the provision. Reservations of a general character shall not be permitted under this Article.

Reservations must therefore relate to a particular provision of the Convention and to a particular law in force at the time; in addition, according to paragraph (2), they must contain a brief statement of the law concerned. Relatively few reservations have been made to the Convention and Protocols, and these are mainly very limited in scope.[2] Any far-reaching reservation would in any event be illegal as being incompatible with the object and purpose of the Treaty.[3]

Applications which must be excluded because of a reservation made by the respondent Government have been regarded by the Commission as 'incompatible with the provisions of the Convention' and rejected as inadmissible under Article 27(2). This seems incorrect; they should be regarded as outside the Commis-

[1] See Article 19 et seq. of the Vienna Convention on the Law of Treaties.

[2] See Collected Texts, 9th edn., section 6. It is curious that at least one purported reservation does not comply with the requirement of Article 64(2) that it should contain a brief statement of the law concerned.

[3] Article 19 of the Vienna Convention; cf. Reservations to the Convention on Genocide, [1951] I.C.J. Reports, p. 15.

sion's competence *ratione materiae*.[1] A reservation must be interpreted in the language in which it is made, not in its translation into one of the languages, English or French, of the authentic texts of the Convention.[2]

The Commission has given a rather extensive interpretation of those reservations which have been made. Thus it has held that a reservation may serve to exclude, not only measures expressly covered by the reservation, but also other related measures.[3] It may extend to exclude a new law which replaces the law in force at the time of the reservation, provided that the new law does not have the effect of enlarging the scope of the reservation.[4] It may extend to legislative and administrative measures to implement the purpose for which the reservation was made.[5] It may even extend to other provisions of the Convention than those expressly mentioned in the reservation, if it is clearly intended to cover the entire operation of domestic law in the field concerned.[6]

An important reservation relates to the Austrian State Treaty of 1955, the Treaty for the Restoration of an Independent and Democratic Austria, which constitutes Austria's peace treaty with the Western Powers and the Soviet Union. The Austrian reservation, made when Austria ratified the Convention and First Protocol in 1958, provides that Article 1 of the First Protocol, which relates to property rights, should not affect Part IV of the Treaty, 'Claims arising out of the War' and Part V, 'Property, Rights and Interests'. A claim for compensation concerned, not the State Treaty itself, but a law of 1958, not mentioned in the reservation, passed in execution of Part IV of the Treaty. The Commission considered that, in making its reservation, Austria must necessarily have intended to exclude from the scope of the First Protocol everything forming the subject-matter of Parts IV and V of the State Treaty; and that the reservation must be interpreted as intended to cover all legislative and administrative measures directly related to this subject-matter.[7]

---

[1] See below, p. 224.
[2] 1047/61, *Yearbook* 4, 356; 1452/62, *Yearbook* 6, 268; 2432/65, *Collection of Decisions* 22, 124.
[3] 2432/65, *Collection of Decisions* 22, 124.
[4] Ibid.; cf. 3923/69, *Collection of Decisions* 37, 10.
[5] 2765/66, *Yearbook* 10, 412 at 418.
[6] 3923/69, *Collection of Decisions* 37, 10; 4002/69, *Yearbook* 14, 178.
[7] Ibid.

Other reservations, made by the Federal Republic of Germany,[1] France,[2] Norway,[3] and Sweden[4] (this last one of many reservations and declarations relating to Article 2 of the First Protocol[5]), and certain proposed reservations of Switzerland,[6] have been considered above.

It is very doubtful whether reservations may be made to declarations under Article 25, accepting the competence of the Commission to receive applications by individuals, or under Article 46, recognizing the compulsory jurisdiction of the Court. Article 46(1), providing for declarations recognizing the Court's jurisdiction 'in all matters', seems to exclude the possibility of a partial recognition, although Article 46(2) provides that a declaration may be made on condition of reciprocity or for a limited period. Further, Article 64 seems to envisage only reservations of a substantive character, relating to a specific law in force at the time of signature or ratification; and a resevation is not permissible where a treaty provides for only specified reservations which do not include the reservation in question.[7] The Commission has nevertheless accepted that declarations under Article 25 may be subject to the proviso that they have no retroactive effect.[8]

Quite apart from this point, it would seem that the Commission has departed from the evident intention of Article 64. That Article refers expressly to laws in force at the time of signature or ratification, and clearly envisages that all subsequent legislation will be in conformity with the Convention. The Commission appears to have gone too far in accepting that a later law in the same field might be brought within the scope of a reservation.

Indeed, although there is no legal obligation in this respect, and no express provision for withdrawal of a reservation, it would be in accordance with the spirit of the Convention, and with its object and purpose, to envisage that laws which necessitated reservations would progressively be amended or repealed to ensure that the Contracting States complied without reservation with all the the Convention's provisions.[9]

---

[1] p. 125.   [2] pp. 90, 209.   [3] p. 144.
[4] p. 174.   [5] See Collected Texts, 9th edn., section 6.   [6] pp. 144, 179.
[7] Article 19 of the Vienna Convention on the Law of Treaties.
[8] See below, p. 231.
[9] Cf. the Norwegian withdrawal of a reservation, above, p. 144.

PART IV REMEDIES

1. REMEDIES BEFORE NATIONAL AUTHORITIES (ARTICLE 13)

Article 13 provides that: 'Everyone whose rights and freedoms as set forth in this Convention are violated shall have an effective remedy before a national authority notwithstanding that the violation has been committed by persons acting in an official capacity.'

It is clear, if only from its place in the Convention, that Article 13 is one of the rights guaranteed by the States parties to the Convention, an alleged violation of which may itself be the subject of an application to the Commission under Article 25.

Nevertheless, there is a certain anomaly in the right to a remedy itself being classed among the rights guaranteed, and this has led to difficulties, not yet resolved, in deciding when the right arises. Should complaints under Article 13 be examined by the Commission at the stage of admissibility, or only on the merits? Or does Article 13 presuppose that a violation of the Convention has already been established by the Court or the Committee of Ministers? This last interpretation is supported, in particular, by the French text of Article 13 (*dont les droits et libertés reconnus dans la présente Convention ont été violés*), and also by certain decisions of the Commission.[1] It would also accord with the interpretation of Article 5(5) adopted by the Court.[2] But on further examination, this interpretation is untenable. It would deprive Article 13 of all effect, for whenever a violation of the Convention has been established, there has necessarily been, having regard to Article 26, a breach of Article 13. The absence of an effective remedy before a national authority is a condition of the admissibility of an application. For obvious practical reasons, too, complaints under Article 13 should be examined on the merits with the rest of the case.

It would seem, therefore, that once a complaint is declared admissible, the Commission should deal with allegations under

---

[1] See, e.g. 1167/61, *Yearbook* 6, 204 at 220.
[2] See above, p. 75.

Article 13 in the same way as the other Articles guaranteeing substantive rights, in the course of its examination of the merits of the case. This was the course in fact adopted by the Commission in the Greek Case. It stated its opinion, in its Report, that the remedies called for by Article 13 had not been fully effective in Greece since 21 April 1967. It found that the courts were not independent, and that in administrative inquiries, in particular into complaints of torture and ill-treatment, the most elementary principles had been disregarded.[1]

Thus, although the absence of a remedy before the national authorities will normally be a matter subsidiary to the principal complaint, it is appropriate that it should be examined separately where it is alleged that, as a general feature of the national law, there is no effective remedy. For example, it may be suggested that if an applicant complains of an invasion of privacy, and if domestic law affords no general remedy in such cases, the complaint should be examined under Article 13 as well as under Article 8.

On the other hand, where the principal complaint is itself the absence of an appropriate remedy under another provision of the Convention, it is unnecessary to consider Article 13. Thus, in the Vagrancy cases,[2] where the Court found that the applicants did not have the necessary judicial guarantees under Article 5(4) to challenge the lawfulness of their detention, the Court did not consider that it had to examine separately the issue under Article 13.[3]

The last words of Article 13, 'notwithstanding that the violation has been committed by persons acting in an official capacity', show that no defence of State privilege or immunity from suit may be allowed. It has been argued that they also show that the scope of the Convention is not limited to persons exercising public authority.[4]

---

[1] *Yearbook* 12, The Greek Case, p. 174.
[2] See above, p. 55.
[3] Para. 95.
[4] See above, p. 12.

II PROCEEDINGS BEFORE THE COMMISSION
Composition of the Commission

The European Commission of Human Rights[1] consists of a number of members equal to that of the Contracting Parties (Article 20), (at present, sixteen) elected for a period of six years (Article 22(1)) by the Committee of Ministers of the Council of Europe[2] from a list of names drawn up in the Consultative Assembly.[3] When a vacancy occurs in respect of a given State, the group of parliamentarians from that State puts forward three candidates, of whom at least two must be its nationals (Article 21). No qualifications for membership of the Commission are laid down in the Convention, which provides only that members shall sit in their individual capacity (Article 23). In practice, the election of Government officials has generally not been regarded as appropriate and most members of the Commission, although nationals of the State in respect of which they were elected, hold independent judicial or academic legal appointments in their own countries.[4] The work of the Commission is part-time; it holds six regular sessions a year in Strasbourg, with occasional special sessions there or elsewhere as necessary; under its Rules of Procedure certain tasks may be performed by delegates or *rapporteurs* (Rules 45 and 51). The Commission, which held its first session in July 1955, deals with about 500 applications a year, compared with about 100 in the first years of the Convention.

[1] For an outline of the functions of the Commission, see above, p. 7. Its tasks are considered in more detail below, p. 218. See further Monconduit, *La Commission européenne des droits de l'homme*, Leyden, 1965.

[2] See above, p. 2.

[3] See above, p. 2.

[4] It has been the practice when a vacancy occurs for the President of the Consultative Assembly to write to the chairman of the national delegation concerned in the following terms:

'National delegations of course have entire freedom of choice when preparing their lists of candidates. In the view of the Bureau of the Assembly, however, it is desirable when the choice comes to be made that the following qualities—essential for any member of the Commission of Human Rights who is to fulfil his duty—be taken into consideration:
(a) high moral integrity;
(b) recognised competence in matters connected with human rights;
(c) substantial legal or judicial experience.

The Bureau has further asked me to call your attention to the difficulties in which a member of the Commission might find himself if he were at the same time a member of a national public service, and to the doubts which might arise in such circumstances as to the impartiality of the Commission.'

Because of the part-time character of the Commission and its heavy case-load, the Commission's secretariat has an important role. The secretariat is provided by the Secretary General of the Council of Europe[1] and its members are qualified lawyers from the Member States, engaged as full-time officials of the Council, with a supporting administrative and clerical staff. Its main functions are to conduct correspondence with applicants and governments, to organize the Commission's sessions, to prepare cases for examination, to advise the Commission on questions of national law and the law of the Convention, and to assist members of the Commission in the drafting of its decisions and reports. The practice has been for a case to be assigned, as it comes in, to a member of the secretariat, who will prepare the case for the Commission, discuss it with the *rapporteur*,[2] and attend sessions of the Commission whenever the case is being examined. In a large measure the quality of the Commission's work, and its effectiveness, depend on the quality of its secretariat.

I
Examination of admissibility

A. Procedure

Examination of the admissibility of applications is one of the principal tasks of the Commission. It is clear from the preparatory work of the Convention that the role of the Commission was envisaged as a screen or filter to sift the expected mass of individual applications, and indeed it is obvious that such an 'organe de filtrage' was necessary in a system which was to be open to the world at large, without formality or expense.

It follows that the stage of admissibility is crucial in the working of the Convention. Quite apart from the interpretation of the rules concerning the conditions of admissibility, a simple and flexible procedure[3] must be devised so that the Commission is not sub-

---

[1] Article 37. See also Rules 11–14 of the Commission's Rules of Procedure.

[2] See below, p. 220.

[3] Thus the Commission has stated that, as an international judicial organ, it 'is not bound to treat questions of form with the same degree of strictness as might be the case in municipal law': Lawless case, *Yearbook* 2, 308 at 326, citing Mavrommatis Palestine Concessions Case, Permanent Court of International Justice, 1924, Series A, No. 2, page 34; Belgian Linguistic Case, *Yearbook* 7, 140 at 154–6.

merged by the number of applications, while at the same time it can be ready to take the necessary action on the isolated complaint, not immediately distinguishable from many others, which requires thorough investigation.[1] The following brief account of the procedure on admissibility must be read with these considerations in mind.[2]

Procedure before the Commission in the examination of admissibility is primarily in writing. Article 25(1), which refers to petitions addressed to the Secretary General of the Council of Europe, clearly envisages that the application which institutes proceedings before the Commission should be made in writing. Most applications originate in a letter to the Commission's Secretary[3] setting out the complaint, and there are no special requirements as to form.

Applications may be made either by the applicant in person, or by a lawyer acting under a power of attorney. An applicant may be assisted or represented by a barrister, solicitor, professor of law, or any other lawyer approved by the Commission.[4] While the official languages of the Commission are English and French, applicants are regularly allowed to use certain other languages.[5]

An application should state the applicant's name and that of the respondent government, the object of the claim, as far as possible the provision of the Convention alleged to have been violated, and a statement of the facts and arguments on which the applicant relies.[6] In particular, the application should include information showing that it satisfies the conditions laid down in Article 26 regarding exhaustion of domestic remedies and observance of the six months rule.[7] To facilitate the applicant's task, he is normally sent an application form by the secretariat of the Commission, but he may submit other documents instead or in addition.

[1] Compare in this respect the use by the Commission of the 'global formula', below, p. 224, and the justification for the Commission's power to reject an application as being 'an abuse of the right of petition', below, p. 247.

[2] See further 'Case-Law Topics', No. 3, *Bringing an Application before the European Commission of Human Rights*, Strasbourg, 1972.

[3] The Secretary is the channel for all communications concerning the Commission: Rule 12(b) of the Commission's Rules of Procedure. On the role of the secretariat, see above, p. 218.

[4] Rule 36(2) of the Commission's Rules of Procedure.

[5] Rules 35(1) and 37. In practice Dutch, German, Italian and the Scandinavian languages are also accepted.

[6] Rule 41(1).   [7] Rule 41(2).

Before the Commission's Rules of Procedure were amended in 1973, individual applications were first referred to a group of three members for a preliminary examination of admissibility, and the group's report was then submitted to the Commission.

If the group of three members unanimously reported that the application appeared to be admissible, it was communicated directly to the respondent government for written observations on admissibility. In any other case, the Commission, taking account of the group's report, could either itself communicate the application or declare it inadmissible without communicating it; in fact, a substantial majority of individual applications was never referred to the respondent government.[1]

When an application was referred to the government, its observations were sent to the applicant for his reply. There would then be a further examination by a group of three before the Commission decided on admissibility.

'Group of three' procedure was replaced in 1973 by a more flexible *rapporteur* system. Under this system, a report on the admissibility of an application is submitted by a single member acting as *rapporteur*.[2] He may request relevant information on matters connected with the application, from the applicant or the government, and sends any information so obtained from the government to the applicant for comments.[3] In any event the application is examined by the plenary Commission.

The Commission, if it does not decide at that stage that the application is inadmissible, may either itself request further information from the applicant or the government, or formally ask the government for its written observations on admissibility.[4]

Before deciding upon the admissibility of the application the Commission may invite the parties to submit further observations, either in writing or at an oral hearing.[5] With a view to shortening the proceedings, the Commission's recent practice shows a tendency to avoid an oral hearing at the stage of admissibility, but a

---

[1] For statistics, see Yearbooks and Stocktaking note. In 1969, 439 applications were filed; 327 applications were declared inadmissible (or struck off the list) without being communicated to the respondent government. In 1970 the figures were 379 and 395 respectively; the latter figure evidently includes applications introduced before 1970. In 1971 the respective figures were 433 and 358. See *Yearbook* 14, 782.

[2] Rule 45(1). [3] Rule 45(2).
[4] Rule 46. [5] Rule 46(2) *in fine*.

case will not be declared admissible without a hearing if the respondent government objects.

Article 33 of the Convention provides that the Commission should meet *in camera*. Consequently, no information relating to proceedings before the Commission may be made available to the public or the Press.[1] The secrecy of the proceedings has been criticized but may in some cases protect both the applicant and the respondent government from harmful publicity. Further, secrecy may facilitate a subsequent friendly settlement, since a government's incentive to settle a case might be reduced by publicity.[2] However, the Commission's more important decisions on admissibility, and its reports, are generally published, and press communiqués on cases of public interest are released from time to time. This does not entitle the parties to the proceedings to disclose further information. Publicity by the applicant might in some circumstances be regarded by the Commission as constituting an abuse of the right of petition.[3]

The decision of the Commission on the admissibility of an application is normally final and there is no possibility of appeal. However, if an application is declared admissible, it is open to the Commission, under Article 29, subsequently to reject the application if it finds, in the course of its examination of the merits, that one of the grounds of inadmissibility has been established. Such a decision can only be taken unanimously. This procedure was used in the Raupp case, where an application was rejected, after having been declared admissible, on the ground of abuse of the right of petition.[4] Article 29 gives the Commission the power to examine at any stage of the proceedings on the merits, *ex officio* and irrespective of any pleas by the parties, the question whether or not one of the grounds provided for in Article 27 has been established.[5]

If the application is referred to the Court, it is possible that the Court may take a different view on the question of admissibility.[6]

If, on the other hand, the application is declared inadmissible by the Commission, the applicant has no means of challenging this decision. He may, however, submit a new application if it

---

[1] 4835/71, *Collection of Decisions* 40, 34.
[2] See below, p. 255.   [3] See below, p. 246.
[4] 5207/71, *Collection of Decisions* 42, 85.
[5] 5100/71, 5354/72, 5370/72, *Collection of Decisions* 44, 9.
[6] See below, p. 263.

contains any relevant new information. If it contains no such new information, but is substantially the same as the previous application, it will be inadmissible on that ground.[1]

There are no fees or charges for applications to the Commission, the expenses of the Commission and the Court being met, under Article 58 of the Convention, by the Council of Europe. Under the Addendum to the Rules of Procedure, the Commission may grant an applicant free legal aid at any stage of the proceedings after the respondent government's observations on admissibility have been received. The applicant must submit a certified declaration of means, showing that he has not sufficient means to meet his costs. Legal aid may be granted to cover the applicant's lawyer's fees, on a scale fixed by the Commission's Secretary, and also other necessary expenses.

The procedure for inter-State cases is broadly similar to that outlined above. However, under Rule 44, any inter-State case is automatically communicated at once to the respondent government for its observations on admissibility.

The Commission has no power under the Convention to order interim or interlocutory measures to safeguard the position of the parties pending a final decision. However, in urgent cases—for example, where there is a possibility of immediate expulsion which might raise an issue under Article 3—the Commission may informally notify the respondent government as soon as the application is introduced, and may request the government not to take steps which might prejudice the outcome of the case.[2]

Freedom to correspond with the Commission, even in the case of persons in detention whose correspondence is normally subject to control, is protected by Article 25(1) of the Convention and by the European Agreement relating to persons participating in proceedings of the European Commission and Court of Human Rights.[3]

B. Conditions of admissibility

The conditions of admissibility of an application to the Commission are governed by Articles 26 and 27 of the Convention.

[1] See below, p. 249.
[2] See above, p. 32, and cf. Second Greek Case, p. 232. See Eissen, Les mesures provisoires dans la Convention européenne des Droits de l'Homme, *Revue des droits de l'homme* (1969), p. 252.
[3] See above, p. 142.

The most important grounds in practice for rejection of individual applications are three. First, as being incompatible with the provisions of the Convention. Second, for non-exhaustion of domestic remedies or non-observance of the six months rule under Article 26. Third, as being manifestly ill-founded, which may involve a finding on the merits. These grounds will be considered separately below.

First, however, something must be said of the relation between admissibility and the question of the Commission's competence; and certain general features of the Commission's practice in taking decisions on admissibility may be mentioned.

Logically, a distinction should be drawn between applications which are outside the competence of the Commission, for example by reason of the time factor (*ratione temporis*), and applications which are within the Commission's competence but inadmissible, for example as being manifestly ill-founded.[1] The distinction between competence and admissibility is not preserved in the Convention itself, and cannot be pressed too far. For example, if an applicant invokes a right not guaranteed by the Convention, it may be difficult to say whether the application is outside the Commission's competence, or whether it is incompatible with the provisions of the Convention *ratione materiae* and so inadmissible under Article 27(2). The normal practice of the Commission is to treat almost all applications outside its competence *ratione materiae* as being incompatible, and to reject them under Article 27(2). It has treated such questions of competence, in other words, as going to admissibility. This approach is justifiable on the view that the grounds on which the Commission may reject an application are listed exhaustively in Article 27.

In inter-State cases, however, the distinction between competence and admissibility retains its importance. Such an application cannot be rejected as incompatible under Article 27(2), which applies only to individual applications. It can be rejected as inadmissible only under Article 26, for non-exhaustion of domestic remedies or for non-observance of the six months rule. Nevertheless it is clear that such an application might be outside the

---

[1] See Chrysostomides, 'Competence' and 'Incompatibility' in the Jurisprudence of the European Commission of Human Rights, Zeitschrift für ausländisches öffentliches Recht und Völkerrecht, 1973, 449.

competence of the Commission, and would then have to be rejected on that ground.

Again, an application which falls under a reservation[1] by the respondent government is outside the Commission's competence *ratione materiae*. It is incorrect to regard it, as the Commission has done,[2] as incompatible with the provisions of the Convention.

It should be possible, in principle, to establish a certain sequence of priority in considering the various conditions of admissibility.[3] Sometimes a complaint may be capable of being rejected on alternative grounds. Thus, a rejection as manifestly ill-founded, which may involve a finding on the merits, should normally be among the last of the grounds considered.

Of the three most important grounds in practice, the question of compatibility should be examined first. Next, if the application does fall within the Convention, the question of exhaustion of remedies, and the six months rule, should be examined. Finally it must be considered whether the application is manifestly ill-founded. The Commission, however, has often been guided by practical considerations in selecting the appropriate ground.[4]

Another example of this practical approach is the so-called 'global formula'. Frequently an application will contain a number of different complaints, which may be inadmissible on different grounds. Instead of examining the applicant's complaints separately, and rejecting them individually for different reasons, the Commission will often, where it considers such a detailed examination unwarranted by the nature of the case, instead reject it as being 'as a whole' manifestly ill-founded.

On the other hand, where an application is inadmissible on technical grounds, the Commission may nevertheless pronounce *obiter* on the substance of the case in its decision on admissibility.[5] Similarly, where there is a procedural defect in bringing an application, the Commission may take its decision on the assumption that the defect had been remedied.[6] Generally, it would be

---

[1] See above, p. 235.

[2] See, e.g. 473/59, *Yearbook* 2, 400 at 406; 1452/62, *Yearbook* 6, 268 at 276.

[3] See Khol, *Zwischen Staat und Weltstaat*, Vienna, 1969, 554–5.

[4] So, too, the International Court of Justice; cf. De Visscher, *Aspects récents du droit procédural de la Cour International de Justice*, Paris, 1966.

[5] 1718/62, *Yearbook* 8, 168.

[6] 3798/68, *Yearbook* 12, 306 at 318.

contrary to the spirit of the Convention to rely too much on technicalities in matters of procedure.[1]

Finally, it is the duty of the Commission to examine an application under any Article of the Convention which may be in issue, even if it has not been invoked by the applicant. Although the Commission can only act when it has been seised of an application, it must, when once seised, examine that application, not only in relation to any rights that may have been invoked by the applicant, but also *ex officio* in relation to any rights which, on the facts and submissions before it, may appear to have been infringed. The Commission must also examine if necessary *ex officio* the different conditions of admissibility, unless this requirement is waived by the respondent government.[2] It may also happen that the respondent government states that it has no objection to an application being declared admissible, either because it regards the decision as inevitable, or because it wants the case to be examined on the merits.[3]

As on questions of procedure, the Commission's approach to the rules of admissibility has been pragmatic. Because of the importance of the admissibility stage in the system of the Convention, it has developed a very substantial body of law on the subject. It has recognized as a general principle that rules restricting its competence should themselves be interpreted restrictively;[4] but the following sections may suggest that it has not always applied that principle.

COMPETENCE OF THE COMMISSION

The competence of the Commission must be considered on a number of planes: in respect of the person by whom, and against whom, the application is brought (competence *ratione personae*), in respect of the time and place of the alleged violation (competence *ratione temporis* and *ratione loci*), and in respect of the subject-matter of the complaint (competence *ratione materiae*).

COMPETENCE 'RATIONE PERSONAE'

The questions to be considered under this head are against whom, and by whom, an application may be brought.

It is clear from Articles 24 and 25 that an application may be

---

[1] Cf. p. 218 n. 3.   [2] See below, p. 236.   [3] See above, pp. 159 and 175.
[4] See, e.g. 214/56, *De Becker* v. *Belgium*, *Yearbook* 2, 214 at 244–6.

brought only against a State which has ratified the Convention, and, in the case of Article 25, which has recognized this competence of the Commission. A further condition, as will be seen below, is that the State must in some way be responsible for the alleged breach. Otherwise the application, even though brought against a State which has fulfilled the above conditions, will be rejected as being outside the Commission's competence *ratione personae*.

It does not follow, however, that an application cannot be brought against such a State, even in respect of violations committed by a private individual. The State may be indirectly liable in some way for the acts of a private individual;[1] or it may be separately liable, for example under Article 13, for failing to provide an effective remedy.[2]

Moreover, no limitation on the Commission's competence which can be derived from Article 25 could possibly restrict the obligation of the States parties under Article 1 to secure the rights and freedoms concerned to everyone within their jurisdiction. The terms of Article 1 are sufficiently wide to impose the duty on that State not merely to respect those rights itself, but to secure them against all infringements,[3] even though such infringements cannot be invoked before the Commission.

On the other hand, there are necessarily certain limits beyond which responsibility can no longer be attributed to a State. For example, the United Kingdom is not responsible for decisions of the Judicial Committee of the Privy Council, in proceedings relating to appeals from independent Commonwealth countries. For, although the Judicial Committee is composed mainly of British judges, sits in London, and is financed by the United Kingdom Government, it is to be regarded, in hearing such appeals, as part of the judicial system of the State from which they come. Hence complaints concerning these proceedings will be outside the Commission's competence *ratione personae* in so far as they are directed against the United Kingdom.[4]

Similarly, the Federal Republic of Germany could not be responsible for decisions taken by the Supreme Restitution Court set up in Germany after the war.[5] Still less could it be

---

[1] See above, p. 11.   [2] See above, p. 215.
[3] See above, p. 9.
[4] 3813/68, *Yearbook* 13, 586 at 598–600.
[5] 235/56, *Yearbook* 2, 256 at 288–304; cf. 182/56, *Yearbook* 1, 167.

responsible for the decisions of courts in the German Democratic Republic.[1]

It is more difficult to determine the extent to which a State may be liable for an infringement by a private individual. This may, as stated in Part I,[2] depend on an examination of the individual Articles of the Convention.

It is clear that the State is directly liable, in an application brought under Article 25, for the acts of the legislative, executive and judiciary. It is less clear how far it is liable for the acts of other public bodies, for example, public corporations with a certain measure of independence. The Commission has left open the question whether the United Kingdom Government is responsible for the British Broadcasting Corporation.[3]

A similar question arose where an applicant complained, under Article 11 of the Convention, of interference with his duties as a shop steward at a Board established in Ireland by statute but largely independent of the State in its operations. Having found that the acts alleged by the applicant fell within the domain of day-to-day administration for which the Government was not directly responsible, the Commission nevertheless went on to consider, first whether the domestic law protected the right in question, and secondly whether there was an adequate remedy for enforcing the law's protection in this respect.[4] Without referring explicitly to Articles 1 and 13 of the Convention, the Commission was thus of the opinion that, even where the acts complained of are acts for which the State is not directly responsible, its responsibility may be involved in these respects.

This decision suggests that, where a government is not directly responsible for an infringement of the rights guaranteed under Section I, it may none the less be liable for a violation of Article 1 or of Article 13, if that right is not secured by law, or if the victim cannot obtain a remedy for the infringement.

The second question to be considered under this head is the question of standing: who may bring an application to the Commission under Article 25? Article 24 presents no problem in this respect; an application may be brought under Article 24 by any

---

[1] 448/59, *Yearbook* 3, 254 at 264.
[2] See above, p. 11.
[3] 3059/67, *Collection of Decisions* 28, 89; 4515/70, *Yearbook* 14, 538 at 544.
[4] 4125/69, *Yearbook* 14, 198.

State, and only by a State, which has ratified the Convention. It may have done so only subsequently to the events which are the subject of the application.[1]

Under Article 25, the Commission may receive applications 'from any person, non-governmental organization or group of individuals claiming to be the victim of a violation by one of the High Contracting Parties of the rights set forth in this Convention, provided that the High Contracting Party against which the complaint has been lodged has declared that it recognizes the competence of the Commission to receive such petitions'. The term 'person' (*personne physique* in the French text) includes only natural persons but an application may be brought also by any corporate or unincorporated body.[2] Thus applications have been brought by companies,[3] trade unions,[4] churches,[5] political parties,[6] and numerous other types of body. Article 25 should be understood as excluding from the right of petition only governmental bodies, whose rights are protected, if only against infringement by other States, under Article 24. A corporate body has some but not all of the rights of individuals: thus it has the right to a fair trial under Article 6,[7] and is expressly granted property rights under Article 1 of the First Protocol, but it does not have the right to education under Article 2.[8] Non-governmental organizations, and groups of individuals, may be restricted both in the extent of their capacity to introduce an application, and in their enjoyment of the substantive rights,[9] but these limitations can be overcome if the applications are introduced directly by the individuals concerned.

There are, of course, no restrictions on the ground of residence, nationality, or any other status. An applicant may be a minor or under some other legal incapacity and is entitled to bring his case in person.[10] Only if the individual applicant does

[1] See above, p. 13.

[2] See Golsong, La Convention européenne des Droits de l'Homme et les Personnes morales, in Les droits de l'homme et les personnes morales, Brussels, 1970.

[3] See above, p. 103. [4] See above, pp. 159, 160.

[5] See above, p. 148. [6] See above, p. 210.

[7] 2076/63, *Collection of Decisions* 23, 74; 3147/67, *Collection of Decisions* 27, 119.

[8] See above, p. 176.

[9] See the submissions of the United Kingdom Government in the First Northern Irish cases, *Yearbook* 13, 340 at 390 ff.

[10] 1527/62, *Yearbook* 5, 238 at 246.

not claim to be a victim, as for example where he complains generally of certain legislation,[1] or where he simply alleges that a fellow-prisoner has been ill-treated,[2] will the application be outside the Commission's competence *ratione personae*. If he does claim to be a victim, that claim is sufficient to give him standing; it is irrelevant whether he is a victim in fact. If he is not a victim in fact, his application may be manifestly ill-founded, but will not be outside the Commission's competence *ratione personae*. Nevertheless, it is convenient to consider here the grounds on which a person may be regarded as a victim in fact.

If the applicant claims to be a victim, the Commission will examine the application on that basis and will consider, if necessary, whether the applicant may indirectly be a victim of the alleged violation. Thus the Commission has accepted that a woman might indirectly be a victim where her complaint related to the conviction and sentence of her son, a minor;[3] and that a woman might similarly be a victim whose husband had been detained in a mental institution.[4] It was therefore competent to examine their applications, but only to the extent that the matters complained of might have affected their own rights under the Convention.

In some cases, a moral interest may suffice. Where an applicant complained that the education of his niece and nephew, with which he had been entrusted, was being conducted contrary to his wishes with the result of estranging them from their religion, the Commission raised, without answering, the question

whether the applicant, although not a direct victim of the alleged violation of the right of his niece and nephew to religious freedom, can nevertheless be considered in the circumstances of the case as having such moral interest in their religious education and as being so affected, albeit indirectly, by the alleged violation as to be considered a victim within the meaning of Article 25.[5]

Again, where an applicant who complained of a radio and television monopoly in Sweden did not allege that he himself or any group to which he belonged wished to establish an independent

---

[1] See above, p. 21.
[2] 2300/64, *Collection of Decisions* 22, 73.
[3] 4007/69, unpublished: see 'Case-Law Topics', No. 3, p. 5.
[4] 4185/69, *Collection of Decisions* 35, 140.
[5] 3110/67, *Yearbook* 11, 494 at 518 f.

broadcasting or television enterprise, but claimed that as a member of the general public he was affected in his rights and freedoms guaranteed under Article 10, the Commission raised, without pursuing, the question whether the applicant, because of this alleged general impact on all citizens, could claim to be a victim as required by Article 25.[1]

Where the Commission finds that the applicant, though claiming to be a victim, could not be so described in fact, the application, as mentioned above, is not outside its competence but will be manifestly ill-founded on that ground. The *claim* to be a victim goes to the question of standing; *being* a victim goes to the merits. But, if the applicant is manifestly not a victim of the alleged violation, his application will be inadmissible as manifestly ill-founded.

The principle that only a victim may bring an application is plainly reasonable. Even within domestic systems, strict rules of standing have been found necessary in both judicial and extra-judicial systems of review of administrative action. They must be reflected on the international plane. They are all the more justified under the European Convention which makes available an *actio popularis* by a State under Article 24.

COMPETENCE 'RATIONE TEMPORIS'

The scope of the Convention *ratione temporis* has been considered above.[2] In accordance with a generally recognized principle of international law, the Convention has no retroactive effect. A different question is that of the competence of the Commission *ratione temporis*.

In principle, the acceptance of judicial settlement, under international law, covers disputes which are referred to the judicial body after it has been established, even if they relate to matters prior to its establishment. In a similar context, the Permanent Court of International Justice stated that 'The reservation made in many arbitration treaties regarding disputes arising out of events previous to the conclusion of the treaty seems to prove the necessity for an explicit limitation of jurisdiction.'[3] Thus, in principle, declarations accepting the Commission's competence are retroactive, unlike the Convention itself, although they cannot,

---

[1] 3071/67, *Collection of Decisions* 26, 71.   [2] p. 12.

[3] Mavrommatis Palestine Concessions Case, cited in 788/60, *Yearbook* 4, 116 at 136.

of course, relate back to a date prior to the entry into force of the Convention in respect of the State concerned.[1]

However, such a declaration may be expressed in terms which are intended to exclude any such retroactive effect. This was the case with the first United Kingdom declaration under Article 25, made on 14 January 1966, which purported to take effect only 'in relation to any act or decision occurring or any facts or events arising' after 13 January 1966.[2] Italy's initial declaration in 1973 was to the same effect. For reasons which have been stated above, it is doubtful whether Article 25 admits of reservations at all.[3] But the Commission has accepted that the United Kingdom declaration has no retroactive effect, and that applications against the United Kingdom are outside its competence in so far as they relate to the period before the date of the initial declaration.[4]

The matter is not of great practical importance. Where the complaint concerns a single event or decision, it will normally in any event quickly become time-barred by the rule that an application must be brought within six months from the final domestic decision.[5] On the other hand, where the applicant complains of a continuing situation,[6] only the date of the application is material. Thus, in the De Becker case,[7] the judgment under which the applicant forfeited his rights was given before the Convention entered into force in respect of Belgium. But the applicant was complaining not of the judgment as such, but of the forfeiture of his rights which was the automatic and permanent consequence of the judgment. Hence there was a continuing situation, the result of legislation still in force, giving rise to an issue under the Convention, and the Commission was competent *ratione temporis*.

In the event of a State denouncing the Convention, the denunciation takes effect, in accordance with Article 65(1), after six months. Article 65(2) provides that: 'Such a denunciation shall not have the effect of releasing the High Contracting Party concerned from its obligations under this Convention in respect of any act which, being capable of constituting a violation of such obligations, may have been performed by it before the date at

---

[1] See above, p. 12. [2] *Yearbook* 9, 8. [3] p. 214.
[4] See, e.g. 4288/69, *Yearbook* 10, 892 at 894.
[5] See below, p. 241. [6] See below, p. 243.
[7] See above, p. 151. Cf. 2717/66, *Yearbook* 13, 200 at 234–6.

which the denunciation became effective.' If an application is introduced after the date of denunciation, but before the date on which it takes effect, the Commission remains competent *ratione temporis* to deal with it. After Greece had given notice of its denunciation of the Convention, but before the six months' period had expired, the Danish, Norwegian, and Swedish Governments brought a further application against Greece. It concerned the trial of thirty-four persons, accused of subversive activities, which was then taking place before a court martial in Athens and in which the public prosecutor had requested the death penalty for one of the accused. The applicant Governments alleged violations of Article 3 and Article 6. The Commission, rejecting the respondent Government's submissions in this respect, held that it was and remained competent to deal with the application.[1] Owing to the exceptional circumstances, however, it subsequently decided that it could not proceed with the case.[2] No death sentence was in fact pronounced. The case illustrates graphically the possibilities, and also the limitations, of the protection of human rights on the international plane.[3]

COMPETENCE 'RATIONE LOCI'

As stated above,[4] the extension of the Convention, by the terms of Article 1, to all persons within the jurisdiction of the Contracting States, is subject to the 'colonial' clause, Article 63. The Convention does not extend to dependent territories unless the State concerned has made a declaration under Article 63(1).

Further, the acceptance of the Commission's competence to receive individual applications is subject to the making of a declaration under Article 63(4). Such declarations have been made by the Netherlands, in respect of Surinam, and by the United Kingdom in respect of a number of overseas territories,[5] although there appear to have been few, if any, applications from any of these territories.

In the absence of such declarations, a complaint against a State in respect of acts in the dependent territories will be outside the Commission's competence *ratione loci*. This was held to be

---

[1] 4448/70, *Yearbook* 13, 108 at 120.
[2] See Stock-taking note, B(73)47, 9.
[3] See below, p. 273.   [4] p. 14.
[5] See *Collected Texts*, 9th edn., 602-3.

the case, for example, in an application concerning the former Belgian Congo. The applicants contended that, at the material time, the Belgian Congo formed an integral part of the national territory, and that the Convention, including the Belgian declaration under Article 25, was therefore in force there without the need for declarations under Article 63 or the corresponding Article 4 of the First Protocol. The Commission considered, however, that whatever the exact status of the Belgian Congo, it clearly came within the category of territories referred to in Article 63.[1]

The correct interpretation of Article 63 would seem to be that it provides for the possibility of extending the Convention to *self-governing* territories for whose international relations the Contracting States are responsible. Since there otherwise is no territorial limitation on the scope of the Convention,[2] it should be regarded as extending automatically, despite Article 63, to all *non*-self-governing territories. But its extension to self-governing territories must be dependent on a separate declaration which could be withdrawn, since such extension would be dependent on the consent of the internal government of the territory concerned.

COMPETENCE 'RATIONE MATERIAE'

A distinction is necessary between inter-State applications under Article 24, and individual applications under Article 25.

Any Contracting Party may refer to the Commission, under Article 24, 'any alleged breach of the provisions of the Convention' by another Contracting Party. It may be a violation of the rights set out in Section I of the Convention. In that event it does not matter whether the victim is a national of the applicant State, or indeed whether there is a victim at all. It would be sufficient that a law of the respondent government was inconsistent with the Convention.

However, the wording of Article 24 seems to go further than this; it may be possible for an applicant State to refer to the Commission infringements of subsequent Sections of the Convention. It could thus refer to the Commission, for example, an interference with the right of petition, under Article 25(1), or a refusal to provide facilities to the Commission under Article 28(a), or a failure to execute a decision of the Committee of Ministers

---

[1] 1065/61, *Yearbook* 4, 260 at 266.
[2] See above, p. 14.

or of the Court under Article 32(4) and Article 53 respectively. An examination of these questions would seem consistent with the Commission's duty under Article 19 'to ensure the observance of the engagements undertaken by the High Contracting Parties in the present Convention'.

The scope of individual applications is more restricted. Under Article 25, an individual applicant must claim to be a victim of 'the rights set forth in this Convention'. These are principally the rights set out in Section I of the Convention. In addition, interference with the right of petition under Article 25 may itself be the subject of a complaint.[1]

It is evident that the Commission cannot deal with complaints concerning rights not covered by the Convention. As stated above, such complaints are normally rejected as incompatible with the provisions of the Convention under Article 27(2).[2]

We thus move from questions of competence to the conditions of admissibility proper.[3]

'INCOMPATIBLE'

Clearly, the Commission cannot deal with a complaint which is outside the subject-matter covered by the Convention.

As has been pointed out above,[4] however, it is not always easy to distinguish, in the Commission's decisions on admissibility, two separate questions. The first is whether the application is outside its competence. The second is whether it is incompatible with the provisions of the Convention under Article 27(2). The clearest example of complaints which are incompatible with the provisions of the Convention, in the strict sense, would be those falling under Article 17;[5] for an application whose purpose or effect was to subvert the rights guaranteed would quite literally be incompatible with the Convention. Where, on the other hand, the Convention is silent, an application would not normally be described as 'incompatible', but rather as being outside its scope. Since, however, Article 27 is apparently intended to list exhaustively the grounds on which an application may be rejected, the

---

[1] See above, p. 141.
[2] But an application brought by a State under Article 24 which is incompatible *ratione materiae* cannot be rejected as inadmissible on that ground: see above, p. 223.
[3] For the distinction between competence and admissibility see above, p. 223.
[4] Ibid.   [5] See above, p. 210.

Commission has treated such applications as incompatible on the ground that, under the terms of Article 1, the Convention guarantees only the rights and freedoms defined in Section I.

It has therefore rejected as incompatible, for example, complaints that a person was denied a nationality,[1] or was refused permission to enter a State of which he was not a national,[2] or was not allowed to appeal,[3] or was not granted a pension.[4]

However, caution is necessary in rejecting a complaint on this ground. Even where the right invoked is not directly guaranteed by the Convention, a provision of the Convention may indirectly protect it. For example, under the Fourth Protocol, while there is no right to a nationality as such, a person may not be refused nationality if the sole object of the refusal is to expel him from the State.[5]

Similarly, while a person has no right as such, under the Convention, to enter a State of which he is not a national, he may not be refused admission if such a refusal were to violate, for example, his right to respect for family life under Article 8.[6]

Again, although the Convention confers no right of appeal, the refusal of permission to appeal, where such a possibility exists, may infringe Article 6 read together with Article 14.[7] And while no right to a pension is included in the Convention or Protocols, interference with acquired rights under a pension scheme might raise an issue under Article 1 of the First Protocol.[8]

In these cases it will often be difficult to find the dividing line between complaints which are incompatible and those which, while not incompatible, are manifestly ill-founded. Both types of decision may involve at least an implicit interpretation of the provisions of the Convention.[9]

DOMESTIC REMEDIES

According to Article 26: 'The Commission may only deal with the matter after all domestic remedies have been exhausted, according to the generally recognised rules of international law, and

---

[1] See, e.g. 288/57, *Yearbook* 1, 209.
[2] See, e.g. 3325/67, *Yearbook* 10, 528.
[3] See, e.g. 4133/69, *Yearbook* 13, 780.
[4] See, e.g. 4130/69, *Yearbook* 14, 224 at 238.
[5] See above, p. 186.   [6] See above, p. 129.
[7] See above, p. 189.   [8] See above, p. 167.   [9] See below, p. 243.

within a period of six months from the date on which the final decision was taken.'

The domestic remedies rule has its origin under general international law in claims brought by a State for wrongs to its nationals. The legal basis of such claims is that 'in taking up the case of one of its nationals, by resorting to diplomatic action or international judicial proceedings on his behalf, a state is in reality asserting its own right, the right to ensure in the person of its nationals respect for the rules of international law.'[1]

It is ordinarily a condition of such a claim for the redress of an injury that the person affected should first have exhausted any remedies available to him under the local law, and Article 26 expressly refers to the application of the domestic remedies rule as it has been developed in the context of general international law.

Thus, the Commission, citing the Interhandel case before the International Court of Justice,[2] has stated that the rule requiring the exhaustion of domestic remedies as a condition of the presentation of an international claim is founded upon the principle that the respondent State must first have an opportunity to redress by its own means within the framework of its own domestic legal system the wrong alleged to have been done to the individual.[3]

Similarly, the Commission has relied on the general rules of international law to show that, while it must normally examine *ex officio* whether domestic remedies have been exhausted, nevertheless since the main object of the rule is to protect the domestic legal system of the Contracting States, the requirement may be expressly or impliedly waived by the respondent government.[4]

The domestic remedies rule applies also to inter-State applications under Article 24, unlike the other grounds of inadmissibility specified in Article 27, which are expressly confined to individual applications under Article 25. In the Pfunders case, the Austrian Government which brought the application submitted that the rule did not apply to inter-State applications, since these were based on the concepts of collective guarantee and

---

[1] Permanent Court of International Justice, Panevezys-Saldutiskis Railway Case, Series A/B, 76, p. 16.

[2] I.C.J. Reports, 1959, p. 27.

[3] 343/57, *Yearbook* 2, 412 at 438.

[4] 1994/63, *Yearbook* 7, 252 at 258–60; Vagrancy cases, 'Judgment of the Court', p. 31.

the public interest, and an applicant State did not have to show any damage.[1] The Commission held, however, that the principle upon which the domestic remedies rule is founded and the considerations which led to its introduction in general international law apply not less but *a fortiori* to a system of international protection which extends to a State's own nationals as well as to foreigners.[2] It accordingly rejected parts of the application, as it had previously done in the Second Cyprus case,[3] for non-compliance with the rule.

On the other hand, the Commission has recognized that the rule has only a limited application in inter-State cases. It applies where the case is concerned, as were the cases just mentioned, with violations of the rights of particular individuals. Indeed it would be unreasonable to suggest that, if an individual has not exhausted the domestic remedies, the Commission can deal with the case if it is brought not by the alleged victim but by a State. But the rule does not apply where the scope of the application is to determine the compatibility with the Convention of legislative measures and administrative practices in general.[4] Here it would be unreasonable to apply the rule, as there is no requirement in such cases that there should be a victim at all.[5] Thus the rule does not apply if the applicant government can show that the treatment complained of constitutes an administrative practice; it did not apply, for this reason, in the Irish Case, to the Irish Government's complaints concerning the treatment of persons in custody in Northern Ireland.[6] But it is not sufficient merely to allege the existence of such legislative measures or administrative practices; their existence must be shown by means of substantial evidence. On this ground, the complaints in the same case relating to deaths allegedly caused by the United Kingdom Government's security forces were rejected for non-compliance with the rule.[7] More questionable is the Commission's decision, in subsequent applications by individuals claiming to be victims, on similar facts, of an administrative practice of ill-treatment, to declare these complaints admissible despite Article

---

[1] *Yearbook* 4, 116 at 146–8. [2] At 150.
[3] *Yearbook* 2, 186 at 190 *et seq.*
[4] First Cyprus case, *Yearbook* 2, 182 at 184; the Greek Case, *Yearbook* 11, 690 at 726.
[5] See above, pp. 7, 233.
[6] *Collection of Decisions* 41, 3 at 85–7. [7] At 84–5.

26 and to join any question of domestic remedies to the merits.[1]

The domestic remedies rule requires that the complaint should have been brought before the appropriate judicial or administrative authorities, and should have been taken to the highest instance available. This requirement may raise difficulties where there are doubts whether a particular course of action would constitute an effective remedy: for example is an applicant in the United Kingdom required to petition for leave to appeal to the House of Lords against a decision of the Court of Appeal? The Commission has not yet rejected an application on such a ground. On the other hand, it has rejected complaints from Germany which have not been taken to the Federal Constitutional Court, although the prospects of success there too might be thought equally slender. The difference perhaps can be explained by the fact that the Federal Constitution contains guarantees similar to some of those set out in the Convention; for example, the right to a fair hearing in Article 6(1) has its counterpart in Article 103(1) of the German Basic Law.[2] Where domestic law offers, despite Article 13 of the Convention, no remedy at all, there is of course no obligation to exhaust: as where a complaint is made against a United Kingdom Act of Parliament which directly affects the situation of the applicant, without the intervention of an individual decision, applying that legislation to him.[3]

In accordance with the generally recognized rules of international law, not all domestic remedies have to be tried, but only those which are capable of providing an effective and sufficient means of redressing the wrongs which are the subject of the international claim.[4] Only a remedy which will redress the complaint as of right need be tried.[5] If the applicant complains of his trial, he must therefore appeal against the judgment, but he is not required to petition for a new trial. Such a petition is normally granted only as a matter of discretion, and, if it is granted, will not of itself redress the complaints. The Commission's decision in the Nielsen case,[6] where it took into consideration for the purposes of Article 26 a petition to the Special Court of

---

[1] *Collection of Decisions* 43, 122.

[2] 2257/64, *Yearbook* 11, 180 at 222 *et seq.*

[3] East African Asians case, Yearbook 13, 928 at 998.

[4] 343/57, *Yearbook* 2, 413 at 436 f.; 514/59, *Yearbook* 3, 196 at 202; 654/59, *Yearbook* 4, 276 at 282.

[5] 214/56, *Yearbook* 2, 214 at 236–8.   [6] See below, p. 242.

Revision in Denmark, appears to be incorrect, and more recently the Commission has indicated that it may decide the question differently in future cases.[1]

Again, if the case-law of the appeal courts shows that an appeal has no reasonable chance of success, the applicant is not obliged to appeal. The question arose in the Vagrancy cases;[2] the Belgian Conseil d'État had held that it had no jurisdiction to hear an appeal against a magistrate's order, and the Commission concluded that there were no domestic remedies.[3] Subsequently, however, the Conseil d'État reversed its former case-law; the Government thereupon requested the Commission to reject the applications as inadmissible for non-exhaustion of domestic remedies, but the Commission declined to do so.[4] The Court, which held that it was competent to review the Commission's decision on admissibility in this respect,[5] rejected the Government's objections on the ground that according to the settled legal opinion which existed in Belgium at the material time, recourse to the Conseil d'État against the orders of a magistrate was thought to be inadmissible.[6]

Where, on the other hand, the case-law of the domestic courts leaves the question open, the applicant must avail himself of the remedy.[7] The Commission has gone as far as to say that the applicant must exhaust every domestic remedy which cannot clearly be said to lack any chance of success.[8] The formulation of the Court in the Vagrancy cases is to be preferred.

A separate question, not always distinguished from that just discussed, is under what circumstances an applicant may be absolved from exhausting a given remedy. He may allege, for example, that his lawyers, or indeed the court, advised him not to appeal because there was no prospect of succeeding. This situation is to be distinguished from the submission that there was, from an objective viewpoint, no effective remedy. Here the applicant acknowledges that the remedy may exist, but submits that on the facts of his case he was absolved from the requirement to exhaust it. The Commission has acknowledged that, under the generally recognized rules of international law, an applicant

---

[1] 4311/69, *Yearbook* 14, 280 at 318.   [2] See above, p. 55.
[3] *Yearbook* 10, 420.   [4] 'Publications of the Court', Series B, p. 94.
[5] See below, p. 263.   [6] 'Judgment of the Court', p. 34.
[7] 712/60, *Yearbook* 4, 384 at 406; 2257/64, *Yearbook* 11, 180 at 222–4.
[8] 2257/64, *Yearbook* 11, 180 at 224.

may in special circumstances be absolved from the domestic remedies rule, but it has not accepted this as such a case.[1]

Nor is an applicant absolved from appealing against conviction or sentence by the fact that he was informed that the Court of Appeal had power to direct that the time spent in custody pending the determination of his appeal should not be reckoned as part of his sentence.[2]

While the question what constitutes a remedy is to be answered by reference to the general rules of international law, only domestic law can determine what is the correct forum for the complaint. Similarly it rests with the national authorities to determine the manner and the time-limits to be observed by the parties in resorting to the competent domestic courts.[3] The Convention also leaves it to the Contracting States to interpret and apply their relevant legislative provisions; the Commission could intervene only if it were established that as a result of such interpretation or application the applicant was a victim of a denial of justice.[4]

It is not sufficient that the applicant has taken his case before the domestic courts of appeal or other authorities. He must have raised before them, if it is possible to do so, the particular complaints which he wishes to raise before the Commission.[5] If he raises only some of his complaints, only those will be admissible. Thus in the Pfunders case[6] one of the complaints was that the trial was not held before an independent and impartial tribunal, by reason of the composition of the courts concerned. The accused, however, had not applied for a change of venue; and the applicant government had not shown that such an application would not have constituted an effective remedy. This complaint therefore had to be rejected as inadmissible.[7]

What counts as a remedy is thus a question of substance, not of form. On the one hand, a remedy which is formally open to the applicant does not have to be exhausted if there is no prospect of its giving him satisfaction. On the other hand, there is no formal limit to what counts as a remedy, if it is capable of giving satis-

---

[1] Ibid. [2] 4133/69, *Yearbook* 13, 780 at 788.

[3] 1191/61, *Yearbook* 8, 106 at 154–6.

[4] Ibid.; on denial of justice see Fitzmaurice, 'Meaning of the Term Denial of Justice', B.Y.B.I.L. 1932, p. 93.

[5] See, e.g. 1661/62, *Yearbook* 6, 360 at 366.

[6] See above, p. 13. [7] *Yearbook* 4, 116 at 166–170.

faction as of right. An isolated decision of the Commission to the contrary, in the sailor boys' case,[1] seems to be incorrect in this respect. The Commission there held that 'mere internal representations to higher authorities within the military hierarchy cannot be considered as an effective remedy within the meaning of Article 26;' and that 'this provision, although not necessarily presupposing a judicial review, nevertheless refers only to a reconsideration by some outside organ which is not part of the decision-making authority itself.'[2] It is clear, however, that an administrative complaint, such as a complaint by a prisoner to the prison governor against the decision of a subordinate officer, or against the decision of the governor to his hierarchical superiors, may be an effective remedy for the purpose of Article 26.[3]

By way of conclusion, some indication may be given of the operation of the domestic remedies rule in practice. The applicant must provide, in his application, information enabling it to be shown that the conditions laid down in Article 26 have been satisfied;[4] if he does not do so, the Commission must examine the question *ex officio*. If the respondent government raises the objection of non-exhaustion, it is for that government to prove the existence, in its municipal legal system, of remedies which have not been exercised.[5] If the existence of such a remedy is established, the applicant must show that he has exhausted it, or that it was unlikely to be effective and adequate in regard to the grievance in question,[6] or that in the special circumstances of the case he was absolved from compliance with the rule. The rules concerning the burden of proof are based, as is the substantive rule, on the generally recognized rules of international law referred to in Article 26.

THE SIX MONTHS RULE

Article 26 prescribes a strict period of limitation: an application is inadmissible if it is not brought within six months from the date on which the final decision was taken. The six months rule is closely related to the domestic remedies rule. As the Commission stated in the De Becker case:[7]

---

[1] See above, p. 41.   [2] 3435/67 etc., *Yearbook* 11, 562 at 590.
[3] See, e.g. 4451/70, *Yearbook* 14, 416 at 440–2.
[4] Rule 41(2) of the Commission's Rules of Procedure.
[5] Pfunders case, *Yearbook* 4, 116 at 166–8.
[6] Ibid.   [7] See above, p. 151.

the two rules contained in Article 26 . . . are closely interrelated, since not only are they combined in the same Article, but they are also expressed in a single sentence whose grammatical construction implies such correlation; . . . the term 'final decision', therefore, in Article 26 refers exclusively to the final decision concerned in the exhaustion of all domestic remedies . . . so that the six months period is operative only in this context.[1]

This interpretation, while plainly correct, may appear to confront the applicant with a dilemma, if he is in doubt whether a particular remedy is effective. If he does exhaust it, and the Commission holds that it was not a remedy to be exhausted, his application may be too late. If on the other hand he does not exhaust it, the application might be declared inadmissible on that ground. His dilemma, however, is only apparent. If in doubt, he has only to introduce his application, at the same time pursuing the domestic proceedings. While as a rule he must exercise the different domestic remedies before he applies to the Commission, the Commission will accept that the last stage of such remedies may be reached shortly after the lodging of the application but before the Commission has pronounced on admissibility.[2] In the unlikely event that the Commission were to reject the application for non-exhaustion because the final domestic decision has not yet been given, that decision will be a relevant new fact within the meaning of Article 27(1) (b) which will entitle the applicant to introduce a fresh application.[3]

Since the final decision is that involved in the exhaustion of domestic remedies, an applicant cannot reopen the period by, for example, subsequently applying for a retrial, as such an application does not constitute a remedy for the purposes of Article 26. In the Nielsen case the Commission departed from this rule, holding that the applicant's petition to the Special Court of Revision in Denmark could be taken into account for the purposes of the six months rule. The decision does not accord with the general rules regarding what constitutes a remedy,[4] and if generalized would have the effect of depriving the six months rule of any real significance.

---

[1] *Yearbook* 2, 214 at 242.
[2] Ringeisen case, 'Judgment of the Court', para. 91.
[3] 347/58, *Yearbook* 2, 407; see below, p. 250.
[4] See above, p. 238.

Despite the wording of the English text of Article 26 ('within a period of six months from the date on which the final decision was taken'), it would seem that the period should start to run only from the date on which the applicant has notice of the decision. The application must be deposited[1] within six months of that date. The Commission has accepted that the period might in special circumstances be interrupted or suspended[2] but there appears to be no example of such a case in the Commission's decisions.

The six months rule has in any event no application where a person complains, as was the case in De Becker,[3] of a continuing situation. In such cases, indeed, the initial act may even have taken place before the Convention entered into force in respect of the State concerned; it is not the initial act, but the present situation of the applicant, which is the true subject of the complaint. Here the problem of the six months period can arise only after this situation has ceased to exist; so long as it continues, it is as if the alleged violation were being repeated daily thus preventing the running of the period.[4] If, therefore, a distinction is drawn between the mere consequences of a prior decision, and a continuing situation, the latter concept is not a real exception to the six months rule.

MANIFESTLY ILL-FOUNDED

Article 27(2) requires the Commission to reject as inadmissible an application which is 'manifestly ill-founded'. It is clear that such a provision is essential to the function of the Commission, as it was originally conceived, as a screen or filter designed to ensure that only complaints of substance were examined on the merits. The concept of 'manifestly ill-founded' has thus played a key role in the Commission's practice, and the evolution of the concept is the clearest single guide to the evolution of the Commission itself.[5]

The requirement that an application should not be manifestly ill-founded differs from all the other conditions of admissibility in that it relates not to form but to substance; it goes, if only a step,

---

[1] 1468/62, *Yearbook* 6, 278 at 322.
[2] See, e.g. 2618/65, *Yearbook* 8, 374.   [3] See above, p. 151.
[4] 214/56, *De Becker* v. *Belgium, Yearbook* 2, 214 at 244.
[5] See below, p. 275.

to the merits of the case. The rule contrasts in this respect with a general principle of international litigation which insists on a rigid separation of form and substance.[1] Broadly, the rule may be interpreted as amounting to a requirement that the applicant must show a *prima facie* case.

However, in some cases a finding of manifestly ill-founded may be closely related to a finding that an application is outside the Commission's competence *ratione materiae* or incompatible with the provisions of the Convention. This is because either finding may involve an interpretation, if only implicit, of the substantive provisions of the Convention.

The main difference between 'manifestly ill-founded' and 'incompatibility' is easily stated, although the distinction is not always easy to apply in practice.

A complaint is incompatible if it is altogether outside the scope of the Convention, so that there is no possibility of going into the merits of the case. A complaint is manifestly ill-founded if, while it falls *prima facie* within the scope of the Convention, a preliminary examination of the merits shows that there is no need for any further such examination. This may be because the applicant has made wholly unsubstantiated allegations, in which case the rule comes close to being a rule of evidence. Or it may be because the allegations which he makes, even if substantiated, would not suffice to establish a violation. For example, complaints by prisoners under Article 3 concerning the conditions of their detention are frequently rejected as manifestly ill-founded on the ground that, even if the matters complained of were established, they would not constitute 'inhuman or degrading treatment or punishment'.

There is no logical criterion for distinguishing 'manifestly ill-founded' and 'incompatible' in cases where a question of interpretation is involved, since it must always be a matter of degree. Where it is patent that the right claimed is outside the scope of the Convention, the application is incompatible. Where, as in the case of treatment and punishment, it is rather a matter of standards, the application is manifestly ill-founded. Where there is doubt whether the complaint comes within the scope of the Convention, the application should be admitted and the question examined on the merits.

[1] Cf. De Visscher, *Aspects récents du droit procédural de la Cour Internationale de Justice*, Paris, 1966, 99 ff.

Although it is essential that the Commission should be able to reject complaints which are manifestly ill-founded, there is no doubt that the Commission has at times taken this provision too far in examining the merits of a case at the stage of admissibility.

It has frequently stated the principle that 'an application should be declared inadmissible as being manifestly ill-founded only when a preliminary examination does not disclose any appearance of a violation of the Convention';[1] but its application of this principle has not always been satisfactory.

The most obvious example was the Iversen case in 1963,[2] which the Commission ultimately rejected as manifestly ill-founded, since here the Commission actually included in its decision on admissibility separate and minority opinions on the interpretation of Article 4. It is apparent from reading the decision itself that, whatever the final judgment on the merits might have been, the case was manifestly not inadmissible on the ground stated by the Commission.

Nevertheless there has been an evolution in the Commission's approach to this question, which may be apparent in the rather larger proportion of cases declared admissible in recent years. This might also be due, of course, to the fact that more meritorious cases are being brought before the Commission. But a comparison of the decision in the Iversen case with that, for example, in Gussenbauer in 1972,[3] which also raised issues under Article 4, will show a positive trend in the policy of the Commission. It may be surmised that if a case very similar to the Iversen case were brought today, the decision would be different.

The opposite fault is also sometimes apparent in the Commission's decisions rejecting applications as manifestly ill-founded. It may not go sufficiently into the merits, with the consequence that its reasoning in support of its decision is inadequate, or sometimes even totally lacking.

It is patently not sufficient to give, as a reason for declaring an application inadmissible, the statement that it is manifestly ill-founded. It has to be stated why it is manifestly ill-founded. In some cases, of course, the reason may simply be that the facts alleged, even if proved, could not constitute a violation. But often

[1] 596/59, *Yearbook* 3, 356 at 368.
[2] See above, p. 37.   [3] See above, p. 43.

more elaborate reasoning will be necessary to show that the complaint has been properly considered.

This is necessary, for example, when dealing with complaints under Articles such as Article 8. Interferences with the rights guaranteed by Article 8(1) must be justified on one of the grounds set out in Article 8(2). If they can be so justified, the complaint is clearly not incompatible, since one of the Convention rights is in issue, but is manifestly ill-founded. But it is of course not sufficient simply to state, as the Commission has sometimes done, that the interference was justified under paragraph (2). It must be shown in each case why it was justified, and how each of the conditions set out in paragraph (2) is fulfilled.[1] If this cannot be done at the stage of admissibility, the complaint must be examined on the merits.

ABUSE OF THE RIGHT OF PETITION

Abuse of the right of petition, as a ground for rejecting an application, must of course be distinguished from the principle of abuse of rights embodied in Article 17. Article 17 lays down, in effect, that no one may be able to take advantage of the provisions of the Convention to perform acts aimed at destroying the rights guaranteed.[2] It is thus concerned with preventing abuse of the substantive rights. Abuse of the right of petition, on the other hand, may arise where the applicant makes improper use of his procedural right under Article 25 to bring his complaint before the Commission. Consequently, in accordance with a rule applicable generally to restrictions on the Commission's competence,[3] the term should not be given an extensive interpretation.

Thus the Commission stated in the Lawless case that 'the fact that the applicant was inspired by motives of publicity and political propaganda, even if established, would not by itself necessarily have the consequence that the application was an abuse of the right of petition'.[4] On the other hand, the Commission appeared to consider, in the Iversen case, that if the applicant gives undue emphasis to the political aspect of his case, this might constitute an abuse.[5] Similarly, the Commission has adopted the practice of warning applicants who may wish to publicize their cases that

---

[1] See above, p. 196. [2] See above, p. 210.
[3] See above, p. 225. [4] 332/57, *Yearbook* 2, 308 at 338.
[5] 1468/62, *Yearbook* 6, 278 at 326.

such publicity, contrary to Article 33,[1] might lead to the rejection of the application on the grounds of abuse. The rule is that while an applicant may of course publicize his complaints, he may not publicize the proceedings before the Commission.

The Commission has also treated as an abuse of the right of petition defamatory remarks made by the applicant against the respondent Government.[2] This interpretation requires some justification. An alternative interpretation, which is supported by the French text, is that abuse of the right of petition means the frivolous and vexatious institution of proceedings,[3] or, within the limits stated above, the institution of proceedings for an improper purpose, such as to obtain publicity. It is also questionable whether the use of objectionable language in the course of proceedings can make inadmissible not only the particular pleading, but the application which instituted the proceedings.[4] The justification of the Commission's interpretation must be that it has no power of committal for contempt of court or any other disciplinary power and that the dismissal of an application on the ground of abuse is the only sanction available for improper conduct of the proceedings.

In the Huber case, the Austrian Government sought to make an ingenious use of this provision. The applicant withdrew certain statements to which the Government had objected as constituting an abuse of the right of petition. The Government then argued that, as a result of the withdrawal of these statements, the remaining parts of the application were insufficient to support his complaint, and that the application had consequently lost its substance. This submission was rejected by the Commission.[5]

On the other hand, there is justification for retaining the ground of abuse, in proper cases, as a ground of admissibility. In the first place, the procedure made available under Article 25 is so remarkable and exceptional in itself that the Commission may legitimately be concerned to protect governments against its abuse. Secondly,

---

[1] See above, p. 221.

[2] See, e.g. 2424/65, *Yearbook* 9, 426; 3934/69, *Collection of Decisions* 34, 27.

[3] See, e.g. 26/55, 169/56, and 244/57, *Yearbook* 1, 194, 195 and 196; 5070, 5171, 5186/71, *Collection of Decisions* 42, 58; 5145/71 etc., *Collection of Decisions* 43, 152.

[4] See Schwelb, The Abuse of the Right of Petition, *Revue des Droits de l'Homme* (1970), 177.

[5] 4517/70, *Yearbook* 14, 572 at 602–8.

such protection is in the interests of the good functioning of the Convention itself, since, as the Commission has observed in recent applications,[1]

> It cannot be the task of the Commission, a body which was set up under the Convention 'to ensure the observance of the engagements undertaken by the High Contracting Parties in the present Convention' to deal with a succession of ill-founded and querulous complaints, creating unnecessary work which is incompatible with its real functions, and which hinders it in carrying them out.

A special case was that of Ilse Koch, wife of the commandant of Buchenwald concentration camp, who complained of her conviction by the German courts. The Commission stated that, although the applicant was imprisoned in execution of a sentence imposed on her for crimes against the most elementary rights of men, she was entitled to the protection of the Convention. The application was inadmissible, partly as being outside the competence of the Commission and partly as being manifestly ill-founded. However, the Commission did not reject the application on these grounds. It held that the applicant, in the circumstances referred to above, and in presenting a series of allegations and complaints that were completely unsupported by the Convention, was seeking merely to escape the consequences of her conviction. The application was consequently a 'clear and manifest abuse' of the right of petition.[2]

ANONYMOUS APPLICANTS

Applications have rarely been rejected on this ground. In an early case,[3] the applicant signing himself 'lover of tranquillity' asked the Commission in an undated letter postmarked in Dublin 'to arrange as soon as possible a Committee of Enquiry into the Irish problem' in order to obtain an all-Ireland plebiscite on the question of relations between Ireland and Great Britain. The Commission found that the file did not contain any element enabling the Commission to identify the applicant and rejected the application as being anonymous.

---

[1] 5070, 5071, 5186/71, *Collection of Decisions* 42, 58; 5145/71 etc., *Collection of Decisions* 43, 152.
[2] 1270/61, *Yearbook* 5, 126 at 134–6.
[3] 361/58 (not published), see 'Case-Law Topics', No. 3, p. 10.

In another more recent case,[1] the application was lodged by the Church of Scientology of California, a corporation, alleging violations of its own rights and/or of the collective rights of its members. The Commission therefore treated the complaints as having been made both by the Church and by its individual members but declared them inadmissible. It found that, in so far as the application could be considered as having been brought by or on behalf of the members, the identity of these members had not been disclosed and it was therefore inadmissible under Article 27(1) (a) of the Convention as being anonymous. The Commission, however, continued to examine the various allegations 'assuming that this procedural defect were to be corrected' and rejected them on other grounds. The question of the procedural correction did not therefore arise.

APPLICATIONS SUBSTANTIALLY THE SAME

Article 27(1) (b) provides that an application under Article 25 is inadmissible if it 'is substantially the same as a matter which has already been examined by the Commission or has already been submitted to another procedure of international investigation or settlement and if it contains no relevant new information'.

There appears to be no decision of the Commission rejecting an application on the ground that it has already been submitted to another procedure of international investigation or settlement. The possibilities of overlap between different international procedures are considered below.[2]

The rule that the Commission cannot consider again a complaint which it has itself previously examined accords with the universal principle that a case once legally decided cannot be reopened. The notion of 'relevant new information' should be construed in the light of this principle.[3]

In some cases an applicant has sought to reopen proceedings after his application has been declared inadmissible, and has alleged errors in the Commission's decision[4] or has introduced further details of the same complaints.[5] Since there is no provision for

---

[1] 3798/68, see above, p. 147.   [2] p. 276.
[3] Cf. 202/56, *Yearbook* I, 190.
[4] 3806/68, *Yearbook* II, 609.
[5] 2606/65, *Collection of Decisions* 26, 22.

reopening a case, it is necessary to treat the new material as a fresh application. Such an application will be inadmissible if, for example, the new material does not affect the substance of his previous allegations.[1]

However, in other cases the new material may affect the ground on which the previous application was rejected. If, for example, an application is rejected for non-exhaustion of domestic remedies, the applicant may still be able to pursue his domestic remedies and then bring his complaint before the Commission again. Having obtained a final decision, he can submit this as relevant new information. A different example was an applicant's complaint concerning his conviction and sentence which the Commission had rejected in a previous application on the ground of non-exhaustion of domestic remedies as the applicant had stated that the final decision in his case was that of the Court of Appeal at Liège. In his new application he showed that he himself had committed an error in that the decision in question had, in fact, not been given by the Court of Appeal but by the Court of Cassation against which there was no further remedy. The Commission considered that this fact, if it had been known to the Commission, would have required a different decision. It found, therefore, that this new information was such as to change the legal basis of its previous decision and was therefore 'relevant new information' within the meaning of Article 27(1) (b) of the Convention.[2] The Commission then proceeded with the examination of the applicant's complaint but declared it inadmissible on other grounds.

Another example of the same type of reasoning was a case in which the applicant, who was detained in prison, complained about the German authorities' refusal of permission for him to leave Germany and live in Poland. This complaint had also been the subject of his previous application which the Commission had rejected as being incompatible with the provisions of the Convention on the ground that no right to reside in a particular country was as such guaranteed by the Convention.

However, when bringing a second application, the applicant was able to invoke the Fourth Protocol, which had meanwhile entered into force in respect of the Federal Republic, and which provides in Article 2(2) that 'Everyone shall be free to leave any

---

[1] Ibid.   [2] 3780/68, *Collection of Decisions* 37, 6.

country, including his own.' Consequently, while the applicant's factual situation had not changed, the legal qualification of his complaint was no longer the same, and so Article 27(1) (b) did not apply.[1] The application was nevertheless inadmissible as being manifestly ill-founded as the provision in the Fourth Protocol is subject to an exception, reasonably enough, in the case of persons in detention.[2]

While there is no provision in the Convention for reopening a case, and no provision for an appeal against the decisions of the Commission, there are two exceptions to the principle that the decision on admissibility is final. A decision that an application is inadmissible can never be challenged, but where the Commission declares an application admissible, it may subsequently decide unanimously, under Article 29, to reject the application if it finds, in the course of its examination, that the conditions of admissibility have not been fulfilled.[3] Secondly, the decision on admissibility may in effect be reviewed by the Court when it deals with the merits of the case.[4]

2

Examination of the merits

If an application is declared admissible, the Commission proceeds, under Article 28, to an examination of the merits of the case. Under Article 28(a), it is required to ascertain the facts of the case; under Article 28(b), it is required to place itself at the disposal of the parties with a view to securing a friendly settlement of the matter. This task is considered in the next section.

The tasks of the Commission under Article 28 were assigned by Article 29 to a Sub-Commission. Sub-Commission procedure, however, was found to be cumbersome, and was abolished by the Third Protocol which introduced a new text of Article 29.

The facts of the case are established by an exchange of written pleadings and further oral argument. The Commission may also call witnesses, carry out a visit of inquiry, or take any other measures which it considers necessary. The establishment of the facts has naturally been most extensive in inter-State cases. Thus in the Greek case the Sub-Commission heard a total of eighty-

---

[1] 4256/59, *Collection of Decisions* 37, 67.   [2] See above, p. 184.
[3] See above, p. 159.   [4] See below, p. 263.

seven witnesses. It visited Athens but returned after hearing fifty witnesses as it considered that the Greek Government had prevented it from hearing others and from visiting an Athens prison and detention camps on Leros.[1] Under Article 28 (a) the States concerned are obliged to furnish all necessary facilities for the effective conduct of any necessary investigation. In the Irish Case,[2] delegates of the Commission heard a number of witnesses at a military base in Norway, chosen for security reasons.[3]

If no settlement is reached, the Commission is required by Article 31 to draw up a report on the facts and state its opinion as to whether the facts found disclose a breach of the Convention. The report is sent to the Committee of Ministers which, if the case is not referred to the Court within a period of three months, will take a final decision under Article 32(1) on whether there has been a violation of the Convention.

Although Article 28(a) refers only to ascertainment of the facts, the Commission must in practice examine also the issues of law raised by the application. This is necessary to enable it to form a provisional view of the merits for the purposes of the friendly settlement negotiations,[4] or if no settlement is reached to enable it to form an opinion on the question of violation. Hence the written and oral submissions of the parties will deal with the issues of law as well as fact.

In sending its report to the Committee of Ministers, the Commission may under Article 31(3) make such proposals as it thinks fit. From the Commission's practice, it seems that such proposals may be proposals for action by the Committee of Ministers, or for action by the respondent Government. In the Pataki/ Dunshirn cases,[5] where the measures complained of were remedied by the Austrian Government during the proceedings before the Commission, the Commission proposed that the Committee of Ministers should 'take note of this report, express its appreciation of the legislative measures adopted in Austria with a view to giving full effect to the Convention of Human Rights, and decide that no further action should be taken in the present cases.'[6]

In the Greek Case, the Commission made ten separate proposals

---

[1] Stock-taking note, DH(73)8, p. 7.   [2] See above, p. 25.
[3] See Council of Europe Press communiqués C(74)20 and C(74)23.
[4] See below, p. 255.   [5] Above, p. 99.
[6] *Yearbook* 6, 718 at 734.

designed to remedy the various aspects of the situation in Greece which it had found inconsistent with the Convention.[1]

The Committee of Ministers has expressed the view that the Commission is not entitled to make proposals in cases where it considers that there has not been a violation of the Convention;[2] the Convention gives no support for this view, and such proposals, even if not formally approved by the Committee of Ministers, might still carry some weight with the respondent government.

In the Pfunders case (*Austria* v. *Italy*) the Commission ultimately reached the opinion that there had been no violation. Nevertheless, without making formal proposals under Article 31(3), it expressed the view that it was 'desirable for humanitarian reasons, among which may be counted the youth of the prisoners, that measures of clemency be taken in their favour.'[3] The youngest of the accused was in fact pardoned.[4]

The proceedings before the Commission on the merits of a case often seem unduly protracted. Sometimes, of course, the complexity of the case requires lengthy examination. In the Greek Case, for example, the whole of the political life in Greece was in issue. The Sub-Commission heard 87 witnesses in all and held one of its sessions in Athens. But in other, simpler cases there seems little reason for the delay other than the congestion of the Commission's agenda.

Excluding exceptional cases, the Commission's examination of the merits usually lasts about two years. Given the length of proceedings on admissibility,[5] and the possibility of further proceedings before the Court, this period is too long. It should be possible to simplify and abbreviate the procedure, especially where the facts have been substantially established in the proceedings on admissibility. However, in some cases the delay is due not to difficulties in establishing the facts, but to attempts to carry out the task, described in the following section, of achieving a 'friendly settlement'.

---

[1] *Yearbook* 12, The Greek Case, 514–15.
[2] Rule 6 of the Rules adopted by the Committee of Ministers for the application of Article 32 of the Convention, *Collected Texts*, section 4.
[3] *Yearbook* 6, 800.
[4] B(73)47, 7.
[5] See above, p. 218.

3
Friendly settlement

After an application has been declared admissible, the Commission is required, under Article 28(b), to 'place itself at the disposal of the parties concerned with a view to securing a friendly settlement of the matter on the basis of respect for Human Rights as defined in this Convention'.

Conciliation is one of the traditional methods of peaceful settlement of international disputes.[1] At first sight, nevertheless, it is surprising that such a method should be expressly recognized in a human rights convention. But it will be seen that this may provide a more effective remedy than judicial determination of the case; and it was therefore to be expected that a virtually identical provision should be included in the American Convention on Human Rights.[2] If it goes too far to say that it is its primary duty, it is one of the major tasks of the Commission to conduct confidential negotiations with the parties and to try to set right unobtrusively any breach of human rights that may have occurred.[3]

It follows from the terms of Article 28(b) that there are two conditions which have to be satisfied for a friendly settlement to be achieved.

First, there must be an agreement between the parties disposing of the case to their satisfaction. Thus in the case of an application by an individual, he must obtain satisfaction, by way of compensation or otherwise, in respect of his complaint.

Second, the settlement must be 'on the basis of respect for Human Rights as defined in this Convention'. It follows that such a settlement must not only be acceptable to the parties; it must also satisfy this requirement in the opinion of the Commission. The applicant may be the victim of a law or administrative practice which the Commission considers, at least provisionally, incompatible with the Convention. In such a case a settlement by way of compensation to the applicant, even if acceptable to him,

[1] See Article 33(1) of the United Nations Charter. The term 'friendly settlement' was adopted rather than 'conciliation' because the latter was considered more appropriate to exclusively inter-State disputes: see Monconduit, *La Commission européenne des Droits de l'Homme*, Leyden, 1965, p. 376.

[2] See Article 48(1)(f); cf. the conciliation procedures provided for by Articles 41(e) and 42 of the U.N. Covenant on Civil and Political Rights.

[3] Cf. Waldock, *The British Year Book of International Law*, 1958, 356 at 362.

would not satisfy the requirements of Article 28; only a change in the law or practice concerned would meet the general interest.

Thus, it may be necessary for the Commission to form a provisional view of the merits of the case before friendly settlement discussions can usefully start.

It is the normal practice of the Commission to indicate to the Government in confidence, and very tentatively, its provisional opinion on the question of violation.[1] If this is affirmative, it is in the clear interest of the Government to achieve a settlement, since it will thus avoid the possibility of a formal finding of a violation, which might in any event necessitate both compensating the victim and making any requisite change in the law.

Even if the majority of the Commission is provisionally of the opinion that there has not been a breach of the Convention, the Government may wish to avoid further proceedings in the case, resulting in a detailed report containing the full facts and the Commission's reasoning, with the possibility of minority opinions to the effect that there has been a violation, and the possibility also of public proceedings before the Court. Even totalitarian governments are sensitive to international opinion on human rights issues. Democratic governments are still more reluctant to be condemned for violations of human rights, especially in the context of a regional human rights system operating with unrestricted publicity and without any marked political bias.[2] From this point of view the great advantage of a friendly settlement to a respondent Government is that no position will be taken on the question of violation.

It is in the interests of the applicant, also, that he should obtain satisfaction at the earliest stage and avoid the uncertainties of further proceedings. In particular, if the Commission considers that there has been a violation, the applicant who refuses to settle a case incurs the risk that the Government will refer the case to the Court, which may reach a different conclusion.

If a friendly settlement is achieved, the Commission draws up a report, which under Article 30 is confined to a brief statement of the facts and of the solution reached. The report is published and that is the end of the case.

[1] See Raymond, 'Comment s'exerce la fonction de conciliation de la Commission européenne des Droits de l'Homme', *Revue des droits de l'homme*, 1969, 259.   [2] See below, p. 275.

A formal friendly settlement under Article 28 has been reached in relatively few cases, although other forms of settlement have been frequent.

In the very first case in which a friendly settlement was reached, there appears to have been no question of a general law or practice being inconsistent with the Convention; it was a complaint concerning an isolated incident. The applicant, Boeckmans, who had been convicted of theft in Belgium, complained that remarks made by the President of the Chamber of the Court of Appeal were inconsistent with certain rights of accused persons under Article 6. The Belgian Government, while stating that the validity of the sentence could not be questioned, agreed to pay the applicant 65,000 Belgian francs as compensation for remarks which 'were such as to disturb the serenity of the atmosphere during the proceedings in a manner contrary to the Convention and may have caused the applicant a moral injury'.[1]

A more complex solution was reached in the Sepp case, where the applicant had complained of the length of criminal proceedings against him in Germany. The applicant, a chartered accountant, had been convicted of fraud. The elaborate terms of the settlement included, among other measures, a suspension of the prison sentence imposed on the applicant, a remission of the costs of the proceedings, and an undertaking that the competent authorities would not object to the readmission of the applicant as a chartered accountant.[2]

The facts of the Alam and Knechtl cases against the United Kingdom have been given above.[3] In the first case, a child was refused admission to the United Kingdom to join his father. Under the terms of the settlement, the Government, which had meanwhile granted the child an entry certificate, agreed to make an *ex gratia* payment of the cost of his air ticket from Pakistan to London. The Commission's report also recorded the Government's statement that it had introduced draft legislation to confer on Commonwealth citizens and aliens a right of appeal against the decisions of immigration officers.[4] The significance of this was that the case had been considered by the Commission under Article 6(1) as well as under Article 8. Under Article 6(1) a question of general interest was raised by the case. It would have been

[1] 1727/62, *Yearbook* 8, 410 at 422.   [2] 3897/68, B(73)47, 23.
[3] p. 129, and p. 90.   [4] *Yearbook* 11, 788.

necessary to decide whether the applicant was entitled to a 'fair and public hearing by an independent and impartial tribunal'. He would have been so entitled if refusal of admission by an immigration officer could be said to constitute a determination of civil rights under Article 6(1), at least in a case where the rights of family life are concerned. As the case was settled, the question was not resolved, but the draft legislation was subsequently enacted.[1]

A question of general interest, going beyond the interest of the individual applicant, arose also in the Knechtl case. The applicant's complaint was that, while detained in prison, he was refused permission to bring legal proceedings. It was not disputed that this refusal was in accordance with the English prison rules and administrative practice in force at the time. The question of general interest was whether this system was consistent with the Convention, if Article 6(1) is regarded as granting the right of access to the courts.[2] In approving the settlement of the Knechtl case, the Commission noted that the system had been modified as described above.[3]

The examples of friendly settlement given above show that their terms may include undertakings by the parties. The question has not yet arisen what the consequences would be of a failure to carry out such undertakings. The correct view would seem to be that the obligations resulting from a settlement are those of international law.[4] If an analogy is to be drawn with the other procedures provided for by the Convention,[5] it should be for the Committee of Ministers to act if the obligations of the Contracting States are not fulfilled.

Some type of settlement not amounting to a settlement under Article 28 has been reached in a number of other cases.[6] The facts of some of these cases, and the resulting settlement, have already been discussed; for example, the case of *Televizier* v. *The Netherlands*,[7] and *Karnell & Hardt* v. *Sweden*.[8] Sometimes, as

---

[1] The Immigration Appeals Act 1969, re-enacted with modifications in the Immigration Act 1971.

[2] See above, p. 90.   [3] See above, p. 91.

[4] See Frowein, The guarantees afforded by the institutional machinery of the Convention, in *Privacy and Human Rights*, ed. Robertson, Manchester, 1973, 284 at 288.

[5] Cf. Article 32(2) and (3) and Article 54.

[6] B(73)47, 25–33.   [7] p. 153.   [8] p. 174.

in the latter case, the Commission has taken note of a change in the system which is the subject of the application.

Where the applicant considers that his interests have been fully satisfied, he may seek to withdraw his application. Before accepting such withdrawal, the Commission will consider whether the general interest is satisfied by the outcome of the case; only then will it strike the case off its list.[1] This may be done either before or after the case is declared admissible. Thus in *Rebitzer* v. *Austria*, where the applicant was claiming compensation for wrongful detention, his claim was satisfied by a settlement concluded between himself and the Government before the decision on admissibility was taken. As part of the terms of the settlement, which was reached under new legislation on the subject, the applicant was to receive 1,000,000 Austrian schillings compensation and undertook to withdraw his application to the Commission. Without taking a decision on admissibility, the Commission struck the application off its list.[2]

Proceedings have also been terminated before the Court[3] and the Committee of Ministers[4] following unofficial settlements.

The requirement, for both friendly settlements and other forms of settlement, that the general interest should be satisfied is not merely a necessary feature of a system designed to protect human rights; it also has a practical justification, since if this aspect of a settlement is neglected, there is the risk that the procedures will have to be repeated in future cases.[5]

Criticisms have sometimes been expressed of the system of friendly settlement. It may be said, for example, that it introduces an extra-judicial, or even a political element into what should be a purely legal process. The very notion of compromise, implied in the idea of a settlement, may seem inconsistent with the concept of human rights. But the formulation of Article 28(b), by requiring that the settlement be based on respect for human rights, and the practice of the Commission in carrying out its functions under this provision, seem to meet the objections. It may sometimes be possible to criticize a particular settlement,

---

[1] 'Case-Law Topics', No. 3, p. 29.
[2] 3245/67, *Yearbook* 14, 160.
[3] De Becker case, above, p. 151.
[4] The Cyprus cases, *Yearbook* 2, 174.
[5] See above, p. 153.

or other form of arrangement, on the basis of its terms. This would be, however, to criticize the working of the system, rather than the system itself. And of course such criticisms may also be made of final decisions or judgments based on purely legal considerations.

It would indeed be possible to argue that the friendly settlement, and other informal solutions of the same type, represent the main contribution which the Convention can make to the securing of human rights. The advantages to the parties have already been mentioned.[1] But from the point of view of the operation of the human rights system, also, it is preferable that governments should co-operate voluntarily in achieving the standards of the Convention, and where necessary amend their existing law or practice, rather than await a formal finding on the question of violation. Voluntary co-operation in the implementation of the Convention is the surest guarantee of its success. Compliance may be less likely, more difficult to ensure, and less effective, where a final decision on the question of violation is necessary.[2]

III   PROCEEDINGS BEFORE THE COURT

Before the Convention was adopted a serious difference of opinion arose on the question whether a European Court of Human Rights should be created at all.[3] Since the proposal to create a Court with compulsory jurisdiction did not receive the support of the majority of States, it was contemplated that it should not be included in the draft Convention. A compromise solution was reached, reflected in Articles 46 and 48 of the Convention, which provide that the Court has jurisdiction only if the State concerned has recognized its jurisdiction by a declaration to that effect,[4] or has otherwise consented to it.

The Court can only deal with a case which has previously been examined by the Commission; which has not resulted in a friendly settlement (Article 47); and which has been referred to the Court by the Commission or by a State Party in accordance with Article

---

[1] See above, p. 255.
[2] See below, p. 266.
[3] See Robertson, *Human Rights in Europe*, Manchester, 1963, 87.
[4] See above, p. 5.

48. A case cannot be referred to the Court by an individual applicant.

When the Convention was drafted, the idea of giving the individual direct access to an international court seemed too revolutionary to be acceptable. Shortly afterwards, it is true, the founding Member States of the European Coal and Steel Community were prepared to give individuals access to the Court of Justice of that Community. That Court, although not an international tribunal for most purposes,[1] was given certain supra-national powers and its decisions were rendered directly enforceable in the Member States.[2] But its jurisdiction was limited, in its early days, to economic matters of a highly technical character, and did not encroach substantially, as does jurisdiction in the field of human rights, on matters touching the dignity of States. One can therefore explain historically, if one cannot justify, the fact that the Court of Human Rights is open only to States and to the Commission.

The Court consists of a number of judges equal to that of Member States of the Council of Europe (Article 38) (at present, eighteen), and not, as in the case of the Commission, to the number of Contracting Parties. Thus the Court has included a French judge since it was set up in 1959, but a member of the Commission was elected in respect of France only after France ratified the Convention in 1974. The judges are elected by the reverse procedure to that laid down for the Commission, namely by the Consultative Assembly from a list of persons nominated by the Governments (Article 39(1)). The candidates are required to be of high moral character and must either possess the qualification required for appointment to high judicial office or be 'jurisconsults' of recognized competence (Article 39(3)).[3] The judges, like the members of the Commission, are normally nationals of the State in respect of which they are elected. They are, of course, independent. This is nowhere specified in the Convention, as it is in the case of the Commission, since independence is deemed to be inherent in the judicial function.

The Court has no fixed sessions apart from an annual business meeting but meets as and when cases are brought before it.

---

[1] See below, p. 280.   [2] See below, p. 266.

[3] This provision is based on Article 2 of the Statute of the International Court of Justice.

The Court, which was set up in 1959, dealt with only two cases in the first seven years of its existence, but in the past few years has given a number of judgments, dealing with many major issues under the Convention.

The Convention provides (Article 43) that for the consideration of each case brought before it the Court should consist of a Chamber composed of seven judges. But in accordance with a provision in the Rules of Court (Rule 48) the Chamber has in several cases relinquished jurisdiction in favour of the plenary Court: in the Belgian Linguistic Case, at the request of the Belgian Government, on the ground that it raised a number of serious questions affecting the interpretation of the Convention;[1] in the Vagrancy cases, at the request of the Commission, on the ground that the Commission had raised certain questions on which it was desirable that the Court should be able to rule in plenary session;[2] and most recently in the Golder case.

The judge who is a national of any State Party concerned sits as an *ex officio* member of the Chamber; the names of the other judges are chosen by lot (Article 43). It might seem that it would have been more appropriate to exclude a judge who was the national of a State concerned, but the inclusion of the judge of the respondent State has the advantage of his acquaintance with the legal system and the background of the case.

The Registrar is elected by the Court;[3] his position differs in this respect from that of the Commission's Secretary, who is appointed by the Secretary General of the Council of Europe.[4] The President is required, however, to obtain the Secretary General's opinion before the Court elects the Registrar.[5] The Court also elects a Deputy Registrar.[6] The Registrar and Deputy Registrar are assisted by a small team of other officials who are appointed by the Secretary General with the agreement of the President or Registrar.[7]

The main function of the Court is to give a final judicial decision on cases referred to it under the Convention.

Where the States concerned have accepted the Court's jurisdiction, it extends to all cases concerning the interpretation and

[1] Belgian Linguistic Case, decision of 3 May 1966.
[2] Vagrancy cases, decision of 28 May 1970.
[3] Rule 11(1) of the Rules of Court.
[4] See above, p. 218.   [5] Rule 11(1).
[6] Rule 12(1).   [7] Rule 13.

application of the Convention which are referred to it, in accordance with Article 45, by a State Party or by the Commission. Normally cases are referred to the Court either by the Commission or by the State which was the respondent before the Commission. A case may also, however, be referred to the Court by the State whose national is alleged to be a victim, or, in an inter-State case, by the State which referred the case to the Commission. To date no inter-State applications have been brought before the Court. In practice it is clearly more probable that a case will be referred to the Court by the Commission; and there can be little doubt that the Commission has not exercised this discretion sufficiently often in the past.[1] The result has been a shift in the balance between the Convention bodies from that envisaged by its founders.[2]

The question has arisen only once whether a preliminary objection may be made to the jurisdiction of the Court. The Court's jurisdiction *ratione temporis* is laid down by Article 32(1) and Article 47, which provide that the case must be referred within a period of three months from the date of the transmission of the Commission's report to the Committee of Ministers. As for the Court's jurisdiction *ratione personae*, the State concerned must have recognized the competence of the Court, normally by a declaration under Article 46 recognizing its compulsory jurisdiction. Such a declaration, once made, has retroactive effect unless express provision is made to the contrary.[3]

The question has not yet arisen whether the Court has jurisdiction if the declaration was in force at the date when the case was initially brought before the Commission, or alternatively when the Commission's report was transmitted to the Committee of Ministers, but has expired at the date when the case is referred to the Court. To date all such declarations have invariably been renewed.

In the Belgian Linguistic Case the Court rejected a preliminary objection by the Belgian Government that the Court was not competent *ratione materiae* to examine the merits of the dispute. The Court held that its jurisdiction *ratione materiae* was estab-

---

[1] See Frowein, The guarantees afforded by the institutional machinery of the Convention, in *Privacy and Human Rights*, ed. Robertson, Manchester, 1973, 284 at 290.
[2] See below, p. 275.   [3] Cf. above, p. 230.

lished once the case raised a question of the interpretation or application of the Convention, and that therefore it could decline jurisdiction only if the applicants' complaints were clearly outside the provisions of the Convention and Protocols.[1] The scope for preliminary objections to the jurisdiction of the Court is therefore severely limited.[2]

However, in the Vagrancy cases the Court held that it had jurisdiction to deal with questions of non-exhaustion of domestic remedies and of delay, as objections to the admissibility of an application, and thus in effect to review the Commission's decision on admissibility when pronouncing on the merits of a case. The Court relied on the wide scope of Article 45 which provides that: 'The jurisdiction of the Court shall extend to all cases concerning the interpretation and application of the present Convention which the High Contracting Parties or the Commission shall refer to it in accordance with Article 48.' A case could, of course, only fall within the Court's jurisdiction if the various conditions specified in the Convention[3] were fulfilled; but once the Court was satisfied that the case did come within its jurisdiction, its competence extended to all questions of fact and law which might arise, including therefore questions concerning the interpretation and application of the provisions relating to the admissibility of applications before the Commission.

The Court's decision is open to criticism,[4] in particular as being contrary to the general structure of the Convention and the elaborate balance between its parts. There is already, with the existing division of functions between the Commission and the Court, a considerable degree of repetition in the procedure on the merits, and it would be unfortunate if this were regularly to extend also to questions of admissibility, thereby protracting still further the already lengthy proceedings. The decision also gives a further advantage to the State by giving it, in effect, the right of appeal to the Court against the Commission's decision on admissibility.

[1] Belgian Linguistic Case (Preliminary Objection), Judgment of 9 February 1967, *Yearbook* 10, 596.
[2] Cf. Fawcett, *The Application of the European Convention on Human Rights*, Oxford, 1969, p. 331.
[3] Articles 47 and 48.
[4] See the forceful separate opinions on this question of Judges Ross and Sigurjønsson, Judge Bilge, and Judge Wold, Series A, pp. 49, 52 and 55 respectively.

However, the Court held, in the Vagrancy cases, that a government cannot raise for the first time before the Court objections to admissibility which it has not raised before the Commission.[1] Further, the correct view would seem to be that such objections cannot be raised as preliminary objections to the jurisdiction of the Court, but must be considered in the proceedings on the merits.

Proceedings before the Court are based on the Commission's report, and on written and oral pleadings by the Commission and the State or States concerned. Hearings are public but may exceptionally be held in private (Rule 18 of the Rules of Court). The Commission is represented before the Court by delegates, States by agents (Rules 28 and 29(1)). However, except in inter-State cases, there are no 'parties' in a case before the Court, as there are in proceedings before the Commission. The individual applicant in an application under Article 25 has no *locus standi* before the Court.

This situation results from the initial reluctance of States, described above, to accept that the individual should have direct access to judicial remedies under international law. It has, however, been partly remedied by the Commission's development of its role in proceedings before the Court.

The Commission's function is to assist the Court[2] and its duty is ultimately to the Convention alone. It must state its opinion in complete independence and impartiality. Its role is therefore close to that of the Advocate-General in the Court of Justice of the European Communities,[3] and is in no way that of advocate for the applicant, even though, where it considers that there has been a violation of the Convention, it may be advancing the claims of the applicant.

In its first case, the Lawless case, the Court held that the applicant, although not entitled to bring the case before the Court, to appear before it or even to make submissions through a representative, was nevertheless 'directly concerned' in the proceedings before the Court.[4] The Commission asked the Court to rule that certain observations of the applicant on the Commis-

[1] Paras. 58 and 59.
[2] Rule 71 of the Commission's Rules of Procedure.
[3] EEC Treaty, Article 166; cf. Langer, *Die Beteiligten in dem Verfahren vor dem europäischen Gerichtshof für Menschenrechte*, Bonn, 1966, 73 f.
[4] *Yearbook* 3, 512.

sion's report were to be considered as part of the proceedings in the case. The Court ruled that they were not, but that the Commission was entitled to take account of these views in the proceedings.[1] Further, the Commission was entitled, under the Rules of Court, to call the applicant as a witness, although it has not made use of this right to date.

In the Vagrancy cases the Delegates of the Commission were assisted on a particular point, despite objections from the Belgian Government, by the lawyer who had represented the applicants in the proceedings before the Commission.[2] Some progress has thus been made to redress the situation whereby the applicant has no standing before the Court. But the time has perhaps arrived for the system itself to be amended.

The Court's procedure is based on the inquisitorial rather than the adversary model. Hence the Rules provide that the Chamber decides whether to hear witnesses or experts;[3] that it may depute one or more of its members to conduct an enquiry, to carry out an investigation on the spot or to obtain information in any other manner;[4] and for various other means of obtaining information.[5] These provisions have rarely been used.

The judgment of the Court is final[6] and, after being read by the President at a public hearing,[7] is transmitted by him to the Committee of Ministers for the purposes of the application of Article 54.[8]

Where the Court finds a violation of the Convention, it has a limited power to award compensation. Article 50 provides that:

If the Court finds that a decision or a measure taken by a legal authority or any other authority of a High Contracting Party is completely or partially in conflict with the obligations arising from the present Convention, and if the internal law of the said Party allows only partial reparation to be made for the consequences of this decision or measure, the decision of the Court shall, if necessary, afford just satisfaction to the injured party.

The Article seems to envisage that it is for the national authorities in the first instance to remedy any violation found by the Court. However, if the applicant is unable to obtain an adequate

---

[1] *Yearbook* 4, 444.   [2] Decision of 18 November 1970, Series A, p. 6.
      [3] Rule 38(1).   [4] Rule 38(2).   [5] Rule 38(3).
      [6] Article 52 of the Convention.   [7] Rule 51(2).   [8] Rule 51(3).

remedy there, he may apply directly to the Court. This was so held by the Court for the first time in the Vagrancy cases, where, however, it found that the applicants had suffered no damage. It was in the Ringeisen case, on 22 June 1972, that the Court for the first time made such an award: it ordered the Austrian Government to pay the applicant the sum of 20,000 German marks in respect of the excessive length of his detention on remand. The question then arose whether the sum might not be paid in Austrian currency, although the applicant was now resident in Germany, and whether it could be attached to meet the applicant's liabilities. In a further judgment interpreting its previous decision, the Court held that that decision meant that the sum was to be paid in Germany and in German marks, and that it was to be paid to the applicant personally and free from attachment.[1]

In accordance with Article 54 of the Convention, the Committee of Ministers is responsible for supervising the execution of judgments of the Court. The Committee of Ministers accordingly considered the matter and found that the Austrian Government had duly executed the judgment. For the first time since the Convention entered into force twenty years before, a case referred to the European Court of Human Rights had gone through all the stages of procedure provided.

None the less, the procedure for executing the Court's judgments cannot be regarded as satisfactory. There is a striking contrast in this respect with the judgments of the Court of Justice of the European Communities, whose judgments are directly enforceable in the Member States of the Communities.[2] There may be difficulties in executing the Court's judgments when these involve, apart from compensation for the applicant, amendments to a State's law or practice to comply with the Convention.[3] It is unfortunate, also, that the drafting of Article 50 seems to envisage the institution of further proceedings to obtain compensation, which makes the Convention machinery more cumbersome; it would be preferable for this question to be dealt with by the Court in its judgment on the merits of the case.[4] Further ex-

---

[1] Subsequently, in a sequel to the Neumeister case (see above, p. 64), the Court awarded the applicant 30,000 Austrian schillings, in respect of lawyers' costs, to be paid by Austria: see Council of Europe Press Communiqué C(74)18.

[2] Article 187 and 192 of the EEC Treaty.

[3] See below, p. 268.

[4] Cf. Rule 47 *bis* of the Rules of Court.

perience in this relatively undeveloped area of the law may suggest possibilities of other reforms.

IV DECISION BY THE COMMITTEE OF MINISTERS

If a case on which the Commission has submitted a report under Article 31 has not, within a period of three months, been referred to the Court, the final decision is taken, under Article 32, by the Committee of Ministers.

The Committee of Ministers, the governmental organ under the Statute of the Council of Europe, consists of the Ministers for Foreign Affairs of the Member States. In practice the Foreign Ministers meet twice a year; at other sessions they are represented by Deputies meeting regularly (and often resident) in Strasbourg. The Committee, which normally sits in private,[1] assisted by the Secretary General, is the executive body of the Council of Europe. In addition to its functions under the Convention, it also has powers in relation to human rights under the Statute of the Council of Europe.[2]

The principal functions of the Committee of Ministers under the Convention are, first, to decide the question of violation in cases not referred to the Court; secondly, to supervise the execution of its own decisions and of the judgments of the Court.

Article 32(1) of the Convention provides that:

If the question is not referred to the Court in accordance with Article 48 of this Convention within a period of three months from the date of the transmission of the Report to the Committee of Ministers, the Committee of Ministers shall decide by a majority of two-thirds of the members entitled to sit on the Committee whether there has been a violation of the Convention.

In deciding whether there has been a violation, the Committee of Ministers acts in a judicial capacity. The Rules adopted by the Committee of Ministers for the application of Article 32 of the Convention make provision for further proceedings.[3] Further, Article 1(3) of the European Agreement relating to persons parti-

---

[1] Article 21(a) (i) of the Statute.
[2] See below, p. 269.
[3] *Collected Texts*, 9th edn., Section 5.

cipating in proceedings of the European Commission and Court of Human Rights[1] extends the provisions of the Agreement to proceedings before the Committee of Ministers under Article 32. But the Rules adopted by the Committee of Ministers are hardly adequate and the Committee is not equipped to carry out the tasks envisaged by the Convention.

In practice, it has normally followed the majority opinion in the Commission and there are no separate proceedings in the Committee to investigate the merits of the case. An unfortunate precedent was set by the Fourons case, concerning the linguistic regulations applicable to teaching in the area of Les Fourons in Belgium. The Commission was unanimously of the opinion, in a report transmitted to the Committee of Ministers in 1971, that the Belgian legislation infringed Article 2 of the First Protocol in conjunction with Article 14 of the Convention. The Committee of Ministers' Resolution merely 'takes note' of the Commission's opinion; takes note of new provisions introduced in Belgium after the adoption of the Commission's report; and 'decides in consequence that no further action is called for in this case'.[2] The Resolution thus conflicts with the express duty of the Committee of Ministers under Article 32(1) to decide whether there has been a violation of the Convention. The correct course would have been to decide that there had been a violation but that the situation had been remedied by the measures subsequently introduced.

If the Committee of Ministers finds a violation, it prescribes a period during which the State concerned must take the measures prescribed by its decision (Article 32(2)); if the State fails to comply, the Committee decides what effect should be given to its original decision and publishes the Commission's report (Article 32(3)). There is no provision for publication of the report in other cases referred to the Committee of Ministers or to the Court, but the general practice has been to publish the reports. The Parties to the Convention undertake to regard as binding decisions taken under Article 32.[3]

The Committee of Ministers is also responsible for supervising the execution of judgments of the Court (Article 54).

Such supervision may be relatively simple where as in the

[1] *Collected Texts*, section 2.
[2] Resolution DH(74)1: see Council of Europe Press Communiqué C(74)19.
[3] Article 32(4).

268

Ringeisen case the effect of the Court's judgment is to award 'just satisfaction' to the injured party under Article 50 of the Convention. It is more difficult where the judgment entails the modification of the legislation concerned. An example of supervision in such a case has been mentioned above.[1]

The Convention contains no other provision for sanctions against a State which fails to comply with a judgment of the Court or a decision of the Committee of Ministers. It is assumed that no State, at least so long as it remains a Member of the Council of Europe, and a Party to the Convention, will default on its obligations. However, in the event of a flagrant breach of the Convention, the Committee of Ministers could use its powers under the Statute of the Council of Europe.

As stated above, by the terms of Article 3 of the Statute, every Member State of the Council of Europe must accept the principles of the rule of law and of the enjoyment by all persons within its jurisdiction of human rights and fundamental freedoms. Before the Committee of Ministers invites a State to become a member of the Organisation, it must be satisfied that that State is able and willing to fulfil the provisions of Article 3.[2] It may request a Member State which has seriously violated Article 3 to withdraw from the Council, and, if the State refuses to comply, may expel it.[3] These provisions, which have no parallel in any other international organization, were invoked against Greece while proceedings under the Human Rights Convention were pending before the Commission in the Greek Case. There could be no legal objection to the proceedings running parallel, since the Convention expressly provides, in Article 61, that it shall not prejudice the powers conferred on the Committee of Ministers by the Statute.

On the initiative of the Consultative Assembly the Committee of Ministers was considering a proposal to request Greece to withdraw from the Organisation when the Greek Government announced, in December 1969, its withdrawal from the Council,[4] and simultaneously denounced the Convention.[5] The Commission's report, establishing violations of numerous Articles of the Convention, including a large-scale use of torture contrary to Article 3, had already been transmitted to the Committee of

---

[1] The Vagrancy cases, p. 55.   [2] Article 4 of the Statute.
                    [3] Article 8.
[4] Article 7 of the Statute.   [5] Article 65; see pp. 27 and 231, above.

Ministers, but the Committee was not yet formally able to consider the report because the three months' interval laid down had not expired. Subsequently the Committee of Ministers took a decision on violation of the Convention following the conclusions of the Commission, but it was unable to take action on the Commission's proposals.

This use of the expulsion procedure has been criticized on the ground that the effect was to isolate Greece from European opinion and to remove the possibility of bringing pressure to bear on the Greek Government. Certainly that Government appears to have gone to great lengths to seek to avoid expulsion, which suggests that ultimately it might have made greater concessions. It seems doubtful however whether any real improvement in the situation in Greece could have been achieved by the Council of Europe acting alone. On the other hand, concerted action with other international organizations, in particular through NATO and the European Communities, might well have had more impact.[1]

Five years later, in November 1974, Greece returned to the fold. After the collapse of the military régime it was readmitted to membership of the Council of Europe. At least two requirements appear to have been imposed on the Greek Government as a condition of readmission: that free elections should have been held in Greece, and that the Human Rights Convention should be re-ratified. The newly elected government consequently re-ratified the Convention immediately after its readmission by the Committee of Ministers.

Quite apart from its functions under the Statute of the Council of Europe, the dual role of the Committee of Ministers under the Convention, as organ of decision as well as organ of execution, is not entirely satisfactory. It is the result of a compromise which emerged at the time the Convention was drafted, when it appeared that some governments were not prepared to accept compulsory judicial settlement.[2] Consequently it was agreed to provide an alternative procedure, so that these States could retain the option not to recognize the compulsory jurisdiction of the Court. In fact fourteen of the eighteen Parties to the Convention have now, in some cases after long hesitation, accepted that jurisdiction, but because of their reluctance, and the reluctance of the Commission, to refer cases to the Court, most cases have been finally

[1] See below, p. 273.   [2] See above, p. 259.

decided by the Committee of Ministers. The system is unsatisfactory in principle, since the Committee of Ministers is a political rather than a judicial body. Further, in the case of individual applications, it is clearly wrong that the respondent Government should participate while the applicant has no standing. These drawbacks, however, should not be exaggerated. The political character of the Committee of Ministers may be an advantage if, as suggested earlier,[1] the principal object of the Convention system is not a final legal decision on the issue of violation. Moreover, difficulties need not arise in practice if the Committee of Ministers respects its functions under the Convention and is prepared to follow the opinion of the Commission.

[1] pp. 254, 259.

PART V RESULTS AND PROSPECTS

The achievements of the European Convention on Human Rights cannot be measured entirely in terms of the results of the decided cases. It is useful, of course, to attempt to assess the impact of individual decisions. It is possible to discern, among the cases discussed in this book, many whose outcome might be described as successful, from the point of view of the effectiveness of the system, in the sense that the individual applicant has obtained satisfaction, or that the law or practice of the respondent State has been modified to comply with the Convention. Other cases, and perhaps especially the inter-State cases, have, for reasons which will be considered below, proved less successful. But even if it were possible to quantify the results of the cases in this way, a balance-sheet drawn up in these terms would be dangerously misleading. A better course may be to try to stand back and survey the impact of the system as a whole.

Certain consequences follow from the fact that the system has proved to be workable at all, however qualified its success. It has shown that the individual can be accepted as a proper subject of international law. It has shown that States are prepared to amend their laws, on matters falling within their domestic jurisdiction, to comply with the opinions and judgments of international tribunals. It has shown that States are prepared to remedy by way of compensation, at the instance of international organs, acts of their own administrative authorities and of their own courts of law.

But to present the issue in these terms is to accept the categories of legal thought which prevailed when the Convention was drafted. It may be claimed that those categories have themselves been modified by the working of the Convention. The readiness of States in more recent years to waive formal objections to admissibility, to accept that applications should be treated on the merits, to cooperate with the Commission in securing a friendly settlement, and to modify their legislation and administrative practice, suggests that governments, though still hesitant, are now increasingly prepared to accept the services of the Convention as an instrument to remedy deficiencies in their own systems of law.

Previous chapters have illustrated the impact of the Convention on the laws of Western Europe. No attempt has been made, however, to assess its influence on the constitutions and laws of States outside Europe, or on the drafting of other international instruments for the protection of human rights. Nor has any detailed account seemed necessary of the reporting system established under Article 57 of the Convention.[1] The reasons for the relative ineffectiveness of this system are plainly to be found in the weak position of the Secretary General of the Council of Europe.[2]

More significant may be an attempt to analyse and explain the reasons for such success as has been achieved by the Convention's system of protection. Three factors may serve to elucidate the question: the role of inter-State cases compared with individual applications; the balance between the different organs of the Convention, with the emergence of the Commission as the key institution in the working of the system; and the system's European dimension.

It will be recalled that ratification of the Convention entails automatically acceptance of the Commission's competence in inter-State cases, while acceptance of its competence to receive applications from individuals requires a declaration under Article 25 expressly accepting such competence. None the less it is clear that the individual application was conceived from the outset as the kernel of the system, and that the inter-State application was a subsidiary means of ensuring the application of the Convention. In this respect the European Convention may be contrasted with the United Nations Covenant on Civil and Political Rights, which relegates communications from individuals to a separate Optional Protocol.[3]

For many reasons, the system of inter-State applications is unlikely to be successful as a means of securing human rights. It is a well-known fact of political life that States are unlikely to be disinterested and to bring applications for purely humanitarian motives. Where they do so as a result of a political difference between them, as in the first inter-State cases between Greece and the United Kingdom over Cyprus, and between Austria and Italy where the background of the cases was the dispute over the

[1] See above, p. 5.
[2] Cf. the statement by the Secretary General reproduced in *Collected Texts*, 9th edn., 1974, 910.
[3] Cf. Ermacora, Über die Staatenbeschwerde in Fragen der Menschenrechte, Mélanges Marcel Bridel, Lausanne, 1968, 169.

Tirol, a settlement of the difference may even be made more difficult as the relations between them may be exacerbated by the running sore of litigation. Similar considerations apply to the Irish Case, where the differences between the United Kingdom and the Republic of Ireland over the status of Northern Ireland were balanced by the fact that the terrorist activities in Northern Ireland faced both Governments with a common threat. The Greek Case, where four governments brought applications against the revolutionary government in Greece, is a case apart. It demonstrates that where a government is pursuing a deliberate policy of full-scale violations of human rights, the actions of other governments can only mitigate, but not cure, the evil. Taken together, the inter-State cases show that the Convention cannot be used successfully where the legal issues are overlaid by political ones. Even where the political issues are ultimately resolved, as they were, at least temporarily, in Cyprus and the Tirol, the organs of the Convention cannot themselves be used as instruments of the settlement, since they are equipped to deal only with an aspect of the whole problem.

It follows that the key to the effectiveness of the Convention on the international level lies in individual applications. The 1969 American Convention on Human Rights has thus adopted a solution more satisfactory in theory, providing for the automatic competence of the Inter-American Commission to receive individual petitions, and an optional competence for inter-State complaints.[1] But it may be for this very reason that the prospects of the American Convention entering into force seem remote. The strategy of the European Convention has proved more successful, by enabling all the member States of the Council of Europe to co-operate in the working of the Convention before they have ratified it. The final instances, the Court and the Committee of Ministers, include members from all these States. Government experts from all of them take part in the inter-governmental work in the field of human rights, and parliamentarians in the work of the Consultative Assembly. Further, the technique of allowing States to ratify the Convention without any legal obligation to accept the jurisdiction of the Court, or the Commission's competence to receive individual applications, has proved itself. States

---

[1] Articles 44 and 45 of the American Convention on Human Rights.

have been enabled in these ways to accept step by step the full implementation of the Convention.

In consequence, under the European system, where most of the declarations accepting the Commission's competence to receive individual applications have been made for a limited period, the role of the Commission is delicate: it must resist the temptation to advance too fast, at the risk of losing the support of the governments which is a condition of its effective functioning.

The role of the Commission can be clearly explained in terms of two sets of statistics: the first is the very low proportion of applications declared admissible by the Commission—although it has increased significantly since 1970; the second is that only a handful of cases have resulted in a final decision, whether by the Court or by the Committee of Ministers, that the Convention has been violated. The cautious policy of the Commission in its early years evidently secured the necessary confidence of the governments. The number of States prepared to accept the right of individual petition has gradually increased, and, despite hesitations, no State which has once made a declaration accepting this right has yet failed to renew it. Renewal of the right of petition has become a political issue of some importance, reflected not only in debates in the Consultative Assembly and in national parliaments, but also among groups concerned with civil liberties and in the Press.[1]

In many of the cases admitted by the Commission, any necessary remedial action has been taken by the State concerned in the course of the Commission's proceedings, obviating the need for any further proceedings. The Commission has thus had the opportunity to control the conformity with the Convention of the measures taken by the respondent State: a form of control which, as already mentioned, may be more effective than would be possible once a final decision had been reached.

A further element necessary to secure the confidence of governments is of course political impartiality. It is in this, above all, that the advantage of a regional system is plain. The Convention speaks with a European voice, and governments may be more ready to

[1] On acceptance of the right of petition in Switzerland, see *Yearbook* 14, 952. On renewal of the right of petition in Norway, see above, p. 40. In the United Kingdom, retention of the right of petition was described by the National Council for Civil Liberties as 'perhaps the key civil liberty issue of the decade': *The Times*, 14 November 1973. See also, among others, *The Times* editorial of 29 October 1973.

listen to such a voice, representing a relatively homogenoeus and like-minded group of States with shared values, than would be the case in a wider or universal system. Much evidence of this has been provided by the various universal systems of protection already in force; the crucial test will be provided by the United Nations Covenant.

The entry into force of the United Nations Covenant on Civil and Political Rights and of its Optional Protocol will raise questions of the co-existence of two independent international systems for the protection of human rights.[1] So far as individual applications are concerned, the effect will be, where the State concerned has accepted both the Optional Protocol and the competence of the Commission under Article 25 of the European Convention, to give the individual a choice between the two systems. He will, however, be precluded from using the two systems cumulatively.[2] His choice may be determined in part by the scope of the rights protected by the two systems; in many respects the Covenant gives wider protection than the Convention. But his choice may be influenced also by the relative effectiveness of the two systems. Here experience alone will show which will be the more successful.

THE CONVENTION AND EUROPEAN INTEGRATION

The Preamble to the Human Rights Convention recites that 'the aim of the Council of Europe is the achievement of greater unity between its Members and that one of the methods by which that aim is to be pursued is the maintenance and further realization of Human Rights and Fundamental Freedoms.'

The Convention does not, however, in contrast with the Treaties establishing the European Communities, and indeed certain other Conventions and Agreements concluded within the Council of Europe,[3] seek directly to promote the unification or harmonization of European law.

[1] See Eissen, 'The European Convention on Human Rights and the United Nations Covenant on Civil and Political Rights: problems of co-existence', *Buffalo Law Review* 1972, 181.

[2] European Convention, Article 27(1) (b); Optional Protocol, Article 5(2) (a). For cumulative use of the two systems in inter-State cases, see Eissen, op. cit.

[3] See for example the European Convention on Compulsory Insurance against Civil Liability in respect of Motor Vehicles, E.T.S. 29.

In this respect, the role of the Commission and the Court is quite different from that of the Court of Justice of the European Communities, which has the task of securing the uniform interpretation and application of Community law. The Human Rights Convention requires only that the contracting States give effect in their own law to the obligations they have accepted.

None the less it is clear that, apart from establishing common standards, a significant indirect effect of the Convention is to secure the harmonization of the laws and practices of the contracting States in certain fields. This process is achieved in a number of distinct ways. The drafting, interpretation and application of new legislation, and of constitutional provisions, will necessarily be influenced by the need to comply with the obligations of the Convention. The laws and practices of individual contracting States may be amended to comply with the opinions of the Commission and with the judgments of the Court, and thus brought into line with the law and practice of the other contracting States. The drafting within the Council of Europe of other conventions and agreements, and of other treaties concluded by States Parties to the Convention, must also take account of their obligations under the Convention. In all these respects, the Convention may properly be regarded as the nucleus of a European constitution, laying down the fundamental principles of a European public law in the field of human rights.

This role of the Convention can also be assessed in political, as well as in legal terms. Although these effects are necessarily more difficult to quantify, many individual illustrations could be cited. A striking example, in the context of the Irish Case,[1] is the Sunningdale Agreement of 1973 (not yet ratified) to set up a Council of Ireland which would be invited to consider, among other matters, 'in what way the principles of the European convention on human rights and fundamental freedoms would be expressed in domestic legislation in each part of Ireland'. More generally, membership of the Council of Europe, ratification of the Convention, and acceptance of its optional provisions on the competence of the Commission and the jurisdiction of the Court, can be seen as a touchstone of the quality of a European government, and even of its title to participate in the general movemetn of European integration, through the European Communities and elsewhere.

[1] See above, p. 25.

THE CONVENTION AND THE PROTECTION OF
FUNDAMENTAL RIGHTS IN THE
EUROPEAN COMMUNITIES

The process of European integration raises problems of a novel type in the international legal order.[1] The most significant of these problems arise from the transfer by the Member States of the European Communities of certain of their sovereign powers to the Institutions of the Communities, which, unlike traditional international organizations, have direct authority over private individuals and corporate bodies within the Member States. The Council and the Commission of the European Communities issue regulations and other legal acts of a general character which are directly applicable in the Member States; the Commission makes decisions and the Court of Justice gives judgments which are binding and executory under national law. Within the areas where these Institutions, rather than the authorities of the Member States, are competent, it is an open question whether individual Member States can any longer be held responsible for any alleged infringements of human rights.[2] Here the protection of the individual is primarily the responsibility of the Court of Justice of the European Communities.

The judicial system of the European Communities embodies two distinct mechanisms: direct actions before the European Court, and references for preliminary rulings by the courts and tribunals of Member States. There is as yet no specific declaration of rights in the Community Treaties themselves, although proposals have been made that such a declaration having legal force should be incorporated in any future revision of the Treaties. The protection of fundamental rights has been developed by the Court of Justice of the European Communities as an inherent part of its duty to ensure that in the interpretation and application of the Community Treaties 'the law is observed'.[3] In the exercise of its jurisdiction the Court has relied on the general principles of law, which it has held to include respect for fundamental rights.[4] Hence

---

[1] See Sørensen, 'The Enlargement of the European Communities and the Protection of Human Rights', *European Yearbook*, 1971, 3.

[2] Sørensen, op. cit., p. 12.   [3] Article 164 of the EEC Treaty.

[4] Case 11/70, *Internationale Handelsgesellschaft mbH* v. *Einfuhr- und Vorratsstelle für Getreide und Futtermittel* (Rec. 1970, p. 1125); cf. Case 4/73, *Nold* v. *Commission* [1974] ECR 491, containing the first express reference to the European Convention. See Pescatore, The protection of human rights in the European Communities, *Common Market Law Review*, 1972, 73.

278

it would be open to the Court, although it has never yet done so, to declare invalid an act of a Community institution which did not respect such rights.

Such an act might be challenged on this ground either in a direct action originating in the Court of Justice,[1] or in a reference to the Court of Justice by a national court for a preliminary ruling on the validity of the act.[2] In a direct action an individual can challenge only a decision addressed to him or a decision which, although in the form of a regulation or a decision addressed to another person, is of direct and individual concern to him. On a reference for a preliminary ruling, however, the Court may review, at any time, the validity of any act of a Community institution.

While the existence of two separate European systems, in the Communities and in the Council of Europe, for the protection of fundamental rights may not ultimately be satisfactory, there are unlikely in the short term to be many cases of conflict, or even of overlap, between the two systems. In the first place, now that all the Member States of the European Communities have ratified the Human Rights Convention, the material provisions of the Convention can reasonably be considered as part of the law common to the Member States of the Communities, even though not all of them recognize the Convention as part of their domestic law. Of more practical importance, there are likely to be few situations where the procedures under the two systems will overlap. Even where the same factual situation arises both before the organs of the Convention in Strasbourg and before the Court of Justice in Luxembourg, the issues of legal principle are likely to differ. Thus in a case concerning the Italian cable television monopoly, which came before both instances, the Luxembourg Court dealt with the questions of State monopolies under Article 37 of the EEC treaty, and with the possible abuse of a dominant position under Article 86.[3] The Human Rights Commission, on the other hand, was concerned with the quite separate question of the right to freedom of expression under Article 10 of the Convention.[4] There could be no question of the Commission rejecting the application under Article 27(1) (b) of the Convention as having

[1] Article 173 of the EEC Treaty.
[2] Article 177 of the EEC Treaty.
[3] Case 155/73 *Sacchi* [1974] ECR 409.
[4] See above, p. 156.

'already been submitted to another procedure of international investigation or settlement', for even if the procedure before the Luxembourg Court could correctly be described as international, the substance of the complaint before the Commission was quite different. In fact the correct view would seem to be that a reference for a preliminary ruling by the Court of Justice of the European Communities is not an international procedure but forms an integral part of the proceedings before the national court making the reference.

While it is difficult to predict the future relations between the different European systems, it seems likely that any further development of European integration will lead to new measures to strengthen the protection of human rights in Europe.

It is appropriate to conclude with a quotation from Max Sørensen:[1]

In a longer perspective the present European set-up is likely to appear less attractive and anything but satisfactory. The various organizations and groupings in Western Europe, resulting as they do from historical accident, involve a dispersal of effort and loyalties which is hardly conducive to the promotion of European unity. Plans for a 'Grand Design' with a view to the reorganization and amalgamation of European institutions have been conceived, but never realized. The rational urge of the human mind and the hard realities of governing Europe will some day breathe new life into these plans and overcome the political obstacles of various kinds which have delayed their realization.

One element in such a 'Grand Design' might very well be an amalgamation of existing judicial bodies on the European level and a corresponding extension of the jurisdiction of a new European Court of Justice to all subject-matters and all persons covered by the separate judicial bodies existing at present. Unity of jurisdiction is to some extent an important element of a fair and adequate administration of justice, and the very ideal of human rights may in this way be harnessed to future moves for the reform of European institutions.

[1] Op. cit., pp. 16–17.

BIBLIOGRAPHY

SOURCES

The *text of the Convention* and Protocols in English and French is set out in *European Convention on Human Rights: Collected Texts* (Ninth edition March 1974) which can be obtained free of charge from the Council of Europe, Strasbourg, France. This volume also contains, among other documents and information, the European Agreement relating to persons participating in proceedings of the European Commission and Court of Human Rights, Rules of Procedure of the European Commission of Human Rights, Rules of Court of the European Court of Human Rights, the Rules of Procedure adopted by the Committee of Ministers for the application of Article 32 of the Convention and the declarations and reservations made by States Parties to the Convention.

A selection of the *decisions of the Commission* is published periodically in the original language, English or French, in European Commission of Human Rights, *Collection of Decisions*. The reports of the Commission on admissible applications are published as separate documents. The *judgments of the Court* are published by the Registry of the Court: Publications of the European Court of Human Rights, Series A, contains judgments and decisions; Series B contains the pleadings, oral arguments, and documents in the case.

The *Yearbook of the European Convention on Human Rights* contains, among other documents and information, all official texts relating to the Convention, a selection of the Commisson's decisions on admissibility, and extracts from the reports of the Commission, the judgments of the Court, and the decisions of the Committee of Ministers. All documents are published in both English and French. The first volume of the *Yearbook* (1955–7) was entitled European Commission of Human Rights: Documents and Decisions. The second volume covers 1958–9. Since 1960 an annual volume has been published. A separate volume for 1969 contains, in English only, the report of the Commission on the Greek Case and the Resolution of the Committee of Ministers relating to this case.

Other publications of the Commission's secretariat include *Stocktaking on the European Convention on Human Rights*, published periodically, and Case-Law Topics: No. 1, *Human Rights in Prison* (1971); No. 2, *Family Life* (1972); No. 3, *Bringing an Application before the European Commission of Human Rights* (1972) and No. 4, *Human Rights and Their Limitations* (1973).

BOOKS

BROWNLIE, I. (ed.), *Basic Documents on Human Rights*, Oxford, 1971.

CASTBERG, F., *The European Convention on Human Rights*, Leyden, 1974.

FAWCETT, J. E. S., *The Application of the European Convention on Human Rights*, Oxford, 1969.

GOLSONG, H., *Das Rechtsschutzsystem der Europäischen Menschenrechtskonvention*, Karlsruhe, 1958.

GURADZE, H., *Die Europäische Menschenrechtskonvention*, Berlin, 1968.

KHOL, A., *Zwischen Staat und Weltstaat*, Vienna, 1969.

MONCONDUIT, F., *La Commission européenne des Droits de l'Homme*, Leyden, 1965.

PARTSCH, K. J., *Die Rechte und Freiheiten der Europäischen Menschenrechtskonvention*, Berlin, 1966.

ROBERTSON, A. H., *Human Rights in Europe*, Manchester, 1963.

ROBERTSON, A. H. (ed.), *Human Rights in National and International Law*, Manchester, 1968.

ROBERTSON, A. H. (ed.), *Privacy and Human Rights*, Manchester, 1973.

VASAK, K., *La Convention européenne des Droits de l'Homme*, Paris, 1964.

See further a very full analytical bibliography published by the Council of Europe, *Bibliography relating to the European Convention on Human Rights*, November 1973, document H (73) 13.

INDEX

Abortion 21
Absconding, danger of 52, 66, 71
Abuse of power 202
Abuse of rights 210
Abuse of right of petition 246
Access to Commission 143
Access to courts 16, 90, 190
Actio popularis 230
Administrative authorities 79 seq.
Administrative detention 47, 53, 54, 58, 72, 207
Administrative law 78 seq.
Administrative practice 25, 27, 237
Alcoholics 55
Aliens 14; admission of, 177, 235 and see Immigration; collective expulsion of, 31, 187; political activities of, 166, 195; property of, 165. See also Nationals.
American Convention on Human Rights 21, 31, 203, 254, 274
Anonymous applicants 248
Appeals 84, 110, 114, 130, 189, 235; and detention on remand, 49, 68; applications for leave to appeal, 85, 110; constitutional appeals, 86; criminal appeals, 85; right of appeal, 190, 235
Appreciation, see Discretion, control of.
Arbitration clause 93
Arrest 45 seq., 127, 169
Assembly, freedom of 157
Association, freedom of 157
Asylum 31, 33

Bail 71, 76
Bankrupts 93
Belief, see Religion
Bias 104
Birth control 22, 164
Births, registration of 149
Blasphemy 155
Blood transfusions 149
Broadcasting, licensing of 151, 156
Burden of proof 111, 113, 206, 241

Capital punishment, see Death penalty
Cassation proceedings 68, 84, 100, 102, 108
Censorship 151, 155. See also Correspondence
Census 149
Charge, criminal 60, 61, 83, 108; determination of, 95
Children, access to 102, 129, 133, 136; custody of, 54, 129, 133; illegitimate, 134, 162
Churches 228
Cinemas, licensing of 151
Civil and political rights 3. See also United Nations Covenant
Civil law 78
Civil rights and obligations 78, 257
Civil servants, disciplinary proceedings 89; trade union rights, 160. See also Public service
Collective bargaining 158
Collusion 67
Companies 228
Compensation 74, 254, 265; for expropriation, 78, 167; for unlawful arrest or detention, 60, 74
Computers 127
Conciliation 254
Conflict of laws, see Private international law.
Conscience, freedom of 143; conscientious objectors, 23, 144
Consent 44. See also Waiver
Continuing situation 231, 243
Convention, authentic texts 15, 213; Preamble, 13, 77, 120, 276; ratification, 2, 4, 12; temporal scope, 12; territorial scope, 14. See also Denunciation; Dependent territories; Derogation; Interpretation; Preparatory work; Reciprocity; Retroactivity; Reservations
Conviction 68, 73, 87; previous convictions, 112
Copyright 153
Corporations 175, 176, 228. See also Public corporations.

283

Prisoners, rights of—*contd.*
labour, 40; marriage, 163; religion, 150
Privacy 18, 125, 152
Private international law 48, 123
Private law 78
Probation 86
Property rights 79, 164, 213. See also Expropriation
Proportionality, principle of 191
Public corporations 227
Public law 78, 92, 277
Public service 82
Publicity, of Commission's proceedings 221, 246; pre-trial, 104, 112
Punishment 26, 30, 137, 203, 244; capital, see Death penalty; corporal, 31. See also Disciplinary proceedings; Sentence, proceedings concerning.

Radio licensing 151, 156
Reciprocity 6, 13, 17
Release, conditional 86; pending appeal, 68; pending trial, 66.
Religion, freedom of 143; and education, 173, 174.
Renunciation of rights 93. See also Waiver.
Reputation, protection of 152. See also Defamation proceedings.
Reservations 90, 125, 144, 174, 179, 209, 212, 224
Responsibility, State 6, 14, 15, 31, 278
Retroactivity, of Convention 12; of declarations, 214, 230; of derogations, 238; of legislation, 120.
Revolutionary government 206, 210
Rule of law 2, 48, 77, 120

Secrets, official 153
Security of person 45
Security of the State 51, 110, 153
Sentence, proceedings concerning 87
Servitude 36
Sex education 174, 177. See also Discrimination; Homosexual behaviour.

Slavery 36
Social and economic rights 4. See also United Nations Covenant.
Social security 40, 82, 167
Solitary confinement 30
Sovereignty 17
Standing before the Commission 227; before the Court, 260, 264.
Sterilization 22, 164

Tape-recording 126
Taxation 82, 167
Television licensing 151, 156
Terrorist activities 211
Thought, freedom of 143
Torture 26
Trade unions 157; applications by, 228.
Treatment and punishment 30. See also Degrading treatment; Inhuman treatment.

UNESCO 188
United Nations Charter 3, 254
United Nations Covenant on Civil and Political Rights 4, 44, 188, 203, 254, 273, 276
United Nations Covenant on Economic, Social and Cultural Rights 4, 188
Universal Declaration of Human Rights 3, 4, 9, 21, 31, 158, 178, 181, 184, 188, 203

Vagrants 55, 197
Victim, concept of 229; requirement of, 6, 7, 22, 233, 237
Vienna Convention on the Law of Treaties 3, 16, 185, 212, 214

Waiver 22, 93, 97; of domestic remedies requirement, 236. See also Consent.
War 195; crimes, 124.
Warrant for arrest 46, 61
Wire-tapping 126
Witnesses 101, 118